WHEN EAGLES ROAR

The Amazing Journey of an African Wildlife Adventurer

JAMES ALEXANDER CURRIE
with BONNIE J. FLADUNG

Illustrated by Margo Gabrielle Damian

UKHOZI
PRESS

D1053923

When Eagles Roar

Ukhozi Press
www.UkhoziPress.com

Illustrations: Copyright © 2014 Margo Gabrielle Damian

Cover Illustration: Copyright © 2014 Jon Hughes/ www.jfhdigital.com

Maps by Peter C. Allen

Poetry of Mazisi Kunene
used by permission of the Mazisi Kunene Foundation

Song lyrics "Too Early for the Sky"
used by permission of Johnny Clegg
www.johnnyclegg.com

Wildlife photo sources for adaptation by our illustrator: Adrian Binns, James Currie, James and Ellen Fields, Clement Jacquard, Adam Riley, Charles J. Sharp, Coke Smith, Warwick Tarboton, Simon van Noort, James Weiss, Jonathan Wood.

I have recreated events, places, and conversations from my memories and the recollections of characters in this book. The combination of time and the ravages of a misspent youth have a way of sneakily distorting facts and sequencing. If this occurs on occasion, I profusely do not apologize. The names of some individuals have been changed or appear unmentioned in order to protect their identity and maintain their anonymity. The names of close friends remain real in order to expose what reprobates they truly are.

ISBN: 0990766004
ISBN-13: 978-0990766001

To my Mum
who left us far too soon
and to
Rockerman Ngubane and Norman Mabika
forever my brothers
—J. A. C.

To Dad
who was always up for a great adventure
—B. J. F.

To Anna-Maria & Michael,   5/2/2015

James

TABLE OF CONTENTS

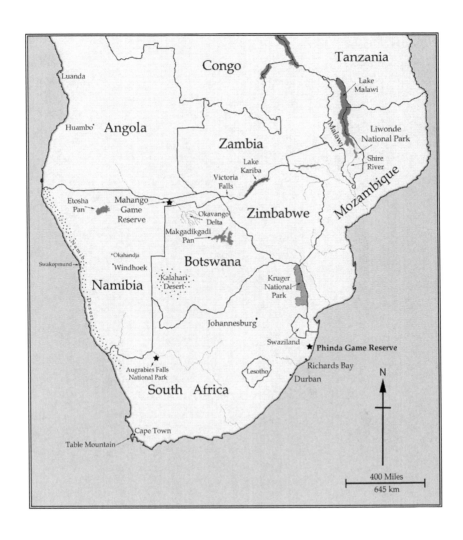

MAP: SOUTHERN AFRICA

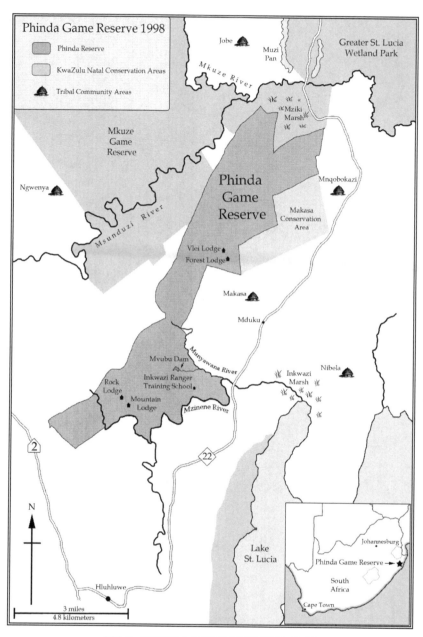

MAP: PHINDA GAME RESERVE 1998

ON THE NATURE OF TRUTH

People do not follow the same direction, like water.
ZULU SAYING

Those who claim the monopoly of truth
Blinded by their own discoveries of power,
Curb the thrust of their own fierce vision.
For there is not one eye over the universe
But a seething nest of rays ever dividing and ever linking.

The multiple creations do not invite disorder,
Nor are the many languages the enemies of humankind.
But the little tyrant must mould things into one body
To control them and give them his single vision.

Yet those who are truly great
On whom time has bequeathed the gift of wisdom
Know all truth must be born of seeing
And all the various dances of humankind are beautiful
They are enriched by the great songs of our planet.

MAZISI KUNENE

PROLOGUE: THE BLACK EAGLE

The great eagle lifts its wings from the dream
And the shells of childhood are scattered
Letting the fierce eyes focus on the morning
As though to cover the earth with darkness.
MAZISI KUNENE,
"The Rise of the Angry Generation"

Umuth' ugotshw usemanzi.
The tree is bent whilst young.
ZULU PROVERB

AN EAGLE SPARKED MY LOVE for adventure and my passion for wildlife, and it was an eagle that nearly took it all away. The attack was swift, fierce, and fatal. I boulder-hopped down to the rectangular-shaped slab and examined the rock surface for any sign of blood or fur. Nothing. Just the granite with its shiny flecks of mica reflected in the sunlight. Moments before, the warm rock had been teeming with activity. Now there was no visible evidence that my life had been changed forever in an instant.

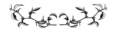

Table Mountain, at the southern tip of Africa, is my playground, and I always look forward to the strenuous hike to the plateau. My parents own the popular restaurant in Kirstenbosch National Botanical Gardens on the eastern slope of the mountain, and because of this I am allowed access before the bustling throngs of tourists arrive. At the top, I overlook my home of Cape Town, one of the most picturesque cities in the world.

The trail to the summit snakes its way up a ravine that is ominously called Skeleton Gorge. To ascend to the top, I wind my way past waterfalls and mountain streams and through dark, shadowy forest patches that open unexpectedly into the blinding sunlight on open stretches of fragrant *fynbos*. I reach a narrow footpath, flanked by large boulders, that departs enticingly from the main trail. Easing my way along the cold granite monoliths, I press my cheek against the hard rock. Below me, the mountainside falls away into oblivion, and my legs twitch nervously as I balance on the narrow ledge.

The giant slabs tower at least three times taller than my ten-year-old frame, forcing me to stretch my hands as high as they will reach to find the subtle finger holds provided by longitudinal cracks in the rock. Now, sliding my hands lower, my fingers touch a soft moist surface, a bright, almost luminous, blob of green moss. Pausing to examine it closely, I see a miniature jungle, complete with understory, soil, and tiny scurrying animals. A different microscopic world in a seriously macro setting. The moss distracts me from my precarious position, clinging to the side of the majestic mountain.

Losing myself in thought, I shiver as I let my hands lead me along the icy curtain of rock, shaded from the soft, caressing fingers of the early sun. Reaching the ragged edge of the boulder and the welcoming golden light, I marvel at the vista below. The narrow, treacherous path has opened into a circular open area, like a box seat above an arena of stunning beauty. I see all the way across the Cape Flats to the distant Hottentots Holland mountain range, the primary travel route to the east coast of South Africa. Immediately below, the mountainside crumbles into a scree of granite boulders, as if a giant had knocked a piece of the mountain away.

I am not alone. Rock hyraxes lie peacefully sunning themselves on the boulders below. These small, rodent-like creatures, called *dassies* in Afrikaans, resemble rats or rabbits but are oddly more closely related to elephants. I sit down, wallowing in a warm pool of solitude and sunlight to watch the hyraxes. Dead quiet. Only the occasional "Willie" call of the sombre bulbul and the gentle breathing of a light wind. I have been here many times, on my own. Just sitting. Just the lazy hyraxes and me.

In an instant, my drowsy daydream is interrupted by a fast-moving silhouette high above, the only thing stirring in this tapestry of calm. A massive black eagle swoops in at lightning speed. I am witnessing one of those rare moments when time slows down, almost intentionally, as if to compensate for the discrepancy between the tortoise-like pace of nature at peace with itself and the speed of reflexes required to ensure survival.

I see every feather, the black tip of the yellow beak, the glint in the eagle's eye. I feel the terror as the hyrax sentries sound the alarm call, rousing dozens of dassies to leap for cover. The aerial assassin is closing in for the kill. The boulders are empty now except for a lone hyrax desperately attempting to nose-dive into a crevice. But it is too late.

For an instant, the dassie is shrouded in darkness as the wings block out all light. The eagle extends its large yellow feet, and black talons the size of bear claws strike their mark, one set over the creature's snout and skull, and the other piercing straight through the major artery in the neck. Death comes instantly to the ill-fated creature as the eagle plucks its victim easily from the rock.

On outstretched wings, the massive eagle lifts the hapless animal effortlessly into the air above, predator and prey covering me briefly in a deathly shadow of unity. Departing as swiftly and silently as it came, I see the prominent white "V" on the eagle's back, signifying victory as it banks away in flight, prey dangling.

I observe all of this in slow motion, leaning against the giant granite boulder in the African dawn. Unmoving and hypnotized by the beautiful brutality of nature. The simple relationship between predator and prey, the hunter and the hunted. Life snuffed out in an instant. Sunbathing one moment, snuffed out the next.

Watching this brings on an instant adrenaline rush. I know at my tender age that I want to chase this thrill the rest of my life. To the ends of the earth.

So my story begins with the sheer power and splendor of the massive black eagle. And it will be the wind spirit of another eagle that almost snuffs it all away.

SO FAR A SAFARI

My Forefathers came
They sent the wind to me and the forest
They caressed me and kissed my forehead
I woke before a long line of horizons
I followed them into the dream
MAZISI KUNENE,
"After a Dark Season"

Isisulu sasendle kasethenjwa.
The solitude of the veld is not trusted.
ZULU PROVERB

IT IS SO PEACEFUL ON the bank of the river. From my resting place under the shade of an overhanging tree, I can hear the sounds of the safari staff in the distance as they prep the evening meal. They are speaking in Chichewa, the language of the lake, a melodious tongue that lulls me further into a sleepy state. I can smell the campfire and hear the clanking of utensils. It doesn't matter what they serve for dinner, a growing twelve-year-old boy is always famished. It feels good to rest in the shade on this hot, sultry day, especially after the morning's lengthy guided nature walk along the riverbank. In my drowsy state, with my eyes half shut, I smell the wood smoke from the campfire mixed with the dry, dusty smell of the veld. I hear the hum of the camp, the soothing sounds of the flowing river, my slow, relaxed breaths.

Hoot! Hoot-hoot-hoot! Hoot!

The call seems to be coming from the forest nearby, a deep repetitive hoot, almost rasping. Immediately alert, I rise to my feet and peer into the scrub. Something green and shiny with a flash of red catches my eye. Flying low through the trees, it lands on a distant branch. From where I stand, I just barely make out a metallic green object concealed among the leaves, but no crimson in view. The colorful bird may have turned its back to me, hiding its red breast, disguising itself as a leaf. Can this be the elusive Narina trogon?

The evening before, Auntie Jan told me to keep an eye out for this colorful bird with the amazing ability to camouflage itself in spite of its shimmering iridescent colors—emerald green feathers, bright red belly, and yellow beak. The bird is especially hard to see, as it is able to remain motionless, completely unobtrusive, blending into the environment. I deduce that this particular bird must be a male, giving off his loud, distinctively sad call either trying to defend its territory or attract a mate. My ability to soak up information about the natural world serves me well, whether it's through my voracious reading, traveling with my aunt, or watching shows like David Attenborough's *Life on Earth* series. And now, on safari in Malawi, I am hearing firsthand the stories of the rangers as they guide us on daily nature walks.

I move closer, and the bird senses my presence. It takes off silently, finding another low branch to perch on about six yards away. I continue to follow, trying to get a closer look. I can still hear the sounds of the camp in the distance as I approach the bird. I really want to get close enough to see its crimson underside, but it keeps eluding me. Flying silently from tree to tree in short spurts, it always lands just out of sight, hidden in the foliage. Its hooting call teasing me and luring me on, I continue to follow my quarry deeper into the bush. I keep my curious eyes focused on the flash of iridescent green, determined to play its little game of hide-and-seek.

Eventually, seemingly tired of flirting with me, it flies off, leaving me alone in the bush. That is when I notice the silence. I stop to listen. There are no more hooting birdcalls. No more babbling river flowing in the distance. It is time to turn back for dinner, but I can no longer hear the humming sounds of the camp. I can't have wandered too far. The bird was flying in short bursts; I just need to retrace my steps. By now, I am sweltering in the heat, as this is one of the hottest, most humid areas of Malawi. Making my way back through the low scrub, I can't wait to tell Auntie Jan about the bird I just saw. I have only been gone about half an hour, so the camp should be nearby. But the landscape all looks the same, every tree like all the others.

I keep stopping to listen for the familiar sounds of the safari camp, looking for my tracks in the sand, sniffing for the woody, smoky smell. But there is only silence, no boot prints to be found and no comforting aroma of food cooking. The gnawing in the pit of my stomach is replaced by the shock, the realization that I am lost in the wilderness, completely alone, with no sounds or smells to guide me. The open veld now feels like a maze of identical scrub trees, the path back obscured in the dusty earth beneath my feet.

"Help! I'm lost! Heeellllp!"

I call out repeatedly. They should hear me. They should be missing me by now. I can't be that far off, I keep telling myself. The more I walk, the more lost I become. I have no water or gear, and it is starting to get dark. I am parched and thirsty, but I know better than to drink any stagnant water. At least until I'm really desperate. At twelve years old, I discover what it feels like to be inexorably lost, that sickening feeling deep in your gut. Back then, we do not have television shows hosted by survivalists like Bear Grylls, featuring the skills and knowledge necessary to survive in the wild. Basic subsistence skills like drinking your own piss and eating beetle larvae. I am totally on my own.

I hear the whooping calls of hyenas in the distance and give in to the sensation of pure panic, that feeling of desperation and utter hopelessness. I start screaming louder, screaming until I am exhausted.

"I am *not* going to France," I told my parents. "I am going on safari with Auntie Jan."

Of course, they relented to my strong will. After all, how much trouble could a preteen boy get into, going bird watching with his beloved aunt?

So it was settled. While my parents and sister went off to enjoy the culture of Paris on one of their first real vacations together, I was headed on a trip into the wilds of Africa. Up until now, my only adventures had been exploring the environs around Cape Town. And explore it I did. Although I didn't realize it at the time, I was fortunate that my extended family chose the most interesting places to live and let me run wild in. I was never in fear of venturing out on my own.

I discovered the beaches and wildlife at my grandfather Jack's wonderful place in Ysterfontein, an old whaling station on the west coast of South Africa near the Cape of Storms, known for its violent seas and numerous shipwrecks. On my maternal grandparents' property at Constantia, deep in the wine country, I set off on real and imaginary adventures with my best friend, Zaron, the family guard dog. But it was on Table Mountain, where my parents managed the restaurant at Kirstenbosch Gardens, that I was often left to explore on my own and had my most memorable boyhood adventures.

It was here where my kindred spirit, Auntie Jan, took me birding, nurturing my early passion for wildlife. She raised horses and dogs and was a member of the Black Sash, an anti-apartheid activist group. The quiet excursions with my aunt taught me important skills of observation at a young age and created a bond that we shared throughout our lifetime. The wisdom she imparted to my youthful spirit extended into the realm of human nature and the equality of all mankind.

Now I longed to see more of the wildlife that was beyond my sheltered home, so Auntie Jan was the logical choice of a traveling companion. We would be spending an idyllic month in Malawi, traveling with an overland safari. This enabled us to cover a lot of territory rather than spend the time in a fixed location. There would be plenty of activity, making and breaking camp, pitching tents, dining around a campfire and planning our forays into the local wilderness. In addition, I would be able to experience some of the local cultures that I'd previously only read about. This was just what my young, adventurous spirit demanded.

The safari followed the path of the Shire River in Malawi, through Liwonde National Park. The famous David Livingstone was one of the first white people to explore this wild and desolate place. He navigated the Shire River all the way to Lake Malawi, which he named the "Lake of Stars," seeing the brilliance of the stars reflected in the calm, clear water. We would be traversing these same riverbanks, which had some of the best locations for viewing wildlife such as crocs, hippos, buffalo, and elephants. Inland were elegant sable antelopes, kudu, and leopards. But Auntie Jan and I were there primarily for the birds. The park was known for some of the best birding in southern Africa.

I came prepared with my binoculars, bird guide, and sturdy shoes. Normally, I ran around barefoot as much as possible when I was at home in Cape Town. But here we would be hiking through flood plains, savannas, and woodlands. The banks of the Shire were teeming with birds big and small, bright and muted, timid and bold. It was like traveling through a giant aviary with no nets or walls.

I filled my dog-eared field guide with penciled annotations as I checked off species I had only dreamed of seeing. Like the Narina trogon, the cause of my current predicament. This bird was named after the Khoikhoi mistress of an eighteenth-century naturalist and explorer. François le Vaillant traveled extensively throughout Africa, collecting specimens and sending the preserved samples back to Europe. Since he was paid by the number of unique specimens he submitted, he sometimes assembled bits and pieces of different birds into new creations. He clearly needed the support and money to fund his seven years of exploring southern Africa.

He would later transcribe his adventures and illustrations into a famous book, *Travels from the Cape of Good Hope Into the Interior Parts of Africa, Including Many Interesting Anecdotes: With Elegant Plates, Descriptive of the Country and Inhabitants*. His interesting anecdotes and observations included not just detailed descriptions about the wildlife he encountered but many details about the natives he met. Including the captivating and flirty Narina, the beautiful Khoikhoi maiden who utterly charmed him. In her honor, the colorful Narina trogon is one of the few birds named after a black African.

Now a descendant of that enigmatic bird had worked its charms on me, luring me far from the safety of the safari camp.

Lost. Alone. No food. No water. No shelter. No weapon.

This is everyone's worst fear, but it's magnified a thousandfold in the African wilderness. Every year many, many people get lost in uncharted areas all over the world. A small percentage do not make it out alive. Except in Africa, where the threat of death is very real. A particularly grisly end awaits the wayward adventurer who becomes spatially disoriented in the massive patches of wilderness, facing an abundance of dangerous organisms. There are too many examples of lost African travelers who have had to be identified by little more than their saliva-encrusted wallets.

Nothing else is left because Africa has a most efficient recycling system. The large predators will bring you down, kill you, and take the lion's share of your edible parts. Then the scavengers will fight over the carcass, even digesting your teeth. If there are any bones left, the giraffes and other ungulates will chew on them for calcium and then drop them elsewhere, distributing your remnants over the terrain. The sun and the rain effectively erase all traces of you.

Traveling safely and staying alive in a potentially hostile environment is an art. Sir Francis Galton, a cousin of Charles Darwin, recognized this and in 1855 created the first of many editions of the definitive manual used by explorers in the Royal Geographic Society. *The Art of Travel; or Shifts and Contrivances Available in Wild Countries* combined knowledge from previous travelers and the native cultures. This handy, entertaining little manual, full of wisdom and advice on survival in strange places, would probably have been found in every early adventurer's backpack.

The practical recommendations from over a hundred fifty years ago still ring true today. The manual states quite clearly what to do when one realizes that one has become lost:

> In fine, if you have lost your way at all, do not make the matter doubly perplexing by wandering further; and be careful to ride in such places as to leave clear tracks behind you.

The Number One Rule is always to stay put. Yet few travelers do so.

I wasn't the first or wouldn't be the last person to become lost because of a bird. Take the disturbing example of Roy Baker, a dedicated participant of a central African birding tour. In 1999, Roy and an international group of fourteen birders traveled to Gabon, looking for a rare cave dweller, the enigmatic grey-necked rock-fowl. The two experienced guides divided the large party into a fast group and a slower group, proceeding up the forested path to the site. Roy initially went with the fast group but en route decided to slow his pace and wait to join the second group, only a few minutes behind. That was the last time anyone saw him. He was never found.

Had a bird called to him, beckoning him to wander off the path just a few steps? Then a few more steps? Search parties looked for weeks, turning up nothing but a towel that he wore around his neck, several miles from where he went missing. To this day, Roy remains lost in the African wilderness. No body, no bones, nothing. It's as if the forest just swallowed him up.

Sadly, the case of Roy Baker is not an isolated example of those who disappear into Africa's mysterious depths, but shows how one's demise can be rather complicated, at least for other people, when no trace of one is ever found. *The Art of Travel* further addresses the mental state of a lost person:

> A man who loses himself, especially in a desert, is sadly apt to find his presence of mind forsake him; the sense of desolation is so strange and overpowering; but he may console himself with the statistics of his chance, viz. that travelers, though constantly losing their party, have hardly ever been known to perish unrelieved.

With today's modern technologies, one would think that the dangers would be minimized, but that is, unfortunately, not entirely true. In a recent tragic case in northern Botswana, an elderly South African couple became lost in 2011 in Chobe National Park. John and Lorraine Bullen were enjoying a drive in the game reserve when their Land Rover ventured into a wilderness area and ended up stuck in thick sand. The couple tried to dig themselves out to no avail and spent the night in the vehicle. Not realizing how far off the path they had wandered, the bush-savvy John set out to look for help, armed with an axe, some provisions, water, and a GPS. His wife stayed put. What sense of desolation had they experienced, Lorraine waiting patiently in the vehicle, John back-tracking through the wilderness, anticipating rescue around every corner? Seven days later, Lorraine was found by other equally lost tourists traversing the same remote road. What happened to John? Even after a massive search, extending over thirty thousand miles, by experienced trackers and aircraft, no sign of John has ever been found. No axe, no water bottles, no GPS. Not even a saliva-encrusted wallet.

One aspect of these tragedies that is all too often unexplored is the psychology of being lost. What causes people to become lost? What can we learn from their experiences to ensure that similar tragedies are mitigated in the future? In *The Psychology of Lost*, Kenneth Hill identifies numerous strategies that people employ to deal with their predicament.

The most common strategy is random traveling, where the person chooses the path of least resistance with the intention of finding something familiar. In many cases, random traveling leads to the traveler becoming even more lost and wandering even farther from a point of familiarity. Most lost persons will stop after a while and employ one of the other more useful strategies like backtracking (carefully following one's signs to a familiar place) or view-enhancing (climbing an elevated object to gain a better perspective of the surroundings). Very few people employ the most useful strategy of all — staying put — until it is, in some cases, too late. Staying put is the single most effective strategy to employ when lost, as long as you are confident that people will come looking for you! This was expressed quite succinctly in *The Art of Travel*:

> Do not go on blundering hither and thither till you are exhausted, but make a comfortable bivouac, and start at daybreak fresh on your search.

Luckily for me, staying put is what eventually led to my being alive today. Although in my case, staying put was not a decision based on choice. It was a decision based on necessity.

I stop screaming for help and calm down completely. My mind becomes clear and I know I need to remove myself from any immediate danger. I now have a goal to focus on—finding a safe place to spend the night. Being out of earshot, my best course of action is to wait until morning and try to retrace my steps in the daylight.

My keen eyes select the tallest tree in the scrub, a mopane tree about twenty feet high, and I scramble up. It is easy to climb with its many forking branches. I don't know it at the time, but this tree is also a source of food. If I had been hungry enough, I could have eaten "mopane manna," the sticky-sweet waxy coating left by molting mopane worms. If I was starving, I could have survived by eating the worms themselves, caterpillars as large as my fingers that are roasted and dried for food but can also be eaten live.

While dinner in the wild is not yet on my mind, it is unquestionably on the minds of others in the area. I hear whooping, unearthly sounds, and the calls keep getting closer and closer. Hyenas. I have been in the bushveld long enough to recognize their distinctive vocal communications, unlike any sound in Africa.

I settle in for the night, planning to stay awake. If I am to be attacked and eaten, I don't want to be surprised. With their excellent night vision and sense of smell, I am an easy target for nocturnal predators. It is small comfort that lions are scarce in the area. A single hyena is unlikely to attack a human, even a child. But large groups of hyena are notoriously brazen and are always on the lookout for an easy meal. If the hyenas get me, there will be nothing left, as they consume every part of their prey with their massive crushing jaws. There will be no traces when the safari guides finally search me out. But hyenas do not typically climb trees, so I must stay alert and not fall out.

My imagination amplifies every noise in the forest. To keep it under control, I concentrate on the immediate environment. Minutely examining up close the coarse bark of the tree, noticing the evening dew as the temperature drops, smelling the sweet, musty grass. Even making a game of guessing the source of the mysterious bush sounds. I use all of my senses to keep my head clear. There will be no more panic attacks for me. I will pass the night waiting, watching, aware of every sight, sound, and smell around me.

What brought me here, all alone and anticipating an untimely, gruesome death? The craving for adventure runs through my veins and can be sparked by the slightest whiff of a scent, by a vision on the horizon or a casual remark that stirs past memories. Visceral memories that perhaps run deep into my ancestral heritage, spurring my curiosity and plunging me headlong into daring exploits. Sitting in the tree, I remind my young heart that I am made of stronger stuff, my blood infused with generations of bravery from my great-grandfather Oswald who hunted elephants in Ceylon, my grandfather Jozef who piloted fighter planes, and my dad who was always off on some new venture.

I climb higher up in the tree, resolving to pass the night alert, awake and waiting patiently for whatever comes. Will it be predator or rescue? I am keenly aware how quickly life can be snuffed out, having so recently witnessed the brutality of that black eagle snatching a helpless dassie on Table Mountain. I become strangely at peace with my fate, both as participant and observer in the chain of life.

I remember reading about the explorer David Livingstone's experience in the grip of a predator. In his case, it was "under the paw of the lion." When asked his thoughts as he was being shaken like a mouse, he replied:

> I was thinking what part of me he would eat first. The shock produced a stupor similar to that which seems to be felt by a mouse after the first grip of the cat. It caused a sort of dreaminess, in which there was no

pain nor feeling of terror, though I was quite conscious of all that was happening.

It is comforting to know that nature provides a natural anesthetic, a dreamy state of shock, when one is being carried about like a rag doll about to have its innards gutted and consumed.

I settle in, anticipating an uncomfortable night in my treetop dwelling. "The forest is a poor man's jacket," the Swedes say. As the sun descends, I feel the first hint of the coolness to come. My rugged shoes, shirt, and shorts are perfect for the heat of the day but surely not enough to provide any warmth against the chill of the African night. I hug the tree closer, nestling near the trunk, wrapping the butterfly-shaped leaves from an adjacent branch around me.

Dusk descends, and it is that time of day when the eerie light and creeping shadows play tricks with your eyes, when everything blends into night, all the sharp edges now merging so it is difficult to tell what is solid and what is shadow. The sounds of an African night strain the imagination, filled with invisible scurrying, cracklings, rustlings, squeaks, and cries.

The hideous yelps of a large group of hyenas are coming closer. These calls are different to the eerie whooping contact calls that I had heard earlier. As if something has brought the hyenas together and stirred them up into an excited frenzy. The sounds are terrifying. I need no better reminder that sleep is a likely death sentence out here.

Instead, I focus on the cramps in my legs, constantly shifting position to ease the pain and stiffness. I again pass the time by playing my bush sounds game.

Good-Lord-deliver-us!

A fiery-necked nightjar whistles its recognizable song and I think how apt its calling is right now.

Whaaaa, whaaaa, whaaa!

The nightjar's song is interrupted by the wailing of a thicktailed bushbaby, its call strangely reminiscent of the crying of a human baby.

Gwok, gwok, gwonk!

Loud pig-like grunting from somewhere close by startles me. Then I remember the call of the giant eagle owl. Something has alarmed it.

I strain my eyes in what's left of the light. A large, loping creature emerges from behind a small mopane tree. Its nose to the ground, it is following a scent trail. My limited knowledge of the African bush screams to me that this is not a good sign and I shout at the animal to get away. Startled, the animal melts back into the darkness. I am relieved, until I hear a cacophony of whoops and eerie shrieks.

Several minutes later, the skulking animal reappears, with another following close behind. And another. Hyenas. Nature's cleverest hunters. Opportunists who are quick to discriminate between the healthy, the sick, the weak, the young and the old. A good tracker can discern the state of an animal by the tracks it leaves behind. Its age, sex, health, mental state. Whether it's injured or lost or frightened. Did my tracks betray me? Do the hyenas sense that I am vulnerable, an easy target?

The prowling animals stick to the edge of my vision range, appearing and disappearing like ghostly hunchbacks. I know that they struggle to climb trees but I'm worried that their sounds might attract some carnivores that can. After what seems like ages, they apparently decide that a boy clinging to a tree is not worth their attentions anymore. As they slink away to seek out easier victims, their eerie calls growing quieter and more distant.

In the renewed tranquility of the evening, my fear-induced fine hearing picks up soft footsteps approaching. Now the bush is neutral, so these could be the steps of friend or foe. I peer through the branches to see what is making a beeline for my tree.

Who is following my tracks now? The cadence of the footsteps seems familiar, almost human. Imagine my relief when I see my rescue party emerge in the form of a local Malawian. I cry out to him for help, but he already seems to know I am up in the tree, his expert tracking skills leading him directly to my perch.

He uses the universal language of signs and motions me to come down from the tree and follow him back to the safety of camp. He speaks to me in his soft Chichewa tongue.

"Chakudza sichiimba ng'oma."

What comes doesn't beat a drum.

Or, you can't always guard against unexpected events.

I was lucky that the Malawian tracker could read my tracks. I was less than a mile from camp and must have walked in circles, completely obliterating my initial trail. I had walked over my tracks so many times.

I wanted to thank my newfound Malawian friend, but he was busy chattering to the other local people in camp. I wished I understood what he was saying, as he was obviously relating his story of my rescue. The Malawians, like almost all Africans, have a tradition of oral storytelling. I was curious to know how he could create an animated story out of liberating me from a tree. Maybe in his version of the story, he fiercely chased away the lurking hyenas. I will never know.

Birding was supposed to be a safe activity. How much trouble could you get into with a pair of binoculars? This would be the first of many life-threatening experiences on my endless journey to see birds. I would be constantly pushing the limits of physical endurance and health, and even straining the personal relationships that meant the most to me. Auntie Jan and the safari team would not be the last people to worry about me. My obsession with birds and wildlife would take me to extraordinary places, each adventure unique and rewarding, each adventure a safari into the unknown.

RANGERS, RIFLES, AND WRATH

We must not retreat from the blue horizon
But leap beyond into the curvature of the earth
Touching the doors of a hidden paradise.
This is where the mind must rest,
Close to the flower.
MAZISI KUNENE,
"After the Crossing"

Ofun' ukuhlakanipha wakh' eceleni kweqili.
He who wants wisdom lives near a cunning person.
ZULU PROVERB

THE RIFLE GOES OFF ACCIDENTALLY. It is a lucky break no one is injured or killed. Accidentally discharging a rifle is akin to the most heinous of crimes. The worst thing that can ever happen. Poor bugger, I will never forget it.

Archer lays into this guy for hours. Insults. Pushups. Lectures. Just hectic. One brief moment of negligence results in endless agony for the unlucky trainee. But it is moments like this that determine your future, because handling a rifle is all about self-control, discipline, cool detachment. An accident could endanger you and all those around you. Could unnecessarily cost a life.

The last few days, Archer drilled us extensively in proper firing techniques and rifle safety. Now Archer is enraged and showing his full fury. The rest of us watch as he harangues and pushes the unfortunate guy to the limits of his endurance. Needless to say, he drops out. Just one of many who don't make it through the course.

Ed Archer is not especially well built or tall, and yet he is the most intimidating badass I have ever met. The *skinder* around camp is that Archer is a former member of the French Foreign Legion which has always had a reputation for creating soldiers who are despised and feared, surrounded by an aura of glamour and mystery. A crazy character, Archer is responsible for teaching us the importance of rifles but yet he runs unarmed in the reserve everyday. Except for the Maasai spear, which he carries like a warrior.

At twenty-five, I am following my lifelong dream of becoming a game ranger at the prestigious Inkwazi Ranger Training School. Applicants are selected from hundreds of resumes, which are further whittled down through personal interviews until a core of twenty-odd applicants remain. Of these, only a few survive the program itself, the most stringent ranger training on the continent.

I had just witnessed yet another trainee quitting, hopes and ambitions dashed. I am more determined than ever to achieve my goal, to become one of the elite.

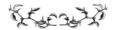

&Beyond, then called CCAfrica, is one of the largest private wildlife tourism companies in the world. No other safari company in Africa has as stringent a ranger training course, recognizing that the success of their luxury lodges hinges almost entirely on the quality of its rangers. Hence, they seek to employ only the very best.

The intensive six-week selection course is a way to determine how badly you want to be a ranger, to push so hard that people drop off along the way. If you are lucky enough to pass, you are then assigned to a specific reserve, working at one of the forty lodges across Africa.

And that's just the beginning. At your selected lodge, you go through up to six months of additional training before you are allowed to drive paying safari guests. But it is the initial six-week selection course that is by far the most arduous part of the learning experience.

I arrived with about twenty others, full of energy and high expectations. While we were a disparate group in terms of backgrounds and physical capabilities, we all shared a deep love and enthusiasm for wildlife. Looking at my companions, it was impossible to predict who would succeed. Some came from big cities like Cape Town and Durban, and this was their first experience in the bush. Some were experienced hunters or zoology graduates. Some wanted the glamour and prestige that came with the title "game ranger." Still others viewed this experience as a challenge to see how tough they were and whether they would make it to the end. And then there was me.

My own path to Inkwazi was a circuitous one. A rebellious youth, I somehow managed to graduate from the University of Cape Town in spite of my days spent surfing at the beach and my

nights partying with my equally wild mates. After graduation, I had a potentially lucrative career mapped out for me in the tropical fish business, importing and supplying fish to aquariums throughout South Africa. Doug, the owner, planned for me to take more control of the day-to-day operations, and I had recently started managing the business.

But I wasn't ready to settle down yet. Something was missing in my life; something was calling me to pursue my dream of becoming a game ranger. I applied to the program and was ecstatic to learn I had been accepted. I remember the day I told Doug I would not be available to carry on and how disappointed he was with my decision to leave.

One day after I had given my notice, Doug left work to play squash, as he often did. He suffered a heart attack and died right there on the squash court at the Kelvin Grove Club. When I later inquired where Doug was, my coworker, Peter, told me matter-of-factly that "the *baas* was now playing squash in heaven."

This was the trigger that reassured me that my decision was the right one. I wanted to pursue my own heaven in Africa's wilderness areas before I got caught up in the rat race of city life. Doug had been somewhat of a father figure to me, and his death emphasized to me how quickly life can be snuffed out.

The word *inkwazi*, which translates to "fish eagle" in Zulu, comes from the same root as the Zulu word *ulwazi* (knowledge). Although the camp name was probably a reference to the iconic fish eagle, whose call could often be heard from the training camp's lofty location overlooking the Mzinene River floodplain, it also represented the place where we would gain the knowledge and expertise for our futures in the African wilderness. It was here at Inkwazi that we would learn the necessary safety, wildlife, and communication skills necessary to guide guests on safari at some of Africa's most prestigious game reserves. Paying guests expected to view wildlife in a luxurious and safe setting, so it was paramount that rangers subscribed to the highest safety standards while catering to their sometimes difficult demands.

Just as each game drive is different and presents unique situations and sometimes unforeseen dangers, each day of the course was designed to throw unanticipated challenges at us. It was our reaction to each situation that would determine whether we would cave in to the pressure or survive another day on the course.

I was looking forward to the upcoming trials at Inkwazi and had a list of experiences under my belt I believed would serve me well on the selection course. I had traveled extensively on a shoe-string budget through sub-Saharan Africa, through Malawi, Mozambique, and Madagascar, where I was forced to think on my feet—whether it was negotiating with a corrupt police officer, finding my way out of a forest, or living off the land when my money ran low. Spending time alone in the bush, learning from the locals, surviving malaria and various tropical illnesses, learning self-sufficiency in primitive environments—these were all experiences that both developed and reinforced my independent streak.

Yes, I thought I was prepared for the stringent regimen that lay before me, and I believed I could handle anything they threw my way.

That first day, I entered the gates of the Phinda Private Game Reserve with one of my fellow trainees, a nice blond girl called Sam. We met up before the course in Cape Town and decided to car-pool to Phinda, a distance of about twelve hundred miles. We drove for two days, all the way from South Africa's southern tip to the far northeastern corner, close to the border of Mozambique. Now we were winding our way through the reserve on a dirt road, following the signs to Mountain Lodge.

We passed zebras, nyalas, warthogs—almost within reach—and caught glimpses of giraffes, wildebeests, and white rhinos through the acacia trees. I was completely mesmerized; the bountiful wildlife could be seen in all directions. At every turn, I wanted to stop and pull out my binoculars, drink in all the sights and sounds. But we were already behind schedule, so we continued straight to our meeting point at Mountain Lodge, where I parked my bakkie for the duration of the course. Observing wildlife would have to wait.

After a quick briefing from our instructors, the group was told to board several Land Rovers. We drove through the reserve, finally scaling a hill and entering the camp that would be our humble abode for the next six weeks. That is ... if we even lasted that long. Most of us had heard stories about how challenging the course was, although there were precious few details. Graduates of this selection course were sworn to secrecy about the grueling details.

The Inkwazi training camp consisted of a minimal set of buildings for classwork and lectures. There was a small mess kitchen, where we would prepare our own meals and do laundry, and simple outhouses. We were provided only the most basic of accommodations: tents pitched on concrete platforms. I would be sharing one of these army-style tents with Brandon, a thickset blond farmer from the lowveld, an area around the world-famous Kruger National Park.

On that first day at Inkwazi, I remember how my eyes were instantly drawn to the breathtaking view.

Perched on a high ridge, the camp overlooked the vast floodplains where big game — lion, elephant, wildebeest, rhino, and leopard — was known to roam. Cheetahs came to the riverbed thickets to give birth, and black-chested snake eagles soared over the fever trees. This idyllic setting, this place of rebirth and highflying hopes, was where game rangers were born.

The instructors were barking orders, abruptly shaking me from my daydreams. The group was directed to immediately drop all our gear and pile back into the Land Rovers. We sat there in silence as they drove for miles, giving us no hint of where we were headed. They eventually dropped us off in the middle of the bush with one of the instructors, a young guy called Brad.

"Stay here. Under *no* circumstances are you allowed to leave," the senior mentors said before they sped off in the vehicles.

We all looked to Brad for guidance, but he was strangely silent, giving no indication or explanation. He refused to answer our pesky questions and propped himself up against a tree trunk, rifle across his lap, radio silent. He closed his eyes and tuned out our chatter.

I surveyed our surroundings. We were in the middle of a drainage line, which was basically a dry riverbed that only runs when extreme rainfall occurs. Tall ficus trees lined the crude banks, and the riverbed was part rocky, part sandy. I remembered learning that these riverbeds are like mini-highways for leopards, providing these secretive cats with unhindered access to hunting grounds while the thick vegetation and the drainage-line walls kept them mostly hidden from view. My favorite of the big cats, I longed to see one of the majestic creatures up close. But not quite yet!

As dark descended, we made small talk and joked about our situation. We were waiting to be picked up at any moment. Maybe the other instructors were having mechanical problems with the vehicles. Or maybe they were sitting up on the ridge, having a good laugh and watching to see if we panicked. As dusk turned to dark, our lighthearted banter became subdued and our thoughts turned worrisome, as it appeared we had a long night ahead of us. Brad's mute presence was not terribly reassuring; he appeared to be quite comfortable tucked under one of the many sycamore fig trees lining the drainage line. He was calm, oblivious to our needs and concerns, obviously waiting for … waiting for what? Or maybe we were just being paranoid.

It's times like this—when people are taken out of their comfort zones—that true personalities come to the fore. Times like this when leaders become leaders and when pessimists reveal their hidden negativity. Some were quiet. Others seemed nervous, having been thrust into the middle of the bush, so different from their comfy city environment.

The long night served its purpose, and the next morning three people dropped out and went home. Just packed up and left. The course was deliberately designed to be a psychological mind-fuck. To stretch us mentally, physically, and emotionally. Constantly breaking us down to see how badly we wanted to be a ranger. Testing our resiliency to contend with the unexpected.

Graham Vercuiel managed the course. Graham was well respected within the company. Soft-spoken and patient, he was an excellent mentor who excelled in teaching us the delicate art of storytelling. The objective of the selection course from a knowledge perspective was twofold.

Firstly, we had to become botanists, zoologists, ornithologists, herpetologists, astronomers, geologists, entomologists. We spent hours studying the correct identification of all things living and soaking up facts pertaining to the wildernesses of Africa.

And secondly, we had to learn how to tell stories. For even if you are armed with all the natural knowledge in the world, this knowledge falls flat if you fail to impart it with a passion for story-telling. Guests don't want facts spewed out to them; they respond much better to interpretive guiding. Stories woven around what an animal is doing and why are far more effective than facts and figures. A good ranger pulls back the invisible shroud that surrounds the African bush and reveals the magic of nature to the guests under his or her care. Picture the scenario below and contrast the two different styles of delivery.

Two rangers are taking their guests on a game drive. They both notice a herd of antelope standing nervously in an open area, snorting and staring in a single direction.

Delivery One The ranger drives up to the animals and keeps his engine running. He's not planning to be there long. He starts talking, and the guests look at the back of his head, struggling to hear what he's saying.

"Those antelope are called impala. They weigh up to one hundred thirty pounds. Only the males have horns. Lion, leopard, cheetah, and sometimes crocodile and even python prey upon them. They are very fast and can run at speeds of up to forty-five miles per hour. They live for up to twelve years. That snorting that you are hearing is normally given when they spot a predator."

The ranger then drives off to find more interesting animals to show his guests. The information he has given his guests is factual. But is there anything here that a guest cannot find in a book? This ranger has briefly touched on the behavior of the animals and imparted that knowledge, almost in passing, right at the end of his delivery.

Delivery Two The ranger sees the impalas, turns off the engine and rotates to face her guests in the open vehicle. She sits high on the steering wheel, commanding their full attention with her authoritative yet friendly voice.

"Close your eyes. Do you hear that sound? That snorting is the sound impala make when they spot or sense a predator close by. A herd member that senses something uses these snorts to warn the rest of the herd. If we just sit here and wait patiently, we may possibly see the techniques that impala use to foil predators.

"First of all, look at their eyes. Look how large their eyes are. They have excellent vision and are able to detect the slightest movement from a great distance. And the advantages of living in a herd are evident because many pairs of keen eyes are better than one pair of excellent eyes.

"Smell the air. What do you smell? Perhaps grass and a general bush smell? Now look at the impala nostrils twitching. They smell something we cannot. You can sometimes see the nostrils opening wide as they almost taste the air. Their sense of smell is as good as their eyesight.

"Feel how this wind is swirling around us. Swirling winds make impala nervous, because they make it harder to isolate where a smell is coming from. And take note of the large ears. You can see how they all have adjusted their ears almost parabolically to zone in on where they think the danger is coming from. Notice how all the impala heads are pointed in the same direction. A collective force of superior senses."

She pauses to let the guests take in this information.

"This herd looks ready to bolt, and if they do you might bear witness to their next level of defense adaptations. Can you all see those black patches on the ankles close to the hooves? Those are scent glands.

"When the impala flee as a group they will spring over thirty feet in a single bound, often jumping over one another in an attempt to confuse the predator. They can also jump over ten feet straight up, and this gives them a great advantage over a chasing predator because they do not have to run around obstacles—they simply leap straight over them.

"Now this is where those scent glands come in. An impala's survival depends upon the herd. During a chase, it is vital for the herd to stay together. They accomplish this in thick bush by clicking their heels together when they jump, releasing puffs of scent from those black scent glands. This ensures that nobody gets lost and becomes an easy, confused target."

She pauses in anticipation that the herd is about to flee.

"There they go!"

And the herd proceeds to do all that the ranger has just told!

This ranger uses storytelling, her knowledge of animal behavior, patience, and anticipation to reveal how incredibly adapted certain animals are to living in the bush. She only relays facts if they are relevant to what is happening or about to happen (leaping thirty-three feet, etc.). And, perhaps most important, she anticipates the animal behavior and shows patience in clearly wrapping up her story and making her guests part of the discovery. They have witnessed all of this with their own senses. They have seen the scent glands, they have heard the impala snorting, they have felt the breeze, and they have smelt the air.

Graham taught us how to use the magic of storytelling to great effect. And he would work through scenarios like the above time and time again to demonstrate how to become effective interpreters of nature.

Working under Graham were specialty instructors who trained us in the various disciplines required to ensure guest safety and increase our knowledge of the African bush and its wildlife. First aid. Off-road driving. Vehicle maintenance. Hospitality training. How to set up a bush breakfast. How to delight guests. And just like a military boot camp, survival, endurance, and rifle training were an integral part of the course.

Some days just never seemed to end. Especially one day in particular. The day we literally walked until we dropped, carrying heavy sand bags. I remember the painful blisters on my feet, the extreme thirst, the severe cramps. But I kept walking. They didn't need to eliminate people after this walk; trainees just quit on their own, thinking they weren't good enough.

But actually, the trainers didn't want to see if you were the last person standing. It was a test to see if you could push yourself to the limit of your capabilities. It didn't matter if you walked six miles or the nearly twenty miles that I actually walked that day. They were watching to see how far you would go, how badly you wanted to be a ranger. So that was how they messed with your mind, and the results were effective. &Beyond has long been recognized as having the best game rangers in Africa.

It was essential to learn as much as possible about nature, wildlife, ecology, conservation, and birds. After an exhausting day of doing various tasks and tests in the bush, we were told to study our books because there would be an examination the next morning. Sleep deprivation was definitely an aspect of the training, and after becoming a ranger, I was able to see why this was important. The job required working long, continuous hours, seven days a week, six to eight weeks at a time, with only five or six hours of sleep a night.

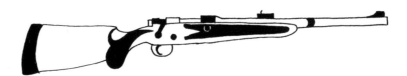

But by far, Ed Archer's weeklong rifle training was the most stressful aspect of the course. We learned how to shoot .375 Holland & Holland Magnum rifles. Designed to bring down elephants and other big game, they can quite easily break your shoulder or collarbone if used incorrectly.

I remember clearly the day that Sam, my companion on the way up to Phinda, first fired a rifle. She was a small girl, maybe one hundred pounds soaking wet. But she also had character, grit, and determination. And she was not going to be outmachoed by any of the guys.

We spent hours at the shooting range in an old disused quarry in the south of the reserve, where the targets were affixed to cardboard boxes some sixty-five feet away. Lined up in rows of four with rifles and ammunition, we learned the safety drills, how to hold and aim, how to chamber a round, and how to use the safety catch.

And now, we would finally have a chance to display our newly learned shooting skills. Or lack thereof. I was standing next to Sam when she squeezed the trigger for the first time. Having never shot a high-caliber rifle myself, I was stunned by what I saw. She squeezed the trigger and the kick sent her hurtling backward, flat on her back. I remember helping her to her feet and seeing her stunned expression.

Nothing can quite prepare you for the recoil of a .375 or .458-Magnum rifle, the rifles used in game reserves across Africa. I was next. I stood with my feet apart, one foot slightly in front of the other. I mentally went through all I had learned and leaned forward a bit to absorb the shock. When I pulled the trigger, the rifle butt jammed into the flesh of my shoulder, and I felt it hit bone. I had failed to lodge the rifle butt securely enough to absorb the impact. My shoulder ached and my ears rang as a puff of blue smoke started to clear. I had not only missed the target but the entire box.

Suddenly I felt a strong arm on my shoulder, and the rifle was ripped out of my arms. Archer had witnessed my errant shot. I think he had been shouting at me but I was half deaf from the rifle blast. He screamed in my face and told me to do fifty push-ups in the dirt. The pain surged through my right shoulder as I attempted the push-ups. Sam was sitting to one side; her eyes welled up with tears. We still had a lot to learn about rifles and shooting.

Archer was constantly giving everyone a hard time and wouldn't let us relax. He strongly believed that a relaxed approach was the catalyst for rifle accidents, and he had zero tolerance for rifle accidents. Archer took his job seriously, filtering out and discriminating among the rookies. Like a Marine drill sergeant, he employed ruthless methods to shape characters into honed fighting machines.

Archer was so in your face, so hectic. One day, to make a point in front of us and his fellow instructors, he took a Bible and threw it down in front of Graham.

"And if you believe all the shit they put in this book ..." he ranted. On and on.

Graham was a devout Christian yet he did not show one bit of shock. Although he was probably deeply offended, his expression was unreadable, and I learnt later that he and Archer were actually good friends. Graham's stoic personality set an example for us all, showing his mental, physical and emotional resilience.

Archer always knew how to shock for maximum effectiveness. He was an expert at breaking you down in public, calling you names.

"You lazy animal!" he screamed at Stephen, a particularly large guy who was scrambling through the makeshift obstacle course of desks and tables.

"You're sweating like a stuck pig!" Archer yelled. "What's your fucking problem? Hold that rifle higher or you're going to fall on your fat fucking face."

Which is exactly what Stephen did, and he was chucked out of the course like a stale Nuttikrust.

For many of the participants, it wasn't the grueling nature of the training that wore you down but the insults thrown at you by Archer. He had the remarkable ability to spot your innermost insecurities and secrets, and throw them back in your face in the middle of your peers. So that when the day was done, you felt as if you'd been horribly violated in some way.

Archer was thin and wiry, with jet-black hair. Smallish eyes. Chiseled, hard, pointed facial features. He would pace like a cat in a cage, saying nothing for minutes. Just pace and watch us. We weren't allowed to look down. We had to look at him. He would wait until people started to become uncomfortable with his pacing and watching. Because the moment you shifted and started sweating, he would pounce and lay into you with verbal insults. He tried to push you off balance and keep you there, weeding out all but the most resilient.

So it was no surprise that the majority of students dropped out under Archer's shrewd tutelage. His job was to drive home the responsibility of handling a rifle and create the muscle memory needed to react quickly in case of danger. I can tell you that, even today, after not handling a rifle for several years, every single word he said is ingrained in me. I can pick up a rifle and use it today. His teaching tactics, although bordering on sadistic, were very effective, and he helped create a band of rangers who knew how to take their jobs seriously.

My time at Inkwazi until now had been harrowing, tiring and inspiring all at the same time. I was one of a select few to make it through the rifle training. I breathed a sigh of relief and felt that nothing could stop me now. I had seen the vision of my future, the life of a game ranger, the chance to be close to the wildlife I loved.

But I was to learn that just living at Inkwazi had its dangers. The bush has its own way of weeding out the vulnerable and unwary. There were far more dangerous creatures than Archer to contend with. When I least expected it, I had a close encounter of the scaly kind.

I have to use the outhouse. It's a number two, so I grab a magazine from the pile. The outhouses are shoulder height, made of *latte*, sticks or reeds placed close together, with gauze up to the ceiling for ventilation. The reading material distracts me from the sounds of the buzzing flies, heat and humidity. As I put down the glossy to make my exit, I am shocked to see an exceptionally large snake coiled up between my feet.

I immediately freeze, as I know enough from my many escapades in southern Africa to recognize a puff adder when I see one, a snake responsible for more snakebites in the region than any other. Puff adders are cryptically colored, and many people are bitten when they step too close to, or on, a camouflaged snake.

I am entirely naked, and there is no way I can pick up my pants for fear of disturbing the snake. Bad-tempered and excitable, puff adders are not shy to strike when cornered. It is well over one hundred degrees in here. The smell of the septic tank merges with the heat and hangs heavy around me. I watch transfixed as the droplets of sweat fall from my brow and land drip, drop on the sluggish snake, coiled just a few inches from my bare feet. I don't know whether to move back and stop the dripping on the snake. Or whether my moving backward will cause him to strike with his front-hinged fangs that unfold like a switchblade.

I am just sitting. Undignified. Hot and paralyzed. Drip. Drop. I am defenseless, vulnerable. I hear the other rangers milling around. Eventually, one of them comes close enough and I risk a hoarse whisper.

"Hey! Brandon. Is that you? Come here!"

My tent mate and I have become good friends over the past few weeks of the selection course. I've aroused his curiosity and he approaches the outhouse.

"Boet, there's a great big snake between my legs."

Through the latte, I can just make out that a couple of other rangers have joined him. One of them teases me.

"Stop bragging, Currie. That's wishful thinking."

For once, I regret being a bit of a joker. I can't get these guys to believe me. No matter how hard I try, all I get in response to my pleas for help are taunts.

"Pervert!"

"We're not checking out your poor excuse for a pecker!"

"Quit your boasting!"

And on and on. To my disgust, they all move off toward the canteen and I can hear their voices, along with the metallic clinking and clanking sounds that emanate from the kitchen.

In times of danger, I seldom panic. Panic is the worst enemy for someone in a crisis. I need a clear mind, keen senses, and the ability to problem-solve. I become captivated by the situation and detach myself from fear and irrational thought. I place myself outside, looking in as if I'm watching from a distance.

So I stare at the snake without emotion, just watching. It is coiled serenely, so close. Yet I feel so strangely removed from any sense of fear or foreboding. The adder is over a yard in length and as fat as my arm. Being larger than most, it is more apt to be lethargic and slower to strike. There are no immediate signs that it is preparing for an attack. Normally, when puff adders are seriously pissed off they fill their bodies with air and hiss, hence their descriptive name. Relying on camouflage to avoid detection, the brownish-yellow-ish color and V-shaped markings on this snake's back blend well into the floor of the outhouse, where it is probably lying in wait for small animals.

I remain motionless, suspended in a trancelike state. Wishing that an unsuspecting frog, lizard, or rodent would wander in and distract the snake.

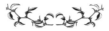

For some reason, snakes loved Inkwazi. This part of the world is home to some of the most dangerous snakes on earth. Mambas, forest cobras, puff adders, boomslangs, and the mfezi, or Mozambique spitting cobra.

We saw snakes on a near daily basis at Inkwazi, in the kitchen or an unzipped tent, everywhere. Perhaps it was because our remote human settlement had zero man-made pest controls. Or maybe they congregated here to feed on the rodents who were drawn to the smells and leftover morsels in the canteen. Or maybe it was the availability of water around the water tanks that attracted frogs and toads, favorite prey of many snake species. Whatever the reason, we shared Inkwazi with a healthy population of slithering serpents.

Mfezis, the feared spitting cobras, were probably the most common. These snakes are responsible for a significant number of snakebites in northern KwaZulu-Natal. And even though they don't have lips or tongues, they are capable of "spitting" venom through a highly evolved mechanism, spraying an accurate stream through a specialized hole in their fang in self-defense. Normally shy and reclusive, they will sometimes enter buildings in search of prey or water. And they are renowned for slithering into warm beds at night.

Which is why one day my friend and fellow ranger Andy was called to coerce a mfezi out of the staff accommodations at Mountain Lodge. Andy was accomplished at handling all types of venomous snakes, but when he entered the building to evaluate the situation, he found he was no match for the instinctive reaction of the cornered snake. As he approached the mfezi, he took a direct hit in his eyes even though he was a fair distance away.

The spitting cobra has the ability to immobilize by directing a stream of venom at the eyes of their victims from up to eight feet away. These volatile and highly-strung snakes are notorious for their extreme accuracy when spitting venom. Expert performers, they will rear two-thirds of their bodies up before directing a seemingly inexhaustible stream of muscle-destroying, cytotoxic venom toward the intruder's eyes. The pain is immediate and excruciating.

Andy was fortunate to be close to supplies and provisions, but even though he washed his eyes out thoroughly with milk and had subsequent treatment, he nearly lost his sight. For weeks his eyes dripped yellow pus and he was in much pain.

My friend Johnny Raw, who managed one of Phinda's lodges, had an even more horrifying brush with a spitting cobra in the dead of night at his home. Johnny had the misfortune of getting into bed with a particularly large specimen. He thought it was a rat biting him multiple times in the chest. I can only imagine his shock when he turned on the light and discovered a fuming spitting cobra. John calmly walked next door for help. Fortunately, his neighbor was Les Carlisle, the group conservation manager at &Beyond. Les lost no time in catching and killing the snake in order to identify it. John knew that he did not have much time, as a bite can be fatal in about ninety minutes. There was a frantic ride to the airstrip, with John nauseous and starting to vomit, then a forty-minute flight to Richards Bay for emergency treatment. Luckily, he lived to tell the tale, but it was a close and harrowing escape.

Forest cobras, another member of the cobra family, are also commonly found at Phinda. These are the largest of all the true co-bra species on earth, reaching up to ten feet in length. King cobras grow much larger, but they are not true cobras (Genus *naja*). For-est cobra venom is highly neurotoxic, shutting down the victim's central nervous system. Ultimately, the nerves that control breath-ing become paralyzed, and death is caused by respiratory failure, sometimes in under an hour. Forest cobras also produce one of the highest venom yields of all the cobra species—enough to kill mul-tiple humans in a single bite. And once driven to bite, they have the nasty habit of refusing to let go. These are the pit bulls of the snake world, and some people have had to sever the head from the body to get the snake to release them. This added fang-time ensures that they release substantial amounts of extremely toxic venom into their victims. Thankfully, few people are bitten by forest cobras, due to their propensity for living in thick forests, away from typical human habitation.

One of the most beautiful and agile of all of Africa's snakes is the boomslang, but its beguiling beauty hides a sinister side. For these snakes possess one of the most dangerous venoms known to man. Unlike cobras that have neurotoxic venom and spitting cobras that have cytotoxic venom, the boomslang has potent hemotoxic venom. This venom affects the body's natural clotting mechanism, resulting in internal bleeding of the organs. It is relatively slow acting, leading many victims to believe that the bite is not serious. Symptoms can take up to twenty-four hours to manifest, but by then it is often too late, resulting in the victim bleeding to death. It's a horrible way to die, oozing blood from the nose and mouth.

Amazingly, in the early 1900s, boomslangs were sometimes sold as docile pets. They are timid snakes, reluctant to bite. Most fatalities occur from handling the snakes unnecessarily, as famed herpetologist Karl Schmidt found out. On a fateful day in 1957, Dr. Schmidt was working in his lab at the Field Museum in Chicago when he was sent an unknown snake by the Lincoln Park Zoo for identification. During handling, he was bitten on the left thumb by only one of the snake's rear fangs. He correctly identified the snake as a juvenile boomslang but due to the snake's small size, coupled with the fact that only one fang had penetrated the skin, he thought he would be fine.

Boomslangs had only recently been found to be venomous and no antivenin was known. Dr. Schmidt famously recorded all his symptoms in his diary until he died twenty-eight hours later from brain hemorrhages.

Dr. Schmidt's unfortunate demise had serious consequences in the spy world in the 1960s. Due to the boomslang venom's imperceptible and fatal properties, international spy organizations, including the CIA, used the poison as a deadly assassination tool. Dimethyl sulfoxide, a transdermal agent, was mixed with the venom to allow the toxin to penetrate the skin unknowingly and with disastrous consequences. Slow acting, difficult to detect and hard to trace, it was the perfect murder weapon.

I saw several boomslangs while at Phinda, identifiable by their short heads and large eyes, but they were always high up in a tree. A snake with similar hemotoxic venom, the southern vine snake, is more common. This exceptionally thin snake is a fast and elegant climber. It will hang motionless for hours from a branch, relying on its camouflage to hide from predators while waiting for its next meal, disguised as a vine swaying in the wind.

Although I never personally came across either species, two types of mambas, green and black, can occur at Phinda. Green mambas are the less dangerous of the two species due to their more docile nature, less virulent venom, and lower venom load. But that does not mean that they are to be trifled with. On the contrary, green mambas, like their black counterparts, possess a mixture of highly potent neurotoxin and a unique cardiotoxin. The cardiotoxin causes damage to the heart muscles, resulting in slower heartbeats or complete cardio failure. And, if that is not enough, the potent neurotoxin shuts down the central nervous system and causes respiratory failure. A double whammy.

Black mambas do not mess around and are commonly believed to be the most dangerous snakes on the planet. Large, highly strung, and inclined to bite. Fast, aggressive and fatal. You know you're in trouble if you see a snake with a coffin-shaped head and jet-black mouth, the perfect delivery system for the "kiss of death." Very, very few people survive a bite. Sometimes the victim does not even realize that he or she has been bitten, as the bite is quick and not necessarily painful. But in that brief encounter, the snake is quite capable of injecting enough venom to kill more than ten men. Without antivenin, their envenomated bites are one hundred percent fatal, and even with antivenin, chances of survival are roughly fifty percent. Their neuro- and cardiotoxic venom is so potent that even a tiny bite or scratch from those short fangs can result in death.

But of all the venomous snakes in Africa, none causes more death and injury than the infamous puff adder. This is not because they have more toxic venom than mambas, cobras, or boomslangs. On the contrary, the venom is much less dangerous if treated early. They are also not the largest nor the fastest snakes. The problem with puffies is that they are common across much of rural Africa. Their paths often intersect with humans as they seek out their next meal. They wait in ambush on footpaths, near water sources and, today, in an outhouse.

I'm sitting in the steamy outhouse for an eternity when one of the guys finally realizes that I haven't been around for a while and that I am still in the toilet. Now, I don't care about being seen naked or undignified. I just want out. Brandon comes over and looks down through the gauze. He sees the snake.

"Fuck me! That's a *moerse* big puffie! I thought you were joking. We gotta get you out of there, *bru!*"

Hallelujah!

Brandon immediately recognizes the danger: an adder once bit him. Not a puff adder but a relative, the night adder. Although less toxic than its larger cousin, Brandon spent a long time in the hospital, and he has a finger that still doesn't work properly and bears the scars of necrosis. Puff adders have cytotoxic venom that destroys muscle tissue rapidly. Although there are few fatalities if the bite is quickly and suitably treated, many people lose entire limbs as a result of the poison. A bite from a large puff adder like this could result in the loss of my leg.

The majority of puff adder bites occur in the dark, and the victim never sees the snake. The bite is so quick that they might feel a momentary twinge, like a twig snapping on their calf. It's not until the limb swells and discolors, within a few hours, that the victim realizes they have been injured. This happens quite often to young Zulu boys who farm or tend the livestock or walk barefoot to ceremonies where they continue to dance after they have been bitten. This activity only serves to hasten the spread of the toxic venom throughout their system. They may first seek treatment from their local traditional healer. When they finally get conventional medical treatment, it's usually too late to save the leg.

If I am the victim of a snakebite, at least I am able to identify the species. I will be able to get the correct treatment, even though the closest hospital with critical care facilities is over sixty miles away. And I am not alone. Others join Brandon when they hear of my plight.

"You're in for a bit of a wait, *boetie,*" Brandon says.

"I've already had my wait, you freak! Can't believe you *okes* just left me here with a meter of leg-rotting toxin! My legs are cramping. Do something!"

Now I am caught in a terrible quandary between not being able to move and having a dozen or so rangers and trainers discuss the complexities of getting a naked man away from a snake.

They all take turns peering down, looking through the latte. Making jokes, even though it is a very serious situation. I listen to their plans with trepidation as they all chime in with various schemes.

"Maybe we should pass him a panga," someone suggests.

The panga is the South African version of a machete, the ultimate utility tool. There is a reason every Zulu male is trained to use a panga and it can be found in every Zulu household. In the right hands, it is a very lethal weapon and has played a key role in many wars and uprisings. It can be used to kill and defend as well as put food on the table. With one carefully aimed swipe, it is possible to lop off the head of any snake. But even if I had a panga, I would need to raise it high enough for a strike and be deadly accurate. What if the snake detected my movement and struck before I was able to decapitate it? What if I accidentally missed and lopped off my foot?

"Keep thinking, guys," I retort loudly. By now, the volume of my exchange has escalated, as I remember that snakes cannot hear; they do not have external ears and sense mostly through vibrations rather than sound. I could probably have shouted at the top of my lungs without aggravating the serpentine coil between my legs.

Their next plan is just as crazy. They want to ease the door open and have a ranger grab each of my outstretched arms. They would just yank me off the toilet in my birthday suit.

"We're big strong dudes," they reassure me. "We'll haul you out of there before that lazy puffie even knows you're gone."

I blanch at the thought of flying through the air at the mercy of my well-intentioned comrades. The snake appears sluggish, but I know my mates are no match for the speed and accuracy of an angry adder. It has the ability to change direction in an instant, and could strike upwards and sideways in a flash. The thought of exposing my naked privates to those long fangs isn't worth the risk of a hasty rescue.

"I'll just wait it out," I say between gritted teeth. It is the only plan that makes sense. Snakes do not attack unless provoked, so I have no choice but to remain still as a stone.

"Right. You survived a week with Archer," they joke. "Should be a piece of cake spending a few hours with a puff adder."

So I continue to sit. Drip. Drop. The sweat falls. I tune out the voices of my companions and steel myself for a long wait. There is only me and a snake with a head shaped like the deadly ace of spades. No warmth in those inhuman, unblinking eyes. Which of us will make the first move?

Eventually the snake uncoils and leisurely slithers away. I watch as it heads back behind the toilet with slow, up-and-down caterpillar-like movements and out through a hole in the wall. As the tail disappears, I quickly pull up my pants and make a relieved, albeit somewhat undignified, exit.

Not all dangerous snakes in Africa are poisonous. The largest snake, the African rock python, has a particularly nasty disposition and is known for its strength, constricting its prey and squeezing the life out of it before swallowing it whole. My fellow ranger and good friend, Mike Karantonis, had the misfortune of socializing with the business end of an especially large specimen.

One balmy afternoon, Mike was driving a Landie full of guests along Main Zinave, the primary access road in the north of the reserve. Unlike most of the other roads, Main Zinave was straight as an arrow, surrounded on both sides by narrow corridors that were kept clear of encroaching trees. The resulting superior visibility and great condition of the road allowed us rangers to drive faster than normal for easy access to the more remote parts of the reserve.

Mike and his guests were enjoying the warm summer wind as it ruffled through the open vehicle, whilst Sipho Zwane sat on the tracker seat, ever alert and present in the moment. He had been Mike's tracking partner ever since the young ranger graduated from Inkwazi. Tall and lean, with clean-cut boyish good looks and a wide smile, Sipho was known to be temperamental. Any mistake from Mike - driving over fresh tracks, positioning the Land Rover too close to thorny acacia trees or getting stuck in mud – could result in a particularly silent and grumpy Sipho. But he was arguably the best tracker that Phinda had ever seen. Sipho began his career at Phinda in the game guard department and worked his way into the tracking team due to an uncanny and almost divine ability to follow tracks. His grandfather, uMakhohlomba, was a potent and well-regarded *sangoma* from the KwaJobe community. Many highly respected South African celebrities, sports stars and politicians travelled to the remote community to seek out the attentions of the old diviner. Legend has it that uMakhohlomba would ask his clientele to reimburse him by going down to the nearest river and throwing the money in the flowing water. People were too afraid of him to ignore his bizarre payment method and it was said that he always received the liquid money transfer. There were whispers that Sipho had inherited his grandfather's intuition and magic, especially when it came to locating wildlife.

A florid plume of dust followed the Landie as it hummed along Zinave. Sipho raised his hand and the vehicle came to a sudden halt. He turned and glared back at Mike, as Mike had stopped too quickly for Sipho's liking.

"*Wenzani wena!*" he reprimanded.

What are you doing!

And then very casually, "*Nants' inyoka …*"

There is a snake.

Mike strained to see what Sipho was pointing at, way down the straight gravel road. Sipho possessed fighter pilot vision and it was only when Mike looked down the road through his binoculars that he noticed a group of agitated baboons surrounding a longitudinal mass that stretched from one side of the road to the other. A massive African rock python, breathtakingly huge and intricately patterned. This was a snake that would enthrall even the most dedicated snake hater.

Mike had always been fond of herpetology and knew that an African rock python sighting was a rare occurrence. He also recognized that the aggressive attentions of the baboon troop could severely injure the snake. Baboons have the longest canines of any African mammal – longer than lion fangs – and the dominant male baboons were giving the snake their full attention. As Mike watched through his binoculars, he noticed a male baboon pounding the snake with its hands. He knew that he was not supposed to interfere with nature but the snake was lying across one of the reserve's major roads, which meant that he could morally intervene and coerce the snake to move off to safer surroundings. He started the vehicle and quickly approached the scene as the primates loped off into the bush.

While the baboons watched from the canopy, and the guests sat entranced in the vehicle, Mike and Sipho approached the colossal snake. The head and tail were not visible, even though the entire body spanned the twelve-foot wide road. Mike's plan was to yank the snake's tail, a maneuver that usually sent a serpent on its way back into the undergrowth. He found the harmless tail and pulled. The python didn't budge, so he tapped on her lower belly. Nothing.

One more step and Mike felt the full force of the snake's one hundred fifty pound body as it struck out in a doubled-up u-shape, latching onto his left hand with its clamping jaws. Within seconds, the serpent wrapped multiple muscular coils around his left leg from groin to foot. His balance compromised, Mike fell back and hit his head hard on the stony ground. The baboons, the guests, Sipho and Mike witnessed first-hand how quickly a python can immobilize a victim using its strong jaws and powerfully built body.

Sipho was quick to recognize the danger. He grabbed the snake's body and attempted to uncoil the ever-tightening compressions around Mike's leg. Mike thought how fortunate he was that Sipho was one of the few Zulu trackers not particularly afraid of snakes. But Sipho's desperate attempt to unravel the snake was in vain. The serpent was simply too strong. The guests on the vehicle started getting increasingly anxious - shocked and frightened by the living nightmare unfolding right before their very eyes.

"Honey, why does Mike have his hand in that snake's mouth?"

The bizarreness of the spectacle had prompted this intelligent response from one particular female guest. Mike remembers chuckling at the comment, knowing full well that the python uses its flexible jaws and recurved teeth, not for chewing but for gripping tight to hold on to the prey as it squeezes the life out of it. Then, it seeks out the head, always swallowing the prey head first, collapsing the body as it moves it down its digestive tract where the strong stomach acids work to break down the meal. Mike had no intention of being that meal, even though his knowledge of snakes reinforced that this particular snake was trying to kill him for defensive, rather than offensive, reasons.

When some species of snakes are stressed, they release a foul smelling liquid as a form of defense. Mike will be the first to tell you that it is one of the most putrid smells that will ever enter your nostrils and, no matter how many times you clean yourself, the stink lingers around for days! Being as large as they are, pythons possess significantly greater quantities of the musky liquid than other snakes. This huge reptile proceeded to empty its bowels all over Mike's leg, now numbed from the muscular spirals. As a last resort, Sipho bravely stuck his finger up from where all of this foul mess was coming from. Like someone incapacitated by a martial arts pressure point hold, the snake went limp and released enough tension for Sipho to start unraveling the massive coils from Mike's leg. At the same time, Mike pushed his hand further down into the python's mouth to put pressure on the trachea, the tube that snakes use to breath when they are swallowing large prey such as impala or reedbuck. A mouth with four rows of hundreds of finely recurved teeth does not allow anything to escape once bitten and this was Mike's only hope to extricate himself from the painful hold. As he carefully worked his hand further and further down, the python started to regurgitate. That was Mike's cue to yank and he dislodged his hand at last.

He and Sipho managed to point the python in the direction of a water hole before attending to Mike's wound, which was bleeding profusely. There are bacteria in the snake's saliva that stops blood from coagulating. Using some whiskey meant for sundowners, he poured it over his punctured, bloodied hand in an attempt to sterilize the wound. Ever the professional, Mike wrapped up his hand and bravely continued with his game drive.

Several weeks later, he experienced continued and severe pain in his hand. A visit to the doctor revealed the presence of five large python teeth firmly embedded in the tissue and tendons. The fangs had to be surgically removed and today they reside in a small bottle of formalin next to his bed, a grim reminder of his brush with the largest serpent in Africa.

Before I scare the living crap out of every potential visitor to Africa, I want to temper the ever-present danger of snakes with the reality of a dangerous encounter. Snakes are useful and beautiful creatures and the risk of harm to a respectful visitor to Africa is nearly zero. In the twenty-odd years that Phinda Private Game Reserve has been operational, there has not been a single guest bitten by a snake.

Snakes are normally shy and retiring. They will often give some kind of a signal; hissing, rearing up, inflating their bodies, spreading a hood to make themselves look larger. Sometimes they may lunge as a warning and bang the intruder with their snout or "dry" bite, saving their lethal venom for prey.

It's easy to vilify snakes, but one must understand that survival in the bush requires a thick skin and tactics that we might perceive as devious. Their highly evolved defense mechanisms are the same as their methods of capturing prey, usually delivering toxic venom with syringe-like accuracy. If a snake is close enough to attack, it is also close enough to be killed, so its reactions must be quick, instinctive. These misunderstood creatures never seek out humans. Rather, it is when their paths collide with ours that they attack. When they are looking for food and water and warmth. When they are threatened or cornered.

The large number of snakes at Inkwazi was definitely the exception rather than the rule, and if you see a snake in the African bush, you can count yourself one of the lucky few.

Yes, snakes loved Inkwazi, but so did I. I dug deep to stay focused in the outhouse. I knew that a snakebite would postpone or kill my chances of ever becoming a ranger. Random encounters with dangerous animals would continue to be a part of the day-to-day life here. It was how I reacted to these confrontations that would determine my fate and the lives of the animals around me.

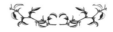

"Who wants to go first?"

As usual, we don't know what to expect, so no one volunteers.

There are only four of us remaining from the original group. This is the last week of the selection course, and we are all wary. Our wits and skills are about to be tested in some crazy scheme; but this time we are equipped with basic ranger skills, along with a rifle and five rounds of live ammunition.

Earlier, we had been ordered to pile into the Land Rover with all of our gear. Once again, Archer and Graham drove us in silence through the reserve to an area that wasn't familiar. We stopped at a drainage line, characterized by unstable treacherous terrain, thick vegetation, and dangerous wildlife.

We are sitting in silence as Archer and Graham size us up, looking at each of us in turn, prolonging the tension. Then they randomly select one of the trainees and escort him out of sight. We wait and listen. After about ten minutes, we hear the loud barking of a troop of baboons. Then silence. And then nothing.

Twenty minutes later, Archer and Graham come back and summon the next person. Again, it is not me. I breathe a sigh of relief. Now there are two of us sitting in the vehicle, just waiting. I attune my sense of hearing to the bush. Maybe I can discern some clue that will help me when it is my turn. Again, after about ten minutes, the troop of baboons starts barking. But this time I hear in quick succession loud shouting followed by a double rifle shot. Then silence for another twenty minutes. Something definitely happened.

Now it is my turn. I am led away from the vehicle, down into the drainage line. Archer and Graham point at the ground and show me fresh tracks. What do I notice about the tracks? They are leopard tracks and there are also smaller tracks. A mother leopard and her cubs.

"Your job is to find that leopard for your guests," they instruct. "Your tracker here, Graham, will accompany you to make sure you find it."

This sounds easy. Graham's experience in the bush and ability to find animals and interpret their behavior is impeccable. How could I miss?

"Let's go bru!" Graham urges. "The sooner we find the leopards, the sooner we can collect our tips."

He heads off down the drainage line, stopping occasionally to read the tracks, sniff the air. I follow into the thick bush, my senses on high alert.

Bogom! Bogom!

The baboons call out from both sides of the dry river, issuing a warning about impending danger. Baboons communicate by vocalization, so I know the males are alerting the troop that there are predators in the area. The leopard family must be nearby, as leopards are one of the biggest threats to baboons.

"Let's wait a bit," I say. "Maybe the leopards will show themselves."

"No, we're on a tight schedule. The guests must be back at the lodge within the hour," Graham says. "It's important to find the leopards. I have many mouths to feed, and a leopard sighting means big tips."

So I carry on, following the leopard tracks until they disappear into extremely thick bush. I have everything I need as a ranger. A live rifle. A first aid kit. My handheld radio. And a confident tracker. Still, I pause. We were taught to be very careful when tracking females with young, whether it's elephant, lion, rhino, buffalo or leopards,

"The tracks are so fresh," Graham says. "They're probably just a few yards away. A mother and cubs, very special. This will mean new shoes for my kids."

I really want to pass this test, delighting my guests as well as keeping my partner happy. And besides, it's broad daylight. Not the typical time of day for leopards to be prowling about, so I stick with Graham and keep following the tracks into the thick bush. Leopards with young are a coveted sighting, so it is important to locate them for my "guests." Everything I studied, practiced, and lived for the past six weeks at Inkwazi were culminating in this final test. After all, my future success as a ranger hinges on my ability to find rare predators in their natural environments.

Then I smell the rotting meat. I hear the buzz of flies. It is now midday. The sweat starts pouring from my brow. The tracks lead right up to the kill. An impala carcass draped over a tree limb. Partially eaten. Just beyond the carcass, the tracks again disappear into thick bush. Yes! Mother and young. Locating the leopard family is paramount; I want to prove that I can do it. As I continue to follow the tracks, every sense is heightened. My entire body is tense, ready for something to happen. I am so absorbed as I look for my quarry that I don't notice that Graham has fallen back, letting me take the lead.

Then I hear it—the low growling of the mother leopard coming from the bush. I can't see shit—nothing. Just hear her. So I start retreating, facing the bush as we'd been taught, and make my way slowly back along my own tracks, Graham now guiding me from behind.

The bushes start rustling and all hell breaks loose. I see something moving at lightning speed in front of me, coming straight at me. I start firing. Chambering and firing. I get off two shots before the "leopard" lands at my feet, still intact with no bullet holes.

"I can't believe it's just a freaking box?"

This is all rigged. I stare incredulously at the improvised "leopard," confused and shattered. I am foiled once again. The cunning instructors rigged everything to lure me into a trap. The baboon calls and the growling leopard sounds are coming from a hidden boom box. Even the tracks and kill are realistically staged to draw me toward the simulated "leopard", a box surreptitiously pulled by a rope from the bush.

What have I done? A few seconds of misjudgment have cost me my career. Graham's greedy tracker persona manipulated me into a very dangerous situation, one I had been warned about many times.

Now I realize why the first trainee's excursion into the drainage ditch had been so short, so uneventful. He had correctly analyzed the situation, maintained the cool calm demeanor that a ranger required, and did not allow himself to be swayed by the sly tracker.

And I have unwittingly fallen under Graham's spell, letting my judgment waver, my guard down, not reading the signs of the bush, ignoring all the training of the past six weeks.

I am devastated.

This simulation of a real-life situation taught me that no matter how much I wanted to please guests and locate an exceptional sighting, I should always read the signs. The thick bush, the recent tracks of a mother and young, the fresh kill were all signs not to interfere. Not to put my life, the lives of my guests, and the life of a wild animal in danger.

This was one of the most important lessons I learned in my life. The final reminder that knowledge needs to be paired with a healthy helping of common sense. Don't mess with the boundaries of wildlife. The first trainee was the only one who interpreted the situation correctly when he refused to follow the tracks. He had passed, but what about the rest of us?

Graham and Archer took a long time over our evaluations, while we sat and cursed our bad judgments. Over and over, I re-played the scenario in my head and what I had learnt about bal-ancing guest expectations, caring for the safety of the tracker and compromising the safety of animal. I had pushed too far with the leopard. Had my foolhardy gung-ho approach cost me my career as a game ranger? The clock ticked off the minutes, then hours.

With great relief, we found out we were all moving on. The course was finished. Graham's dedicated teaching and Archer's hectic rifle training course had equipped us with the skill-set that we required for the next phase of our training. Those of us left were asked which lodge we wanted to be placed at to continue our dreams of becoming game rangers. One guy chose Londolozi, ad-jacent to Kruger National Park, another chose Ngala Private Game Reserve and Brandon was stationed at Madikwe, close to the Bo-tswana border.

I will always be grateful for Graham, his dedicated spirituality and the way he freely shares his passion for the African bush. I love this quote from the man who fledged so many young rangers across Africa and at &Beyond's lodges in India:

> How many people work so long and hard for some perceived future that it eventually eludes them? Don't wait until you are too old to live the life you dream of. This life in the bush, for whatever length of time one chooses, defies that fate. To live here is to become satu-rated with the natural world: to watch seasons change; vibrant life subdued by drought; first green after the rain; miraculous birth; brutal killing; brilliant design; and winter's silent night sky. I cannot imagine a life more invigorating and real. The morning sunshine and

the eyeballing from a predator walking by, the sound of thunder as you are drenched in the open vehicle; and the fire's heat on your face in the cool night.

It's all so simple and yet so perfectly good for the soul. One cannot help but be changed by it all, to emerge with heightened senses and a thoroughly richer view of the world around us.

In the end it is the shared experience that makes it mean so much more. I see it in the eyes and smiles of others and it magnifies the excitement I feel. I watch new rangers discover it all in their own way and know that they, too, will be forever changed. What a pleasure.

The cities will always be there, with careers always available as people clamber over each other heading for the top. Cynical I know, but there is some truth in there too. Wild places are under threat. Every year [that] we spend outdoors exploring these beautiful landscapes and the life that inhabits them is a year to be treasured.

– Graham Vercueil, &Beyond group field manager

I had found paradise at Phinda, deep in the heart of Maputaland and was ecstatic to hear from Graham that Phinda needed rangers. The remaining trainees embarked on their journeys to their respective lodges and I stayed where I was planted.

MY BELOVED PHINDA

When ultimately we cut the links of our past,
It is only to trace the path of our deeper beginning.
MAZISI KUNENE,
"Breaking Off from Tradition"

Imbew' ihlalel' ihlanga layo.
The seed waits for its old ground.
ZULU PROVERB

I HAVE FALLEN IN LOVE WITH Phinda. In Zulu, the word translates as "the return." And I shall always return here. This place is so special to me that I have always fantasized that when I die, my mates would lay my body out in the Phinda bush and let the wild animals dispose of me that way. A more traditional burial would probably be easier on my family.

What makes Phinda so special? Depends on who you ask.

The guests would likely say that it's the perfect safari package. From the moment you arrive, everything is set up to be enchanting. Phinda has five lodges, each designed to be unique and to meld with the African landscape. The staff is trained in the art of hospitality and the attention to detail is outstanding. All &Beyond lodges pride themselves in guest delight. The commitment of the hospitality staff to come up with ingenious ways to surprise guests never ceases to amaze – whether it be a romantic breakfast in the middle of the bush for a honeymoon couple, a bush dinner for the lodge guests complete with hundreds of fairytale lanterns or a birthday bottle of champagne placed on the rim of a rose petal filled bubble bath. The food is excellent, all prepared by professional chefs and served by people from the local community. Phinda is one of those unique places to view the Big Five up close, to hear the stories and witness the restoration of endangered habitats and species, to set foot in the African dream. Simply put, a visit to Phinda is a life-changing and unforgettable experience.

If you ask the local community, they would tell you of the many ways they benefit from having a world-class destination in their neighborhood. The reserve provides steady employment for lodge managers, trackers and rangers, restaurant workers, housekeepers, hospitality, and retail staff. Many wealthy tourists come looking for their adventure of a lifetime but leave with a view into the vast poverty in the area. They donate generously to Africa Foundation, a nonprofit partner with &Beyond that provides support for local community-driven projects. Africa Foundation funded the construction of over one hundred classrooms and several clinics, started small businesses, granted bursaries, and conducted kids' conservation lessons.

The founders would be more than happy to elucidate the history of their vision. It was no small feat to bring their idea for a private game reserve to life. They targeted the heart of Maputaland, the area between the Mkuze Game Reserve, the Sodwana State Forest and the St. Lucia Game Reserve that comprised seven natural habitats. These visionaries saw the potential for restoring Africa's biodiversity and cobbled the reserve together from derelict farms and ranches. It took years of blood and sweat, hard work and dedication, funds and commitment from investors to make this a viable enterprise. The complete story is told in a book, *The Return: The Story of Phinda Game Reserve.*

As rangers, we were trained to interpret the dream, to bring it all together for the guests. Trained in every aspect of wildlife knowledge and hospitality, we were responsible for making each guest's stay a delight. Not just talking about the vision of the founders, but visibly demonstrating every day how the reserve works to support the environment, the local community and the wildlife. Because everything focuses around the wildlife. Phinda is one of the only places on earth where you can dive with dolphins, manta rays, turtles, and whale sharks in the morning and view lions, leopards, rhinos, and giraffes in the afternoon. Where else can you do that?

"Are you ready for your final evaluation drive, bru?" Morty asks me.

"Ready as ever," I reply confidently. "Bring it on."

Morty's real name is Andrew Mortimer and he is the head ranger, the one who coordinates the daily duties of all of the rangers assigned to the different lodges and administers disciplinary actions. I guess today is my big day, the day I must prove I can handle guests and all that the reserve throws my way.

My assigned "guests" will not be the typical visitors from international destinations who come to learn about the wildlife. Today's guests will be a select group of managers, senior rangers, and staff from the reserve who attempt to be as difficult as possible, simulating situations that a new ranger will actually encounter when he or she gets to drive real guests. These people know every nuance that will make life challenging when dealing with the high expectations of guests who have perhaps invested their life savings in the safari adventure of a lifetime. All my skills, both practical and intuitive, will be evaluated.

I anticipate the possible scenarios they will present. Like asking to return to the lodge mid-drive when the vehicle is full of other guests who want to go on. Or demanding a more leisurely pace while others in the group want to see as much as possible in the allotted time. Or ignoring safety rules during a Big Five sighting. I need to know when to facilitate conversation and when to listen, catering to the different needs and personalities of a disparate group, make an adventure out of every mishap, and all the while providing a safe, educational, and entertaining experience for each guest.

I should be nervous, but I'm not. Very few trainees pass their first evaluation drive. So I plan to just do my best, share what I have learned in the past few months, and keep an open mind to the challenges that arise. I know that one of my key strengths is my ability to interpret the environment, to present a unique perspective, to share my knowledge and passions. I will use my flair for storytelling to my advantage, presenting a colorful backdrop to everything we see.

I also recognize that my questionable organizational skills are a big weakness. So I carefully pack the Land Rover and mentally run down the checklist. Snacks, drinks, binoculars, rain jackets, rifle ...

Rockerman, my assigned Zulu tracker for the day, helps me with every detail. Even though he is my age, he has been tracking at the reserve for quite a few years. I worked closely with him these last few weeks, and his experience has been invaluable. A final check, and then I place the vehicle keys in my pocket. I do not want any of my fellow rangers to play a prank on me, stealing the vehicle and hiding it in the bush. This drive is too important to be foiled by practical jokes.

I walk over to greet my guests. It is late afternoon, and they are having tea in the outdoor dining area. I see an assortment of people waiting, managers and senior staff, some of whom I recognize. Old hands who will have fun with me, pretending to be newly arrived guests. I plan to have fun with them as well, giving my best performance as a seasoned game ranger. I walk up and introduce myself, welcoming them to Forest Lodge and their "first" game drive. Even though I have been on multiple game drives during my training at Phinda, it is important to treat each and every drive as a unique experience, each and every guest as special. Even if special means "especially difficult"!

"*Sanibonani!*" Rockerman greets them with a big smile and a traditional Zulu welcome, exuding confidence and warmth. Together, we escort our charges to the waiting Land Rover.

These vehicles are the most dependable transportation available and have been specially modified to enhance the safari experience. Behind the driver's seat are three seats, tiered so that everyone has a great view of the terrain. I notice that one of the managers, who has been especially critical of my performance these past few weeks, takes the seat directly behind me. He is just out of my field of vision although he is capable of hearing my every word, seeing my every move. He is encumbered with binoculars and cameras, so I'm hoping he will stay busy with his toys and not give me too much trouble.

I start the engine and wait for Rockerman to take his place. In front of the passenger seat, on the front left bumper, is a unique seat, probably the most important seat on the vehicle, the seat for the tracker.

"Time to go into my office," Rockerman says as he hops into the open seat. This is where he will be conducting business for the next few hours. I chuckle at Rockerman's comment and hope that, should I qualify, he will be assigned to me as my tracker partner one day. The success of every game drive is closely tied to the tracker's keen observational skills.

From this exposed perch, the tracker can easily communicate with the driver. Telling me when to stop to examine tracks, when to slow down for difficult road conditions, when barriers need to be removed from our path. From here, he can spot the largest game and the smallest insects. Although Rockerman and I have been working together for only a few weeks, we have already established a strong bond, so that we can communicate silently, can almost read each other's thoughts.

I turn to check on my guests and make sure everyone is comfortable. Then we are off, heading out into the ancient sand forest, which speaks to me. It is now my turn to speak for it, to tell its stories, reveal its secrets.

Forest Lodge at Phinda is located in the north of the reserve, set deep in a rare sand forest. Only several thousand protected hectares of sand forest are left on our planet. The lodge was built with every care to protect the environment and consists of luxury guesthouses rising above the ground on stilts, the decks literally built around the trees. These Zulu Zen-style minimalist structures, with their walls of glass, floated within the cathedral-like sand forest, one of the rarest ecosystems in the world.

In contrast to the luxury guest accommodations, my housing would be sparse, I was to learn on arrival. They were short of ranger accommodations, so my lodgings consisted of a simple wooden hut with no indoor toilet or bath facilities. It was the size of a large box, with only room for a bed and side table. I had to go outside to use the separate outhouse and shower. There would be no air conditioning, just a fan to offset the one hundred percent humidity. Wouldn't be forever, they told me, just until more space was freed up. I didn't mind living like a monk, because most of my time was spent outdoors, learning the routines of the safari lodge and forming friendships with rangers who would become my close mates.

But more important, always absorbing knowledge and preparing for the final tasks that would certify me as a game ranger. It was here at Phinda that I met the eccentric characters who would shape the core of my experiences for the next few years.

Morty had been the head ranger for about a year before I arrived. Short and stout with an angelic, youthful face, he was fair but strict. He had the rare qualities of a true leader, someone who was friendly and approachable, yet commanded respect. And you did what he said. Morty had spent his earlier years as a paramedic on the streets of Johannesburg and witnessed just about every gory permutation of shooting, car accident, or disaster that this notorious city could throw at him. He had seen it all. A chain smoker and habitual Coca-Cola guzzler, Morty always went red in the face when one of us idiots managed to tick him off, something I would manage to do on a frequent basis.

The moment I met Fraser Gear, I knew I wanted to be like him. The perfect complement to Morty's pragmatic management style, Fraser was the senior mentor in the ways of the bush. He was the guy all the other rangers admired. He'd been there the longest, ever since he took his head away from schoolbooks when he left high school and went bush crazy. Fraser had exceptional knowledge for a white guy and was an unbelievable tracker of big game. He understood the African bush like no one else I'd ever met. His innate talent of being able to tell great stories made him popular with guests. But he was completely nuts. If a rogue elephant came into camp, he was the guy who would be off in a flash, his tall, lanky frame moving at lightning speed. Running after it, no shirt, his blond hair reflecting the sun, he would chase it away from camp and out of the vegetable garden. Absolutely zero fear.

After his morning game drive with the guests, Fraser would sacrifice his three hours of free time between lunch and the late afternoon game drive to take me out and teach me the ways of the bush. As a fledgling ranger, this was when I had my first intimate experiences with big game. The senior rangers purposely took me on walks to get up close to rhinos, buffalo, and lions. Whatever was out there. This was when the training began in earnest. And Fraser was the guy who took me out every day.

"No" was never an option with Fraser. There were days when I would try to tell him I was tired. Fraser's responses would always be "Life's too short for sleeping. Get your lazy ass out of bed." Even on occasions when Morty had asked me to do a specific task, Fraser would aggressively scream at me, "Screw Morty! This is more important." Fraser basically had carte blanch to do what he wanted at the lodge. Because orienting new rangers to the ways of the wild was much more important than office work and maintenance. He knew that the menial tasks would always be there and somehow they would get done.

He taught me how to track, read the animal's behavior, anticipate the warning signs. Fear was not an emotion that Fraser was familiar with, and we had far too many close encounters with lions, elephants, buffalo, and other dangerous animals. He was one of those people who expected everyone else to be naturally just like him, and he would be genuinely surprised if anyone questioned a potentially hair-raising adventure.

Like Fraser, Benson had years of experience. His extensive military experience meant that he had some of the safest hands when it came to firing .375 Magnum rifles. One of the few Zulu rangers at the time, he lived five minutes from the reserve in the village of Mduku. Benson and I would have many harrowing experiences, and I became close to his family.

Then there was Richard White. The trackers named him Doctor Mhlophe. The Zulus believed that anyone who wore glasses must be a doctor, and *mhlope* means "white." The rest of us knew him as just Doc. In contrast to Fraser, Richard was one of the most unlikely naturalists or game rangers you'd ever meet. He had an irrational fear of elephants, calling them the "gray fear." Richard would only view elephants from a far distance, much to the frustration of his guests, who wanted to see them up close.

Before becoming a game ranger, Richard was the lead singer for a heavy metal rock band called Throat. He was a punk rocker who applied for the ranger-training course with zero knowledge of the African bush. But he turned out to be a pretty darn good ranger. Most rangers had a specialty, and Richard was the "go to" guy when any of us had questions on botany.

Richard was actually banned from driving guests until he got his shooting right. He had terrible eyesight and was not comfortable around guns. He'd often walk into the ranger room dry-firing his rifle at an imaginary target, practicing. At the rifle range, Richard's shooting was so bad that he would regularly miss not only the target but also the paper the target was printed on and the box the target was affixed to. He'd blow big holes in the sandbank and shoot over the top of the range.

After a few months living in the sparse wooden shack, I had the opportunity to move into Richard's house. I now had a room albeit shared, and the luxury of an en suite bathroom. Richard and I got on incredibly well. Like tobacco and aloe, which the Zulus mix to create snuff, we were a potent combination. And like the powerful snuff, we were always getting up to no good.

Richard was short tempered, and for an unassuming small guy he was totally crazy. One time while on leave in Cape Town, we got into a bar fight with a bouncer and the owner of a nightclub. It was then that I saw the wild and dangerous side of Richard. He would pick up anything—bottles, tables, metal pipes. And inflict damage on people. The two of us single-handedly emptied out the popular Cape Town nightclub, fucked up the owner and his bouncer, and tore their premises apart. All because the bouncer prevented an evidently intoxicated Richard from relieving himself in their bathrooms. When the French-speaking owner backed his bouncer and told Richard he can "no pee-pee" in his establishment, Richard went berserk.

"Shut up, you French fuck! You French frogs fucked Gabon, you fucked Madagascar. And now you're trying to fuck with *me*?!!!" yelled Richard, right up in the guy's face. As the bouncer lined up a punch, I was left with no choice but to defend my inebriated buddy. Things went from bad to worse for the nightclub and its patrons.

But Richard's wild side was balanced with an incredible sense of humor. He was always laughing, always smiling, always seeking out a bit of mischief. Life with Richard was never boring. Richard always used to say that the forest has ears. "A house is a trap" is an old Zulu proverb, meaning that you can never tell who may be listening outside, as we were to find out during an encounter with one of the reserve's managers.

He must have heard us laughing and making strange noises, because one day he came into our shared room unannounced. Just opened the door and walked in without knocking. Not the smartest move considering he caught us in mid-throw, pitching knives. When he shut the door, he noticed that not only were we throwing knives at the back of the door but at a crudely hand drawn picture of him tacked to it. The entire back of the door had been destroyed.

He was livid. We got into a lot of trouble. Yes, we disliked the manager. He confirmed that the forest did indeed have ears and the house was a trap.

In contrast to Richard, there was Gavin Foster, a Zululand farmer's son. A typical straight-laced, very conservative guy, he had farmer-boy good looks and did not have a mean bone in his body. The jock of the bunch, he excelled at shooting. While not a great storyteller, he took his ranger job seriously. Whenever we were out together, he was always the one saying, "Guys, I don't think you should be doing this." Those would be the last words he would say before he was swept along with us doing something forbidden.

Once you became a full-fledged ranger, you were randomly assigned a tracker. It was amazing how all the ranger tracker teams were almost mirrors of each other. Chemistry was vital, since often your life depended on the other, and somehow these chance pairings seemed oddly predestined.

Fraser's tracker partner was a guy called Thembinkosi. He was the darkest black guy I had ever seen in my life. He had the biggest smile and this highly animated voice. He was always bubbly, happy to see you. White eyes and white teeth were always flashing under his semi-Afro hairstyle. Fraser and he had a strong bond. Thembinkosi had the weirdest sense of humor. He named his son China because the kid was born with squinting eyes.

Gavin's partner was Sifiso. The black version of Gavin—tall, handsome, fit, and conservative. Always the last to do something wrong, of course.

Richard worked with a small and wiry tracker called Bheki. Those two were a great team. They were always laughing, and Bheki had one of the loudest laughs, one of those guffawing, no-holds-barred laughs.

I remember working with Bheki one day. We were driving with a Land Rover full of guests, and Bheki spotted something whitish gray on the side of the road. He told me to stop and reverse. I asked him what he saw, and he started laughing. Off to the side of the road, he picked up a dead vervet monkey by the tail. He couldn't stop laughing. The eyes had been eaten out by ants, leaving two large ringed holes, surrounded by the white fringe of hair on its face.

"Look James," said Bheki. "It's Doctor Mhlope."

He pointed to the empty eye sockets, resembling the glasses that Richard wore on a daily basis. I remember laughing till my stomach muscles hurt.

Morty worked with the head tracker, Aaron, a Goliath of a Zulu guy. He was always grumpy, with a bad temper, and known to everyone simply as Shakes. He had a chip on his shoulder about being black. Aaron was a serious mobilizer of the other trackers, and not always in a good way, like getting them to go on strike. He was notoriously difficult to work with, and Morty often struggled with him. For some reason, Aaron and I got along quite well. One day I returned from leave to learn that Shakes was dead. No one had a clue as to why or how he died. He simply dropped dead one day while out visiting his homestead. There were whispers of *umthakathi*, a strong Zulu belief in witchcraft, and Shake's name was seldom spoken aloud by the other trackers.

It was into this crazy community that I came as the sole trainee ranger. In the beginning, I was assigned the menial tasks. I was the one linking out late arrivals to other rangers, picking up guests from the airstrip, beach, and other activities, and performing routine office work. I was always the ranger on standby. Between all these tasks, I was like a sponge, absorbing information from the other rangers, the trackers, the staff, and even the guests.

One of the best ways to learn was to go on a "bumble," or staff game drive. This was a great opportunity to travel the terrain and learn the roads, since there are over a hundred different road names in Phinda. We'd pile up a Land Rover full of staff from the lodge. Toss in a cooler full of beer and other alcohol, snacks, and *biltong*. Then head out in the late afternoon on those rare days when the lodges were not busy. A bumble was the perfect activity to glean knowledge from those who knew the lay of the land, a fun way to pass the hours in a low-pressure setting.

And so the days passed. Practicing, shooting, developing everything. Until the day Morty asked me to go on my evaluation drive. Now it was important that I not bumble, that I pull together all my knowledge and experience, that I totally finesse this drive.

I head away from the lodge with my distinguished guests. Even though we are about a hundred miles away from the ocean, I drive through thick sand, a reminder that this land was once under the sea. The late afternoon sunlight dapples the forest, illuminating this magical fairy-tale land. We pass rare and beautiful tree species that dominate the landscape, like the rough-barked Lebombo wattle, the giant of the sand forest. The torchwood is also tall and has a smooth fluted trunk and a history of magical and medicinal uses. Its dry kernels were used as torches, hence its name.

I stop the vehicle under the canopy of one of these towering torchwoods. It is here that I will light a spark, that I will bring the African theater to life. It is here that I begin to tell the story of tragedy and hope.

"This is what it was like thousands of years ago," I motion toward the forest. "The sand forest is a dry forest for most of the year. The substrate is real sea sand and evolved from dune forest from a time gone by. The sea used to go right up to the Lebombo mountain range to the west of Phinda. As the sea retreated at various intervals, it left exposed dune ridges where sand forest took root. If you are fortunate enough to fly over the area, you can clearly see the evidence of longitudinal dune ridges running parallel to the coastline."

I speak powerfully, inviting my guests to look and listen. I point out an orchid, high in the tree. This environment supports a dazzling diversity of epiphytic orchids, including the largest orchid in the world, the leopard orchid. Its name derives from the black rosettes on the bright yellow flower that are strangely reminiscent of the rosettes on a leopard's coat. This massive orchid can grow to the size of a Mercedes Benz.

"The entire orchid becomes so heavy that it sometimes breaks the bough of the tree that it is living on, in sharp contrast to the smallest orchid in the world." I gently finger the tiny delicate white flowers of a plant clinging to a nearby Lebombo wattle and impart the orchid knowledge that I had gleaned from Richard. "Unlike the leopard orchid, the *microselia* orchid has a tiny, pure white flower the size of a pinhead. This is a land of contrasts, large and small."

My story is interrupted by a distinctive sound.

Krook-krook-krook-krook!

I pause as Rockerman locates the source, a bird in a nearby tree. A purple-crested turaco, one of the most beautiful birds in the area, is poised on a branch, blending into the foliage in spite of its glossy violet-blue, green, and red feathers. I explain how the Zulus call this bird *igwalagwala*, an onomatopoeic reference to their loud, guttural calls. The colorful plumes are used in the decorative headdresses distinguishing Zulu royalty. The Zulus, proud people who inhabited this land long before we arrived, have a central part in this story of redemption.

"This sand forest is one of seven ecosystems that comprise Phinda, a small part of the area known as Maputaland. The Maputaland plain was once a paradise with an incredible diversity of wildlife. But about a hundred years ago, most of the wildlife that you will see today was wiped out. And the land became barren. So how did this happen? And who brought the animals back?

"If you asked the animals and they could speak, they would each tell you a different story of how they came to be a part of this dreamscape. They would tell the stories of their ancestors, who roamed freely in vast herds over the Maputaland grasslands, of the natural selection process that prevailed, of living in balance with their predators and prey, of living in harmony with the local ama-Thonga people before these peaceful people were assimilated into the more dominant Zulu nation.

"Then their stories would turn dark, as their land was invaded by the 'great white hunters' with their powerful guns. The balance was shifted in favor of those who could hunt from a distance, those who were not dependent on reading the signs of nature, not aware of the delicate equilibrium that existed. People who looked at the game as conquests, independent of the complicated relationships between species, the tenuous links between animals, plants, insects, and man. The peaceful land was now riddled with the pounding of hooves attempting to escape, followed by the sound of gunshots and the triumphant cries of the hunters. Many of the game animals became gun shy, even teaching their young to avoid man. Subtle changes in behavior that would upset the balance and trust that had existed for thousands of years.

"Casting an even darker shadow, their natural habitats and breeding grounds started to disappear. The colonial powers brought in their culture and expectations of cultivating the land and raising domestic livestock. Taming the land and creating man-made barriers and boundaries where there had once been only rivers, mountains, wetlands, lala palm velds, broadleaf woodlands, and ancient sand forests.

"And this was just a precursor of what was to come. An invisible killer, a parasitical disease transmitted by the tsetse fly called nagana, set upon the newly introduced domestic animals. It was suspected that wild game were carriers of this deadly parasite. Instead of eliminating the tsetse fly, the government launched an intensive campaign in 1917 to eradicate the large game. The only populations spared were the rhino, hippo, and nyala.

"By then, the damage had been done. In just over a century, a once beautiful and diverse area had been reduced to an area of great poverty. The nagana was gone, but the wildlife populations were also decimated. Zululand had been carved up and the Zulu people forcibly removed from their lands and resettled in unfavorable areas. What was left of Maputaland consisted of run-down cattle farms, struggling pineapple plantations, islands of natural habitat, and impoverished people.

"How do you repair one hundred years of damage? How do you convert a wasteland back into a dynamic wilderness? How do you create a place where wild animals not just survive but thrive? How do you bring life and hope back to the once-proud people who inhabit this land?

"It started with a dream, a vision. *Phinda izilwane.* 'The return of the wildlife.'

"The Phinda reserve was created with a vision to unify fragmented ecological habitats, to restore the wildlife, to become a model for economic development as a partnership between the local communities and the tourism industry that made Africa the adventure continent of the world. One by one, the great predators were reintroduced in a carefully orchestrated plan. Not all the wildlife had been eliminated from the area. Resilient species like leopard, hyena, nyala, and reedbuck still held on in the small pockets of natural bush that had been spared. But lions and elephants had not been recorded in the area reliably for several decades. Now every attempt was made to restore and manage the natural predator/prey dynamic.

"The electric fence was erected to keep the animals confined to the reserve, eliminating fear and friction with the neighboring communities. The lowest railing is for lions, the mid-level railing for rhino and buffalo, and the highest railing for the elephants. There is no railing for leopards, as these big cats roam where they will, not deterred by fences.

"One by one, the Big Five had returned to the Phinda area. Today we will venture out and see Africa as it was always meant to be."

I feel pretty good about my waxing lyrical of the history of Phinda until the manager sitting behind me opens his mouth and brings me back to reality.

"I'm not the slightest bit interested in the history of this shithole," he bleats. "I am here only for one day, so get on with it. I paid a lot of money to see the Big Five on this drive, and you have been wasting my time."

Luckily for me, I am prepared for the difficult guest scenario.

"Yes, we will now head toward the savannah," I calmly reassure him. "Would you and the rest of the group like to go looking for lions?"

It's always best to seek consensus, and everyone nods in agreement. It is clear that this particular "guest" is going to push my patience to the limit. I start the engine, curse the dick-head manager under my breath, and we head out of the sand forest to search for lions. I know that the chances of seeing all of the Big Five in one game drive are slim to none, but a guaranteed lion sighting will certainly earn me points.

The North pride had been located that morning at a wildebeest kill on Charcoal Clearings in the north of the reserve. Well-fed lions don't like to move, so the odds that they are in the same location are strongly in my favor. Along the way, we pause to enjoy a sighting of white rhinos, a mother and calf. I relay a brief history of the conservation of this species in Zululand, making sure that my "guests" realize the gravity of seeing a conservation miracle right before their eyes. Some members of the group quiz me about the reproductive cycle and poaching activities, making sure I can answer any questions a tourist might have. The difficult manager is mercifully silent, snapping away with his camera. He is busy playing the role of the over-zealous guest who is only too happy to tick one of the Big Five off his list.

In good time we arrive at Charcoal Clearings in the north of the reserve near Mziki Marsh, and Rockerman taps on the hood, an indication that he has spotted the cats. Game drive protocol dictates that the ranger must insure that the tracker is well and truly within the vehicle during a cat sighting. It is simply too dangerous for the tracker to be exposed on the tracker seat in close proximity to big cats. I reverse about thirty yards, out of sight of the lions. Rockerman jumps off and climbs inside the vehicle—a most important safety decision—and I mentally congratulate myself on remembering this vital detail. Neglecting to do so would mean instant failure and a serious reprimand.

I position the Landie perfectly at the lion sighting, not too close, with the sinking sun behind me. It's hard to see the individual lions well, as they are all lying down in a thicket, gorged on wildebeest meat. I know that this will probably be the last sighting of big game before we have a drink stop and make our way back to the lodge for dinner. How do I talk about sleeping, sated lions and make this interesting? I could spew random facts, but my examiners would not appreciate my lack of interpretive guiding. I take a gamble and recreate the scene of last night's hunt, when these lionesses made the decision to seek out their prey in the clearings.

"The North pride lioness is one of the largest lionesses on record. Just look at the size of her!" I exclaim and point to her languid form under a guarrie bush.

"Lions are considered opportunistic feeders, meaning that they will kill anything that comes their way. However, certain prides also specialize in tackling a specific kind of animal. Unfortunately for the wildebeest here in the north of Phinda, they have become the special focus of the North pride. That dominant lioness has been known to kill three wildebeest in one evening, so she is no slouch when it comes to the gentle art of wildebeest population control!

"Look closely at the carcass over there—" I point to what's left of the morning's meal. Most of the meat has been eaten and all that remains intact is the animal's head.

"What happened here last night is the equivalent of a Shakespearean tragedy. You will notice that the horns are large and joined by a mass of bony material called the boss. This tells us that the unfortunate victim was a mature bull wildebeest. And this is where the tragedy comes in.

"I have been in awe of this particular bull ever since I came to this reserve. He was always alone, guarding his patch of paradise from other bulls. These clearings were his kingdom, his domain to rule and enjoy. Just two days ago, I watched this bachelor as he corralled a breeding herd of females. This Romeo had his choice of Juliets, and in the height of the rutting season, he was not about to let any of them disappear from his sight."

In the middle of my story I notice that the North pride lioness has stood up, displaying her massive frame and is staring intently at us. I follow her line of sight and am horrified to see that the pesky manager is climbing off the vehicle on the opposite side to the watchful lioness. He is poised to take a close-up photo of the pride. Holy smokes! I was so intent on my story that I made a serious lapse in judgment, allowing someone to attempt to leave the safety of the Land Rover. I act quickly, telling Rockerman to grab the errant manager and haul him back in the vehicle. I know that my failure to act earlier has probably meant that I have failed this evaluation drive. There is only one thing left to do.

I turn the radio to Channel Three, which is used for reception or general radio. Channel One is reserved for game drives only, Channel Two is for the conservation staff, and Channel Six is reserved for line-of-sight conversations between game drive vehicles.

"Reception, come in," I radio Octavia at the desk.

"Go ahead, James," she answers.

"Octavia, please can you get hold of the stand-by ranger and ask him to contact me on Channel One?"

Octavia responds affirmatively.

Next, I turn to my naughty guest.

"You were told to remain seated and quiet during a Big Five sighting," I tell him calmly. "You have put the entire vehicle at risk. I have no choice but to send you back to the lodge."

He knows I am right to remove him from the vehicle, but he protests anyway.

"This dumb ass sitting next to me was hogging the view with his big head," he gripes. "I was only out for a minute. This is my best chance to see lions up close and get a good photo, proof that I was actually here. Besides, you have a gun. What danger could there possibly be for me?"

On and on, but his words fall on deaf ears. My earlier briefing was very clear — do not stand up or leave the vehicle, do nothing to break the outline with a single human figure or call attention to us.

I hear the radio come to life on Channel One.

"James, come in." It's a relief to hear Richard's voice; he is on stand-by today.

"Richard, can you please head over to Charcoal Clearings? I need you to please come pick up one of my guests. He needs to return to the lodge ASAP."

"Sure, I'll be there in fifteen." This time, it is Richard's turn to come to my rescue, and I know he will not delay.

I turn to face my guests, sitting on the steering wheel so I can see each and every one of them. Any more stupid moves will not be overlooked. Without missing a beat, I continue my story, which has become much more animated, courtesy of the now very awake pride of lions.

"So Romeo is watching over his group of nubile Juliets. As the dominant bull, he feels obligated not only to sow his oats as efficiently as possible, but also to protect the herd. And he is about to be tested like never before."

I point out the drag marks showing where the lions dragged the carcass, explaining that the wildebeest is one of the heaviest of all the antelope species, and can weigh close to six hundred pounds. I indicate how strong the lioness must have been to drag it this far. I start the vehicle and we slowly follow the drag marks, backtracking for about fifty yards to a recently burnt area of the clearings. Every ten yards or so I show my guests where the lioness stopped to rest before carrying on with the arduous task of dragging the bull to a suitable feeding site.

"This is where the bull made his last stand," I point to a particularly disturbed patch of ground.

"Imagine the scene. It's early morning, and the breeding herd of wildebeest is out in the open, grazing over there. They sense the approaching lionesses and instinctively start making their way toward the thicker woodland behind them. But the bull remains in the clearing, snorting at the approaching cats. He clearly sees two of them, the North pride lioness's adult daughters, and he is sure of his safe distance, the distance required to safely outrun a charge from the lions. What he does not notice is the North pride lioness on the edge of the woodland right over here. In spite of her size, she has stealthily positioned herself for an ambush just out of his sight, nestled deep in the undergrowth."

Rockerman sees where I am going with this, and he indicates where the lioness had lain in wait under a terminalia tree.

"Romeo taunts the approaching lionesses with an assortment of snorts and grunts. How dare they interrupt his lovemaking and chase off his Juliets? He allows the lionesses to come remarkably close before he turns and runs. He darts straight past this terminalia, and wham! The dominant lioness leaps from cover and latches onto his broad neck. The daughters close in on his hindquarters as he fights bravely to stay on his hooves. Within seconds, the combined weight of three felines smothers him, and he crashes to the ground, thrashing wildly.

"From the security of the woodland, the Juliets stop and turn to watch the macabre scene, silent witnesses to the bull wildebeest's final moments. His bellowing subsides as viselike jaws clamp down on his windpipe. The tragic story of Romeo is complete; his days of mating and procreating are over. He faced death in the prime of his life, defending his lovely Juliets. Is one or more of them carrying his offspring? The breeding season is not yet finished. The Juliets turn and make their way, single file, away from the killing grounds toward the marsh where another Romeo surely awaits them, more than happy to fulfill the role of surrogate suitor."

As I finish my monologue, Richard pulls up in his Land Rover, and I ask him to escort my wayward guest back to the lodge. He pleads his innocence but Richard, with a wry smile on his face, is only too happy to oblige. I finish my drive minus one very difficult guest, knowing that I've probably failed but that I certainly didn't let the disagreeable manager get off scot free.

After about an hour of deliberating, my evaluation committee decided my fate and called me into the ranger's room. Morty went through all the things I did well and explained the things that counted against me. I had driven a little quickly at times. I had failed to keep an eye on my guests in a Big Five sighting. But my interpretive stories had saved me.

Somehow, I passed on my first drive! I would like to believe that it was because everyone on the vehicle secretly loved how I handled the misbehaving manager. More than likely, it was because the lodge was desperate for new blood to fill the ranger shortage, alleviating the need for working long work-cycles with few stand-by days. Burnt-out, pissed-off rangers were never a good thing for the company's bottom line. Whatever the reason, I left that room elated, knowing that I just had one final test to complete before becoming a fully fledged member of an elite ranger team.

ALMOST IS NOT EATEN

He asked the spider to reveal his magic words,
To teach him to follow the wisdom of the sky.
Through the patient fingers of the chameleon, he waited.
MAZISI KUNENE,
"Patience and Wisdom"

Ingw' idla ngamabala.
The leopard eats by means of its spots.
ZULU PROVERB

THERE IS A SAYING IN Africa.
"Every morning an impala wakes up knowing that it must outrun the fastest lion if it wants to stay alive. Every morning a lion wakes up knowing that it must outrun the slowest impala or it will starve. It makes no difference if you are a lion or an impala, when the sun comes up in Africa, you must wake up running."

And so it was important for me to wake up running if I was to pass the final hurdle and successfully hunt and kill my impala. I needed to be as patient as a lion, as stealthy as a leopard and as agile as a cheetah. I needed to get inside the minds of these great hunters, become the ultimate predator. Just as their survival depended on their hunting skills, so would my continued existence at Phinda.

This was the last test before I was properly welcomed into the ranger team, before I became officially recognized as a full-fledged game ranger. The final initiation step seemed easy enough: I had to go out and shoot an impala.

Of course, it wasn't as simple as going out and shooting an impala. Like everything, the powers that be had to make it extremely tough. The rationale behind having to seek out and kill something was that many rangers take on the job because they love animals and wildlife. But if it came down to it, faced with a choice of shooting an animal to protect your guests, would you be able to do it? Would you be able to act in the moment, without emotion or attachment, and pull the trigger?

This last exercise was specifically designed to determine your fate, because the fate of so many lives would be in your hands. It was a solitary mission, and each future ranger had to face his or her own inner scruples. Those who grew up hunting were able to complete the task with no compunctions. But there were stories of others who just couldn't. After going through this entire process, all the grit and sweat, physical and mental challenges, they couldn't complete the final trial. One of my fellow rangers, Bryan, was a confirmed vegetarian and pacifist, who struggled to shoot and kill a wild animal. He thought his dreams of becoming a ranger would be forever thwarted by his moral compass. But, after wrestling with his inner convictions for weeks, Bryan finally brought himself to do it. Having completed what was without doubt one of the most difficult tasks of his life, he bore witness that he would not like to face the decision again some day, should a potentially dangerous animal come bearing down on him and those under his care.

Then there were stories like Jacqui's. Sometimes the environment, the time and place can work against you. Jacqui was one of the first female rangers. She successfully stalked an impala, but as she closed the gap, she caught a movement in the bush nearby. A lioness was pursuing the same impala. Without hesitation, she climbed the nearest tree and, from her elevated position, she glanced down and realized that she had left her rifle at the base of the tree. She was stuck with no form of defense, except a sound horn, which she blew on repeatedly until help arrived and transferred her safely into a vehicle.

To understand the difficulty of this challenge, one needs to appreciate the survival instincts of the impala, a common antelope on the South African savannah. Nimble, quick, and graceful, they have some of the keenest senses of any animals in the bush. With an unbelievable sense of hearing, and impeccable eyesight, they are capable of leaping ten feet straight up, running forty-five miles an hour, and clearing over thirty feet at a jump. They are the ultimate shooting challenge, because once in motion it is difficult to predict their speed and direction. Off they zigzag, their lithe bodies leaping far, springing high, running fast.

And they are beautiful. The males have distinctive lyre-shaped horns, which can grow up to three feet long. Their large eyes and slender faces impart a regal air, the golden brown fur perfectly accented with subtle black and white markings as if painted by an artist. They have shiny, glossy coats, with an unrealistic luster as though wrapped in cellophane, a result of allogrooming. Special grooves in their teeth function like a comb, removing the dirt, parasites, anything in their fur. They literally brush each other's hair with their teeth, the saliva giving their coats a glistening appearance.

So that was my target, a common animal seen on almost every game drive. But there were stringent guidelines for killing on the reserve. The impala had to be a male older than two years with fully developed horns. It couldn't be a herd ram with a harem of females, but had to be a lone ram or a member of a bachelor herd. Location was important and the ram couldn't be shot coming down to drink at a water hole, an easy target. It had to be more than two hundred yards away from the nearest road and over a mile from the nearest lodge. The rules immediately eliminated more than half the impala you were likely to see on the reserve.

And there were limits on the hunting strategy. You were only allowed five rounds of ammo, so each attempt to shoot must be well planned and executed. The entire pursuit must be completed entirely on foot. Last, you had to carry the entire impala back to the lodge. No small feat, since a male impala can tip the scales at one hundred thirty to one hundred eighty pounds.

These rules were strictly enforced and there was no leeway for breaking them. Drew, a fellow ranger, found this out the hard way. He went through all the exhausting work, relentlessly seeking out the perfect impala, stalking it, successfully shooting it and then carrying it most of the way back. But as he was nearing the lodge, a staff member drove by and offered to give him and his cumbersome impala a lift. He hopped in and traveled the last few hundred yards in comfort. As he was off-loading his prize, he was busted by one of the lodge management and immediately driven back out into the bush with his impala to complete the task again!

In spite of the strict rules, I was filled with optimism. How hard could it be to hunt and shoot an impala? The cheetah has an impressive fifty percent chance of getting its prey each time it hunts, the leopard a forty percent chance of success, and the lion secures its meal twenty-five percent of the time. With my knowledge of the bush and my high-powered rifle, surely I could beat their odds.

For those three predators to coexist, they developed specific skills and survival tactics. The cheetah with its loose and lanky build is the fastest animal on land. It uses its claws to dig in for traction and hunts by day in open country where there is enough cover for stalking and enough open space for running. The leopard hunts alone at night, the master of the stealthy ambush. It uses the trees for resting, hunting, and conserving food. The lionesses stalk dusk through dawn in groups, creeping up on their victims before launching a coordinated attack.

I would need to find my place in this carefully crafted ecosystem, as we would all be seeking the same target, the nimble impala. At the same time making sure I did not become the victim, the distracted ranger trainee.

Unlike the large cats, I was not possessed with grasping claws, spine-snapping teeth, camouflage, finely honed senses, or incredible speed. My tool of destruction was not something I was born with but something I would bear: the Holland & Holland .375 Magnum rifle. This rifle was introduced in 1912 and remains today one of the best, if not *the* best, calibers for accuracy, reliability, trajectory, and stopping power.

Having practiced my shooting for many weeks now, I had become used to the vicious recoil that had knocked Sam flat on her back during training. The bruising on the inside of my shoulder had long since healed up, and the sound of countless shots fired without protective hearing gear had left my ears dulled to the deafening blast of a shot. I carried with me a killing tool, a weapon more deadly than any of the big cats' macabre attributes.

But like centuries of hunters before me, I would discover that hunting isn't just about going out and killing. It would be a humbling experience, requiring me to master the environment and to overcome great physical, mental, and emotional challenges, thus mastering myself. I joined in an age-old dance. Both predator and prey moving in synchronous steps, advancing and retreating, depending on feedback from each of our senses.

I strike out just before daybreak with my rifle, radio, first aid kit, and pack. The luminous stars are still visible. I see what is left of Orion's Belt, three bright stars fading into the clear blue sky. This constellation was named after the legendary great hunter of Greek mythology. Perhaps Orion will bring me luck today, my first day out on my quest for my impala.

Impala are so common—I have seen hundreds when driving guests around. I know where several herds gather, so I head out of the lodge grounds and make a beeline to where I saw them yesterday. But nothing is guaranteed.

How often is it that when we are specifically looking for something commonplace, we can't find it? Do they sense I am out stalking them? This should be easy; I see traces of their recent spoor. I follow the trail, but they manage to stay out of sight. I walk and walk. I should see them soon; the tracks indicate a fairly small herd, probably males. But there are no signs that they are still in the immediate area. My confidence eventually turns into annoyance. I am ready to return to the lodge without seeing one impala the whole day. A whole day spent traipsing around in the intense heat.

As I turn to go back to the lodge, everything magically aligns. I find the perfect group of bachelor rams, right in the middle of a block far from the road, far from the lodge. They are behind a termite mound, and I can see them so clearly. I line up a large ram in the sight of the rifle. But I just can't pull the trigger. I love animals too much.

Why am I out here? What am I doing? Is it necessary to take a life to prove that I can do it? My mind floods with thoughts and doubts. I hate to kill an innocent animal unnecessarily. Logic says if I merely pull the trigger, the hunt will be over. I will have no chance of finding it again if it senses my presence. So I must pull the trigger.

But something prevents me from shooting. I hesitate, and the herd dashes off, leaving only a termite mound filling my rifle sight.

This happened two or three times when I went out, just watching the impala move out of my sight as my emotions got the better of me. I resolved to still that inner voice and just complete the task. In spite of my efforts to contain my emotions, there was no guarantee that the environment would cooperate. The rules sounded easy, but the reality of actually finding my impala in the right place at the right time was extremely difficult. Overcoming my reluctance to kill was a different matter. It took me a long time.

It finally got to a point that it made me so fricking enraged, I started to hate them. Here I was sweating, getting stung by insects, stuck by thorns, covered in mud. It was all their fault for putting me through pain and hardship. It got to a stage where I wanted to kill these things off just so I would never have to go out again. They frustrated me more and more and more. I thought about all the times I had them in my sights, all those missed opportunities that rarely presented again.

My mind started to play tricks. I was alone out there, and I needed to stay sane, not just to complete the task, but to ensure my own survival. Mentally I would run through what I needed to do. Go for the heart. That was how to bring down an impala. Use soft bullets and shoot behind the shoulder blade. Tune out the heat, the flies, mosquitos, the loneliness. I would concentrate until I got a headache. Concentrate so hard to follow the herd, all the while keeping aware that I was not the only predator out there. There were others also trying to make a kill. I would need to be careful not to unwittingly stumble upon lions, leopards … what else?

My mind would get fried. Sensory overburden, severe head-aches. The constant vigilance. What if I got lost? I was so engrossed in following the herd, I would lose track of space and time. Then there were snakes, all the poisonous varieties. I was just another predator in the circle of life, and I could easily become prey. There were so many things that tripped me up.

Don't think, just walk, crawl, ignore the pain of the thorns. Keep leopard-crawling on my elbows, through the bush. Ignore the acacia thorn that just pierced my arm and drew blood. Don't scream out, stay in control or the impala I'd been tracking all day would hear me.

Now it was time to rise up and walk. But it wasn't a normal walk. I needed to place each step carefully starting with the outside of the heel and rolling the foot in. Roll in. Step. Roll in. Stealthily, I crept up behind the herd. Everything was perfect. I raised my gun to fire.

What was that sound? A troop of baboons in a nearby tree started barking, sending out a warning that I was in the area. Why didn't they bark ten minutes earlier? Why were they playing this cruel joke on me? I watched helplessly as the herd ran off in unison like a school of fish, their heels kicking up and exuding scent, their gossamer coats shining in the sunlight. Once again I returned to the lodge completely frustrated, no prize in tow.

A few days later, I had them perfectly in sight. Everything was great, and I was at the ready to pull the trigger. It all imploded in a second when they caught the glint of the rifle moving in the sunlight. An impala snorted a warning and off they all pronked. The slightest thing could startle them. The impala inhabit the open grasslands and count on their many sets of senses to detect predators. Moving as a herd, that meant many pairs of eyes, many pairs of ears acutely attuned to the environment. My subtle movement of lifting the rifle up after seven hours of pain was for nothing. They ran off into the evening, and I once again walked back to the lodge to try again another day.

On my next attempt, I could have sworn I killed it. The impala was in my sights and I pulled the trigger, using up one of my precious rounds. I was so relieved to have finally shot it. I went to look for the blood trail. But in a split second, between the time I pulled the trigger and the time the bullet fired, the impala had instinctively known to jump or move. They were that quick. I was so sure that I had killed it. I was an accurate shot from all the practice at the firing range and not accustomed to missing my targets. Everything had been perfect. How could I shoot the animal and have the bullet go straight through and not find the blood trail? Was I delusional? I knew I had shot the impala, I was sure of it. If only I could find the body. …

Dejected, I continued on, anticipating that the herd must still be close by. Yes, there they were, across the road. Too late, I heard a vehicle approach. A fellow ranger with a group of guests was out for an evening game drive. But they had spotted me as I ducked for cover! We were supposed to stay out of sight of game drives. I could hear the ranger explain, "It's just one of our trainees in the bush …" How embarrassing to be busted by guests on a vehicle! Another day lost.

My frustrated attempts blurred into a series of unfortunate

episodes. There was the time I took my rifle out, ready to put the rounds in the chamber. But I had no ammo. In my rush to start the day, I had forgotten to bring it when I retrieved the rifle from the safe. *Isidingidwane!* What a foolish thing to do! No wonder my pack seemed so light! I could neither shoot an impala nor defend myself against predators. Another wasted day … another long walk back to camp. …

Then there were the elements I could not control, like the wind, which would shift unexpectedly. I spent the entire day with one bachelor group, leopard-crawling through the bush. I followed, heart beating in anticipation. Which direction would they go? I checked the wind with a bag of chalk or a handful of dust. Surreptitiously, I threw it up in the air and wiggled back under the bush to watch it. I was constantly anticipating, using every bit of cover. I was enduring thorns in my flesh from crawling through the thick bush. It was a painstaking process and so dependent on the wind blowing in the right direction. I must be downwind, hidden in the bush and ready to shoot. But a swirling wind came from nowhere, carrying my scent to both the antelope and the other predators. I was in hiding in the thick bush, but the whirling wind was betraying me. Not a safe day to be out, time to return to the lodge.

I started getting worried I wouldn't qualify. I had sailed through all those weeks of training, all those early successes, all that studying, even the dreaded final game drive with the managers. I was already driving guests unofficially part-time, along with Rockerman, because we were so busy. I needed so desperately to pass this final hurdle and become a fully anointed ranger. I was still the only ranger in training, bottom guy on the totem pole, and it looked like that was where I would remain. Every time I went out, I returned empty handed. Every time, the other rangers would mock me.

"Didn't get it again?"

"Missed it?"

"Waiting for the big one?"

By now I had used four of my rounds and missed. I was experiencing an unbearable level of frustration and failure. This quest for the impala had become an obsession. Even in my dreams, I could see them frolicking about and taunting me. Skipping past me so playfully while I lay there immobilized, just watching them vanish into a hazy mist, too tired to follow. Then I would wake up and think that this was the day I would get that impala, end the struggle. Week after week, I would go out on my free day. One week quickly turned into eight weeks. Everything had come so easily to me before this. Why was this so difficult? I became restless and angry. But I did not give up.

I wake up early, pack my gear, and glance up at the stars. Orion's Belt remains fixed in the sky, a reminder of all the hunters who have gone before me. This is my eighth attempt, my eighth day in just as many weeks, tracking down my impala. *My* impala. Somewhere out there is an impala with my name on it. Just waiting for me.

By now I am familiar with most of the roads through Phinda, so I quickly disappear into a block and traipse off road on the chance that I will stumble upon a herd. My intuition steers me north, far away from camp, up near the pans where the elephants and other large game come to drink. I spend most of the morning walking north in the heat, looking for spoor and other signs of impala.

I stop midday for a break, near a patch of acacia trees. A tower of giraffes is off in the distance, a group of females with young and an older male. They are munching on the sweet acacia pods, and I watch the neck action as they eat, swallow, and regurgitate. They are the world's largest ruminants, animals that chew their cud.

My mind is taken back to Inkwazi where I learned about the many special adaptations required by the tallest animal in the world. The giraffe has a specially designed network of arteries and veins at the top of the neck to prevent excessive blood-flow to the brain when it stoops to drink and a one-way valve in the jugular prevents the back-flow of blood to the brain when the head is lowered. The massive twenty-five pound heart must work twice as hard as the human heart to maintain blood pressure. The two-foot long, prehensile tongue is covered in special papillae, providing protection against the acacia thorns that it relishes.

Giraffes are "taller than the trees," hence their Zulu name, *ndlulamithi*. Antelope and zebras are known to congregate nearby, taking advantage of the giraffe's height and ability to detect predators from a distance. I scan the vegetation surrounding the journey of giraffes, but today there are no impalas in sight. Only a young male giraffe approaching the group. I watch to see if he will challenge the old guy and provide a brief distraction from my hunt. But his attempt to make the older male jealous is futile. In a battle where the neck is used as the primary weapon, the advantage would sometimes go to the smaller male, who could swing lower and harder. The older male knows better than to engage in battle with the young interloper and moves his herd away, avoiding conflict.

I am left alone in the bush once again and continue to head north. It is getting late in the afternoon as I approach an area of mixed woodland. I stop on the edge and decide to wait a few minutes, using my senses to scout the terrain.

Immediately to my right, I see a golden orb spider waiting perfectly still on a giant web between two bushes. The web silk she manufactures from her inner reserve is one of the strongest materials in nature, creating a deadly trap for unwary insects. It has taken her many hours to create this large wheel-shaped web, spinning each strand from within. Her patience and hard work pay off when unsuspecting insects are ensnared in her death trap. Even the male spider is not immune from her clutches, as the female spider has a reputation for cannibalism, preying on the male after mating. Today, all is still as she waits calmly for a meal to appear.

Beyond the spider web, I spot the silky golden color of a herd of impalas off in the distance. They are in a clearing, near a natural embankment. Like the spider, I must be patient if today is the day to fulfill my quest. I approach stealthily, creeping up behind, watching the wind. I see that it is a bachelor group, not young rams but large males with big racks. I am about eighty yards away.

There is no hesitation, no self-doubt, as I dig deep in my own reserves and chamber my rifle. I select a particularly large ram in my rifle sight. Yes, this one has my name on it.

Instincts take over, no emotions, no thoughts. Somehow, all that time in the bush, immune to my own pain and suffering and focusing on a sole target, something makes me hardened. My soft feelings disappear and my killer instinct kicks in. It's a primeval reflex, a compulsion. I slowly raise the rifle and nestle it snugly into my shoulder. Not wanting to risk the movement it will take for me to move the rifle to a dead-rest position, I hold the H&H steady with my left hand and stroke the trigger with my right pointing finger. I line up the bead on a mental mark just behind the shoulder and raise it ever so slightly to account for the eighty-yard distance. I feel the sweat starting to pool on my brow and know from experience that when it drips into my eyes it's all over.

Without hesitation, I coldly pull the trigger.

The sound of the gunshot causes the rest of the herd to immediately kick up their heels and flee. I cannot see anything but empty landscape. There is no way that I could have blown this on my last round. As I run closer, I see the ram exactly where I saw him before I squeezed the trigger. Only now the impala is lifeless on its side, as if in a deep slumber.

I approach the lone animal and see that his rack of horns is even bigger than I thought at first. A magnificent specimen. If I return with a small rack, I would no doubt be ridiculed, so this is a huge plus. Any male over two years is an acceptable kill, but you earn extra respect if you shoot an older one. I feel immediate pride that I managed to shoot a big ram, about one hundred fifty pounds. This will definitely make up for all my previous failed attempts and put an end to all the teasing.

But then I feel a sense of remorse, as I approach closer to the lifeless body. Confronting the impala, I can see his beautiful eyes staring at me from an eerily still face. My exhilaration is quickly replaced with a pang of guilt that shoots through me and makes me shudder. Running my fingers through the perfectly groomed coat, I am proud that I managed to secure the animal that evaded me for so long. But actually touching this graceful beast just lying there wrenches me out of my obsessed state. I break down and cry, thanking this animal for providing me with my selfish personal pursuit of happiness and apologizing for his unnecessary loss of life. Through salty tears, I curse Morty, my training, the lodge, the company. But mostly, I curse the cold-blooded killer that I have now become.

The rapidly growing darkness snaps me out of my grief, and I sharply realize the need to complete my task. I am a fair distance from camp, about three miles. And this large male is way, way heavier than a younger animal. Somehow, I have to carry the carcass back to the lodge before I face the same fate as Jacqui. I do not want to surrender my prize to even more motivated hunters.

I work quickly. To make it lighter, I gut it and leave the entrails in the bush for the hyenas and other predators. I then make an incision in each of the front legs, close to the hooves. Through these incisions, I draw the back legs up to the scent glands on the ankles, creating a natural closure. Now I have created an ingenious backpack.

I carry the bloody animal on my back, its head bobbing over my shoulder. I radio the lodge and tell them I am coming back with my kill. Covered in blood, I march back, making sure my hands are free to reach for my rifle if necessary. Suddenly I realize the futility of this arrangement, as the shot that took the impala down was my last round.

Tired and focused on returning in one piece with my trophy, I do not notice the wasp. Disturbed and decidedly pissed off, the insect takes out its anger on me, stinging me near my eye. I brush it away, but it is too late. My eye quickly swells shut.

I know that this is the time of day when the big cats come out.

And here I am with my senses totally compromised. I can only see out of one eye, I am dragging this long trail of fresh blood through the dark, and I am out of rounds. I need to keep my wits about me. I persevere through the growing darkness. It takes me two long hours to walk back.

I finally see the lights of the lodge and arrive around 9:00 p.m. Everyone is waiting for my triumphant entrance. I am quite a sight, with my one eye swollen shut, this large impala draped over my body. But I am just so happy to be back.

"*Hawu! Utholile inkunzi nkhulu kakhulu!*" Rockerman exclaims. "Wow, you have got a really large ram!"

A sense of accomplishment overwhelms me, and I feel the tears coming back, an outpouring of relief at the realization that I'm being relieved of my burden. The trackers immediately take my prize from me, as they have first dibs on the best body parts. It is more than the weight of the impala that is lifted off my shoulders. My initiation is complete. My life in paradise at Phinda is assured.

Heading toward my room to clean up, I glance toward the starry sky with my good eye. I can see Orion, the mythological hunter who had also been blinded and had recovered to become a great hunter. Somewhere between the stars and Earth, I have developed an even greater respect for the wild animals that inhabit this world and my responsibility to protect them.

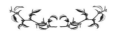

To celebrate, there was a massive big party that lasted all night. We prepared and served the meat to our guests. I made sure that I gave the testicles, the most prized part of the impala, to Rockerman. My first gift to the man that I entrusted my life to every day. I even risked a taste of these Maputaland oysters after downing more than a few celebratory drinks. They were surprisingly good with a gamey, grassy taste.

We had fresh impala meat for the next week. Whatever was left over was made into stews or dried for *biltong*. No part of the animal was wasted. The skin and tail would be used for various things. Rockerman even made me a bracelet out of the hide.

I was completely humbled when I calculated that my actual hunting odds were far less than the patient lion, the stealthy leopard, and the agile cheetah. Eight days. Seventeen stalk attempts. My odds came out at less than six percent.

Yes, I was shown to be the incompetent predator that I am, even with a deadly firearm. It's not as if I had to grab the impala by tooth and claw. Still, I kept the horns outside my house as a reminder of my participation in the age-old dance and my place in the circle of life. This would not be the last animal that I shot in the wild, but it would be the first and only healthy kill I ever made.

ODE TO THE LONGNOSE

Their memories enter the body of the mountain
And they are possessed by the ancient poets
They sing for us their poem
They narrate the story of our beginnings.
MAZISI KUNENE,
"The Great Ones"

Akundlovu yasindwa ngumboko wayo.
No elephant ever found its trunk too heavy.
ZULU PROVERB

AFRICA IS NOT FOR SISSIES. On many occasions she has captured me, torn into my chest cavity like a hungry lioness, removed my heart and eaten it. And then just as quickly my life-organ has been regurgitated, put back in its place, and the chest sewn up again. And I have been free to go. Until the next episode of catch and release. …

There is no favoritism toward celebrities at Phinda. All guests are afforded the same high standard of service regardless of what famous songs they might have written or in what movies they might have appeared. This indifference is probably one reason that celebrities and other notables are frequent visitors. They can be themselves, let their hair down and just fit in. South Africans seem to be immune to celebrity adulation. We know that some of our guests are well known, but to us they are just regular folks. They come to withdraw from the spotlight, to learn more about wildlife and conservation, to tick an African safari off their bucket list of expensive vacations.

And some come to make films here. The African experience can best be told firsthand on African soil, in African settings that cannot be duplicated in a studio. It is a place where the actors are inspired and infused with the sights and sounds of Africa. A place where the settings of the stories they are telling have not changed much over time. Lions on the savannah and leopards in the trees look the same today as fifty years ago, one hundred years ago, one thousand years ago. It is real.

Quite soon after I bagged my impala, in the beginning of my ranger duties, I learned that two productions were being filmed at Phinda and the neighboring reserve. A German crew was at Phinda shooting *A Day in the Life of a Game Ranger*. We often are asked, "So what's it like to be a ranger, to live on a reserve, to have intimate knowledge of the wildlife? It must be awfully exciting and fun. It sounds like a dream job." The camera crew was following one of our most experienced game rangers with the goal of answering these questions. Karl, a quiet guy with ginger-brown hair and freckles, had the enviable task of being the "star." His quiet demeanor belied the steely nerves earned from his many years of participating in game capture and wildlife research. The two German filmmakers were shadowing Karl's every move, creating a documentary about our day-to-day lives.

Coincidentally, the neighboring reserve of Zulu Nyala was the setting for the filming of *I Dreamed of Africa*, based on the book by Kuki Gallman, the Kenyan environmental activist and conservationist. This big-budget Hollywood production brought big name Hollywood stars to Phinda. One day, an A-list film star couple had a free afternoon, and I was assigned to take them on a game drive in a private vehicle.

The V-8 Land Rover purrs to life as Rockerman and I head out with our celebrity guests. I drive down the twisty track, flanked by cathedral-like torchwood trees and towering Lebombo wattles. The guests are silently taking in the beauty of the African bush from their elevated perch behind me. It's a late winter's afternoon, and we're going out looking for elephants. The "gray fear," as Richard calls them. But I am always excited to search for the ellies, and I do not share his overt trepidation. At least not yet.

As we emerge from the sand forest into broadleaf woodland, I am thinking about this day's safari and the best place to take the celebrities for an unforgettable elephant sighting. Although Rockerman and I have only been guiding together for a few weeks, we have formed a strong bond. We often speak in Zulu, both to entertain our guests with the musicality of the language and also to create a plan that will surprise and delight them.

"Bathole izindlovu ekuseni eduze ne-airstrip. Ngicabanga sizozama laphaya," Rockerman says.

They found the elephants this morning close to the airstrip. I think we should try over there.

I drive to where the ellies were seen earlier this morning and start circling the old airstrip. From his tracker's seat, Rockerman gives me the unspoken sign that I should stop. We hop off and examine the mass of tracks crossing the road. To the casual observer, elephant tracks appear like a disorganized mass of saucer-shaped imprints. But a closer look reveals the clear differences between the circular front feet and the cylindrical hind feet. The direction of the tracks can be ascertained by noting the scuffmarks that the hind feet kick up with every step.

I show my guests how, in soft sand, the sole of an elephant's foot leaves an intricately marked mosaic pattern and explain how the feet expand after they touch the ground like massive marshmallows being squished between forefinger and thumb. As the foot is lifted, it contracts again, a most useful adaptation for walking through mud, as the contraction allows for the foot to be extracted more easily with each step. The marshmallow feet also enable elephants to walk with incredible stealth, the cushioning soles minimizing the sound of dry grass or twigs underfoot. Like human fingerprints, the pattern of wrinkles left in fresh tracks is unique to each elephant, and experienced trackers can differentiate between individuals.

I am pleased that we have found the tracks so quickly. We note the direction of the herd and slowly circle the block to make sure the elephants have not crossed outside the perimeter. From his perch up front, Rockerman is constantly scanning the ground, looking not just for signs of the elephants but for other viewable wildlife as well.

The radio crackles to life.

"All mobile units. Repeat all mobile units. I'm zoning the block between Zinave, Qondile, and Airstrip East. I'll be down for a walk for about an hour."

I recognize Karl's voice and the implied meaning of his words. He is also tracking this herd near the airstrip and is planning to take his film crew into the block on foot to view the elephants.

I explain to the film stars that we are going to have to delay our elephant sighting. This is a safety issue. When a ranger is on foot with potentially dangerous game in the area, it is important that other vehicles keep their distance for several reasons. The vehicles can disturb the animals, or even worse, create a situation where the animals are trapped between the vehicles and the people on foot. Additionally, the ranger needs all his senses at their peak when approaching wildlife close up without the means of a quick getaway. The sound of a vehicle could be a costly distraction.

I decide to wait on the outskirts of the block until Karl comes back on the radio to green-light the area again. To pass the time, I talk to my guests about trees and other fauna, interpreting some of the vegetation and smaller wildlife around our vehicle. A loud cackling sound punctuates the air. A group of red-billed wood hoopoes is in the canopy of a marula tree. I explain how the Zulus call this bird *ihlekabafazi,* which literally translates as "the chattering women." The couple are acute listeners, absorbing every detail. They seem to be enjoying their time at Phinda and are easy guests to entertain, interested in everything from the Big Five to the comical dung beetle.

Meanwhile, deep inside the block, Karl and his tracker, Simon, are getting ready to leave the vehicle for their walk with the two cameramen. Simon is one of the most promising trackers on Phinda — so much so that he has conducted safaris as both a ranger and a tracker. His excellent command of English and happy-go-lucky demeanor make him an instant hit with guests, and his outgoing personality is the perfect complement to Karl's quiet restraint. They have sighted the breeding herd about one hundred yards away. After checking the wind direction, Karl gives a safety briefing. Running is the surest way to get killed in the bush. Nearly all dangerous game can easily outrun even the fastest human. So consciously staying behind the rifle at all times is key to a successful safari on foot.

Tracking elephants, especially a breeding herd, requires the utmost care and focus. For exceedingly large animals, they can be remarkably quiet. Their unrivaled sense of smell, excellent hearing and intelligence all combine to make stalking elephants on foot one of the most dangerous pastimes in the world. And elephants, especially the older matriarchs, seem to possess an additional sixth sense when it comes to detecting humans, even when tracking conditions seem perfect.

"If anything unexpected should happen, whatever you do, do not run! Look at me and I'll tell you exactly what to do."

This mantra is repeated whenever we leave the vehicle with guests. It is so drilled into us that few rangers will forget it over the course of a lifetime.

"If anything unexpected should happen, whatever you do, do not run! Look at me and I'll tell you exactly what to do."

Karl and Simon lead the two cameramen toward the distant herd, Karl in front and Simon at the rear. They walk in single file, like a military exercise. A walk in the bush is not a walk in the park, and they need to be fully present in the moment.

The matriarch of this herd had always been a bad-tempered, overly protective elephant. In fact, a week earlier I had been out with Mike, my fellow ranger who had the encounter with the African rock python. We had been viewing the same herd from our respective vehicles, parked in tandem with guests, a safe distance away. Without warning, the matriarch came crashing through the trees, trumpeting and charging, heading straight for us.

Then, just as suddenly, she stopped, reversed into the thick bush and melted away. The air fell silent, as if her screams had canceled out every other living thing. No bird chirped, no cicada buzzed. The only sound was that of collective human breath, exhaling a combination of relief and fear.

And then the impenetrable bush erupted as she came hurtling at us again, flapping her ears and holding her trunk up high, making a beeline for Mike's vehicle. Mike grabbed his rifle, stood up on his seat, and screamed.

"Fuck off, you bitch. Fuck off!!!"

An elephant charge was no time for niceties. I was a new ranger, fresh out of training school, and I remember trying to scream at her to support Mike's efforts. But I had lost control of my voice box.

She retreated again but then charged once more. Only this time she had her trunk curled up and her ears flattened, a sure indication that this was no mock charge. Mike and I, reading these telltale signs, chambered our rifles and braced to shoot. She came within fifteen feet and then dropped to her knees without breaking stride. A cloud of dust hung suspended as the matriarch aimed her head underneath Mike's vehicle to try and flip it.

It is very difficult to turn a serious elephant charge. Almost impossible. But something stopped her, so close to the vehicle that the guests could have reached out and touched her. Maybe it was Mike's cursing. Maybe she felt she had sufficiently made her point. How I did not pull the trigger that day is still a mystery to me. Mike exercised the utmost restraint, somehow realizing at the last possible second that she would stop.

After the dust had settled and we had driven off to an open area to recover, Mike and I unchambered our rifles, relieved and drenched in sweat. A guest had filmed the entire incident from underneath his seat, holding the camera high above his head. Watching the dramatic and shaky video later, we could see just how lucky we all were.

This kind of behavior was not entirely unexpected among matriarchs of elephant breeding herds. But generally, elephants that reside in protected parks, and are not persecuted by hunting or excessive poaching, are much more relaxed around vehicles. This particular female suffered from intense negative human interactions as a result of her relocation to Phinda from the Kruger National Park, one of the largest game reserves in the world. She was part of a herd that had been culled as part of Kruger's controversial elephant management plan. The disturbed female had witnessed her aunts, sisters and probably even her babies slaughtered before her eyes. For an animal with unbreakable social bonds, a vibrant memory and high intelligence, it is not unreasonable to assume that this traumatic life-event caused severe and irreversible psychological effects. She displayed zero trust of humans and treated them with absolute disdain.

In order to fully understand the overly protective nature of certain matriarchs and the severe effects that the relocation had on this particular one, it is important to delve deeper into the nature of elephant society. Most elephant breeding herds comprise a closely knit group of aunts, sisters, daughters, and their young. Sisters form strong, lifelong bonds, as do mothers and daughters. In each breeding herd there are clearly defined female roles. Protective, larger females lead in front and bring up the rear of each family group as it feeds or moves. Other females are tasked with taking care of the youngsters, making sure they do not get into too much trouble.

The matriarch is the most dominant female in the group, often the largest and oldest member of the herd. She is responsible for the decision-making and is respected by the others as the sole leader. She is usually the most protective female in the herd, especially when she has a young calf. Whereas certain bull elephants will display overt aggression when they are injured or in musth, a heightened breeding condition, females generally reserve their aggression purely for the protection of the herd or their young.

That day of the charge on Mike's vehicle, we had been careful to carry out all that our training had taught us. Always have an escape route, check your wind direction, keep your guests quiet, respect your distance. Somehow we still got ourselves into a sticky situation that could have ended tragically.

Karl checks the wind again as he leads the group to a small copse of trees about a rugby field's length away from the elephants. They can see the mothers and young milling about.

The wind starts to swirl. A rare gust blows through from the opposite direction of the prevailing breeze. The matriarch picks up the human scent, and without hesitation, breaks away from the herd. Seeing the group of intruders, she heads straight toward them.

Her overwhelming instinct to protect the herd and her young calf is paramount. Her patience with humans has worn thin. Four tons of angry pachyderm trumpet and crash through the brush. This trumpeting is not musical. Rather, it is like an orchestra of demonic banshees. Few sounds can so concentrate the human mind.

A disastrous chain of events unfolds. The two cameramen peel off at right angles from Karl, ignoring the all-important mantra from earlier.

"If anything unexpected should happen, whatever you do, do not run! Look at me and I'll tell you exactly what to do."

Even armed with this knowledge, the overwhelming instinct is to flee when charged by an elephant. And they both flee. Simon manages to grab one of the men and stays with him. But the other breaks rank and runs in absolute terror.

The matriarch singles out the fleeing man and gives chase. A charging elephant can run at twenty-five miles per hour, easily out-pacing the quickest human. Sensing that the elephant is quickly gaining on him, he selects a termite mound flanked by two trees. He runs up between the trees, which are each about a foot in diameter. She relentlessly hunts him down, charging the termite mound and snapping the pair of trees like toothpicks. The two trees cracking in unison resounds through the forest.

The terrified man trips and stumbles down the other side of the mound. The enraged matriarch follows his same path, and she too loses her footing on the far side of the termite mound. But the cameraman cannot recover in time from his fall. Maybe he is paralyzed with fear. Maybe he realizes that to try and rise up is futile. He resigns himself to his fate as the elephant recovers and closes the gap. The helpless man is an easy target, as the elephant drops to her knees and crushes him into the dirt with her head.

With his rifle chambered, Karl races around the other side of the mound to face every ranger's nightmare. The bloodied man crawls a few paces toward him, pure adrenaline moving the unmovable. He is done. The matriarch charges again. At this stage, it is unclear if she is trying to finish an already finished job or if she has now turned her attentions to Karl himself.

In the split second he has to shoot, the steely ranger notices things he has never noticed before. The elephant's irises, firmly fixed on him, are surrounded by strange white circles that accurately depict the animal's rage and fear. The frightful eyes are surrounded by eyelashes surprisingly long and thick. With a trumpet so ear-splitting that it nearly knocks the rifle out of Karl's hands, she lumbers forward. The massive ears are now held flat against her head, and her trunk coils up against her neck like a massive python primed to strike.

Now the lumbering bulk morphs into a simply astounding turn of speed as clumps of grass and debris explode from her feet like grenade shrapnel. Karl has precious little time to act on what has been drumming in his head for all of a thousand milliseconds.

"Kill or be killed."

He fires. The gargantuan head hardly seems to register the puff of gray dust that rises like smoke from the base of the trunk. The front legs buckle, falling forward over toenails that bury themselves in the dirty earth. Four tons of muscle, bones, tusks and blood crash to the ground as her right shoulder absorbs the impact of the fall. The matriarch teeters from her side onto her back, nearly flips completely over, stretches out all four legs as if reaching for the heavens, and then thuds down onto her side once again.

Karl has dropped her with a well-aimed shot straight through the brain, not an easy shot to take under any circumstances. Undignified, her hulking mass lies prone next to the body of the man who had come to film a documentary on a day in the life of an African game ranger. Karl fires a safety shot into the elephant's lifeless body.

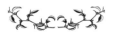

Back at our waiting vehicle, we hear the terrible trumpeting, the ear splitting trumpeting, of a single elephant, then a distant gunshot followed by another. Then more trumpeting, screaming and shrieking as nearly a hundred elephants express their rage at the loss of their matriarch. They are in a panic. The din becomes louder, and there are sounds of bushes and trees being snapped and pushed down. A stampede. Angry, panicked elephants are exceedingly bad news when you are seated in a vehicle that they can toss around like a toy or crumple like a tin can.

Staying here could mean a lot of explaining to millions of angry and mourning fans of my esteemed guests. But trying to outpace a panicked herd through thick woodland is probably even more foolish. I immediately start the engine and decide to cut across the woodland to my left, at right angles to the deafening sound of pachyderms thundering through the forest. The V8 roars as we speed away from the advancing gray avalanche, which is mowing down quite a few saplings in the process. We reach an open pan where the din subsides. I explain to my stunned guests that it is best to stay out of the way of advancing elephants.

I'm not sure if my guests know exactly what is going on. Maybe they don't register the exact severity of the situation. Perhaps they think that elephants just behave this way sometimes. Most visitors to the reserve rightly expect a safe safari and trust their ranger's and tracker's instincts to interpret the foreign environment for them.

As we drive away from the area, Rockerman and I know that something terrible and unexpected has happened. We exchange glances and wonder what transpired in the block, but we dare not discuss it in front of our guests. Not even in Zulu. We don't want our guests to panic. Then the ominous radio message comes through, calling for the immediate return of all vehicles to the lodges.

"What the fuck? Why me? I'd rather gargle wasps!" Richard protested under his breath. He knew that Morty would not waver on this one.

It was ironic that Richard, who was terrified of elephants and would only view them from a distance, was selected to help retrieve the man's body. He would see firsthand how violent an elephant attack could be, and afterward he described it as like nothing he had ever seen before.

"The guy had no back. His entire back was gone."

Richard's words stick with me to this day. The enormity of the attack. The finality of it. I had never seen Richard so distraught about anything. Richard's intuitive respect and fear of elephants had been justified, and it was a difficult realization for him to bear.

Very few people survive an encounter with an enraged elephant. The size, weight, speed, and agility, combined with lethal tusks and crushing feet, make an effective killing machine. When an elephant attacks, it will gore and trample, smash and mangle. Viewing the scene and the remains only solidified everyone's respect for these great creatures. We all emerged with deep reverence for the power that can be unleashed so swiftly and with such brutal force.

The next day, I tagged along with Karl, Morty, Fraser, Richard, and internal investigators for the official inquiry to recreate the details of the attack. If it weren't for the slumped elephant carcass near the termite mound, nobody would have guessed that this had been the scene of a brutal double killing. Karl walked everyone through the scenario. He pointed out where the elephants had been foraging in the thick woodland and showed exactly where he and the others had paused to watch them at a safe distance, careful not to intrude into their comfort zone.

We gawked in wonder at the snapped balanites tree on the left side of the termite mound and the other broken tree on the right side. The crippled trunks revealed the true fury of the mother elephant. As we walked the tracks and listened to Karl's interpretation, I remember feeling like I was simultaneously reliving both the matriarch's rage and the panic that the four humans must have felt. I remember asking myself over and over, "How had it come to this?"

It was a very sad story for everyone involved. The herd abandoned the matriarch's calf. While other females will often try to care for an orphan, it is not always possible if they are not lactating or have their own calves to nurse. Their social ties are deep, but they do what is necessary, making difficult decisions for the survival of the herd. Having lost its mother and deprived of milk, the calf quickly lost strength. About three weeks later, it was found in the extreme south of the reserve, showing signs of severe and irreversible dehydration, indicated by the lack of a vein in the ears. Karl had the unenviable task of shooting the calf, putting an end to this chapter in the story. The double loss of the matriarch and her calf was heartbreaking for the elephant clan.

Back at the lodge, we all went through counseling. This could have happened to any of us. The winds that carry our words and warnings cannot guarantee they will be heeded. Those same winds can betray us when they spin and eddy, carrying our sounds and scents with remarkable speed to distant spaces. We could all identify with this tragic situation.

Our tight knit group lost valuable members as the circle of tragedy grew. Simon started having vivid nightmares and visions. These affected him so seriously that he just disappeared one day, relinquishing his budding career as an excellent tracker and an even more promising ranger. Karl was in a state of shock. He lived to tell the gory tale of every ranger's worst possible guest scenario. The episode continues to haunt him, although five years after, he found some measure of closure after visiting the victim's family in Germany.

These accidents can happen to the most experienced rangers and trackers. Every time we go out, we face a very fine line between showing guests wildlife and impacting the lives of animals. On several occasions I have done stupid things in the bush. Things that could have turned out badly for the animal or me. However, I have been careful not do foolish things with guests. I'm relieved to say that all of the rangers I've worked with have put the safety of their guests first.

Karl certainly did. He was a most experienced and careful ranger, who conducted his safaris by the book. But even when conditions seem perfect, nature can turn in an instant and reveal the most careful tracking party to the wildlife that they are following. It is a fine line that we walk every day. That matriarch was doing what she did best. She was doing her job. Karl was trying to do his. A fine and dangerous line.

This incident changed the ways we conducted our walks, and we were prohibited from walking guests into breeding herds. Safety of the guests is always paramount, balanced with the need to protect wildlife.

We continued on. At the beginning of every game drive, the

start of every walk, we looked each guest in the eye to get their attention. Then we would recite the mantra.

"If anything unexpected should happen ..."

If there is a poem in every story, then the lyrical music in mine would be the elephant. Of all the animals in the African bush, the longnose is my favorite. I have had so many experiences with these loving and amazing creatures—some tragic, some intimate, all very deeply personal. My respect for these large animals only grew stronger the more I observed their behaviors and even participated in their antics.

Elephants share so many characteristics with us that it is hard not to appreciate their humanity. Like us, elephants form complex social relationships. Mothers nurture their young through a long period of childhood. Constantly teaching, guiding, and protecting. They suckle their young from two very human-like mammary glands situated between the front legs, where a woman's breasts would be. Elephants go through puberty at roughly the same age as humans and have similar longevities.

Elephants are known for their brainpower and ability to remember. Their brains are not fully developed when young but continue to grow from birth to adulthood. They exhibit individuality, personality, and cleverness. People who know elephants believe they are self-aware. They have an incredible ability to show emotions like anger, grief, joy, and rage.

There are lessons that we can and should learn from elephants. When some dominant elephant bulls reach old age, young elephant bulls will guard and protect these old bulls. Guiding them through the last years of their lives. These young bulls are called *askaris*, a Swahili word meaning "warriors." The exact reasons for this unlikely pairing between old and young is uncertain. But I like to believe that, in return for their services, the old bull passes on vital knowledge and experience to the younger bulls. Kind of like the male mentor that we should have more of in our human society.

And then there is the strange affinity elephants have for their dead. When elephants come across old bones of their kin, members of the herd will gather around the skeleton. Picking up bones delicately, touching, smelling. Mourning? They have been known to cover their dead with branches and leaves, a ritualistic form of burial.

My experiences with elephants can only be described as instructive, enlightening, and even mystical. They have taught me a lot about myself, and I will always be grateful for the time I spent with these magnificent beasts.

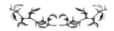

To witness the death of a single elephant is to experience the sadness of the loss of decades of wisdom, magnified a thousandfold when reflected through the eyes, ears, and voices of the herd. Their sheer size amplifies the magnitude of the many tragedies that take place on the African stage in real time. But then the pendulum swings back, balancing the heartbreak with the joy of the unexpected. Special insights that come from being in the right place at the right time. Even though it could just as easily have been the wrong place at the right time.

It is one of those balmy evenings in front of the fire, where beer and talk flow effortlessly with my buddy Greg. We are wrapping up the day at Vlei Lodge, where I am assigned to drive guests for several months, as well as train and mentor Greg. One of the newer rangers at the time, Greg has a larger-than-life personality and a booming laugh that could be heard from hundreds of yards away. One of those infectious laughs that would have you laughing at his laugh.

As I see the full moon coming up over the horizon around midnight, I realize that I stayed later than usual. I need to get some rest if I am to be up at 5:00 a.m. for another day of ranger duty. It's time to return to my quarters at nearby Forest Lodge. Rockerman left with the Land Rover hours ago, so the golf cart is my sole means of transport.

Vlei Lodge is very exclusive, with only six rooms. It is located on the edge of the sand forest, in a big open area that's seasonally inundated with water. This evening, the bright light of the rising moon is reflected in the marshy pools, the few trees casting long shadows on the flat plain. I am enjoying the alcoholic buzz as I bounce along in the little cart. Forest Lodge is only about two minutes away, and I know I have to be up very early. I pushed the evening too late, but there is still time for a few hours sleep.

A ranger is trained to always be on alert. Even in my inebriated state and above the hum of the golf cart, I sense something. First it is a dull shaking of the ground, then noises like trees rustling and branches crackling. I am fringing the open area between the two lodges. The full moon is now completely up, and the sky is filled with stars. Skirting the edge of the sand forest and the wetlands, I scan for the source of the commotion.

Out of nowhere, dozens upon dozens of elephants pour out in front of me. Now I know that a golf cart is no match for elephants; it offers no physical protection, nor can it accelerate faster than an elephant can run. My only choice is to abandon the cart and sprint to a nearby tree.

I scramble up the closest tree to the topmost branches. On closer inspection, I can see there are about a hundred elephants in the clearing. This is a breeding herd, where many splinter groups come together during the mating season. There are bulls, matriarchs, mums, and babies. Every size and shape of elephant is coming closer, multiple shades of luminescent gray approaching my tree.

It is pure serendipity that I find myself at the top of a female marula tree. Elephants are particularly drawn to the female trees, as they produce a sweet, mango-like fruit. There are tales in Zulu folklore about elephants getting drunk from eating the fermented fruit. They will travel for many miles to feast on the fruits of this tree. Perhaps like me, this herd was looking for a little boozy high that night.

The elephants surround the tree, sniffing and reaching up with their trunks. They smell me, try to touch and examine me. Someone is in their favorite tree, his scent mixed with the foliage, bark, and fruit of their marula. I can only look down at this magnificent herd and observe the contrast of their various proportions, colors, and textures in the light of the moon and shadow of the tree. I admire at close range the bright reflection of their coveted ivory tusks against the camouflage gray of their hides, tinted in muted hues by the different colors of dust and dirt they had recently bathed and rolled in. I become aware of a low rumbling sound, which comes from somewhere deep in their bellies. They are communicating with each other in their own private language, consisting of low frequency vibrations that can carry for miles and are pretty much inaudible to humans.

Three hours later, and they are still sniffing and milling around, curious about this stranger in their midst. I spend most of the night in the tree, now sobered up and ever vigilant. From my perch, I closely watch the various social interactions. The protective mums with their babies, the family groupings melding and separating, the affectionate adults often entwining their trunks, the bulls constantly trying to smell and grasp me.

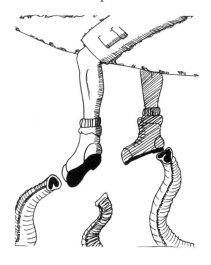

Most of the elephants move off after satisfying their curiosity, until only a few bull elephants remain below me. They continue to inquisitively explore and reach for me, their trunks snaking silently about in the night air, trying to decipher my scent. They may detect the lingering smell of alcohol on my breath with their sensitive trunks and wonder if I have come to join them for a bit of a midnight tipple. These males are huge, and I must lift my legs up several times out of reach of their probing trunks.

Eventually they all move off, except for one big bull that stays behind. With incredible strength, he rubs against the tree, shaking it and knocking off dead branches. Elephants can easily down a tree. And female marula trees are often victims, as the elephants seek out the sweet yellow fruit on the highest branches. Maybe he considers me a threat to the juice in his personal shebeen. I feel the full force of his efforts. But his goal is not to destroy the tree or get more fruit, just send me a message while satisfying a niggling itch.

The large bull decides to show me how strong he is. He lumbers over to the golf cart, wraps his trunk around the roll bar and lifts it like a toy. He proceeds to carry it off about twenty yards. Then he looks around at me as if to say, "Come and get your golf cart!"

He stares at me defiantly, his ears flaring, daring me to come down from the tree. It is a standoff, and he is getting the last word in. He finally shakes his head, turns, and follows the rest of the herd. He made his point.

I wait to make sure they are really gone. As I sit at the top of the marula tree, in that ethereal place between the stars, the moon, and Earth, I wonder how often events like this pass by just a few feet from the lodge. While I sleep in my sheltered bed, many other scenes of courtship, battles, birth, and death play out with only the night sky as their silent witness.

I remember the last time I was caught in a tree at night, when I was lost as a youth on safari on the Shire River. If the Malawian had not rescued me, who knows what visions I might have seen. Maybe my destiny would have required me to play a more active role in the darker side of the African drama, a tasty morsel for hyenas, my leftover bones picked clean by vultures.

After about twenty minutes of reverie, I climb down from the tree and cautiously make my way over to the cart. I examine it for damage, thankful the elephant hasn't turned it over and rolled it. There are a few dents, which I hope I won't have to explain in the morning.

As I drive back to my quarters, the moon is now descending and the light of dawn appears on the horizon. There will be no sleep for me that night, just an indelible memory of magic in the moonlight.

It wasn't just by chance that a herd of elephants was wandering through Phinda that night. The Phinda elephant reintroduction in the early 1990s spared at least some of the elephants from the culling in Kruger, one of the oldest national parks in the world. Elephants reproduced rapidly there, one of the few areas in South Africa where they could roam freely. However, the growing elephant population reached a crisis point. The elephant numbers were negatively affecting the vegetation in the reserve and, as a result, the entire ecosystem began to suffer, turning the park into a desert.

Elephant culling was deemed the most effective way to control the burgeoning population of pachyderms. However, a lucky few were offered respite at nearby reserves like Phinda, where elephants hadn't been seen for years. Although some of the Phinda trackers told me they remember the odd elephant walking through the local communities in the 1970s, the last remaining herd of indigenous elephants in KwaZulu-Natal exists about eighty miles north of Phinda in Tembe Elephant Park.

A team of conservationists, wildlife technicians, and veterinarians was assembled. Their goal was to relocate breeding herds from Kruger to Phinda, minimizing the stress to the elephants. Game capture and animal relocation can be a difficult process, and great care was taken to ensure their safety during transport. Karl, as a part of this core team, was instrumental in caring for their well-being as they acclimated to their new habitat in the introduction *boma*.

Typically, adult elephants become attached to their home range for their lifetime, which is around sixty-five years in the wild. The matriarch retains in her memory the location of food and water sources, sometimes for decades, as it's her responsibility to protect and provide for her siblings and offspring. When a breeding herd is uprooted to new territory with barriers, the established matriarch can become frustrated in her attempts to lead her extended family back to known feeding grounds.

Even though Phinda was less than one one-hundredth of the size of Kruger, conditions were ideal, and the newly introduced elephants multiplied rapidly. The carefully orchestrated reintroduction created widening social circles. Breeding herds headed by a matriarch. Splinter groups. Bachelor herds. And the occasional renegade. These social circles often intersected with the human population as we encroached on their territory and they trespassed on ours. If you look closely at an African elephant, you will notice that the ears are in the shape of the continent of Africa. It's funny how when you are a game ranger in close proximity to an inquisitive or angry elephant you remember bits of trivia like this.

I am the ranger on standby when the call comes in on the radio around noon.

"James, we have a situation at Forest Lodge. That aggressive male elephant is wandering about between the pool and guest quarters, preventing the guests from walking to the lodge for their lunch. Can you please handle this?" asks Morty.

I know exactly which rascal he is referring to. He comes to

Forest Lodge and Vlei Lodge often to harass the guests. The exclusive rooms at Vlei Lodge each have private plunge pools, and the elephant treats the pools as his personal water source. He especially likes to sneak up on skinny-dipping honeymoon couples, as best as a five-ton elephant can sneak up. The shocked guests would make a quick retreat into their room. We would hear their shrieks and know that this curious young bull had interrupted another romantic poolside interlude.

One day, he decided to chase a newly arrived guest as she departed the shuttle vehicle. The lady was in the process of retrieving her baggage from the Land Rover. When he approached, she quickly abandoned her luggage and ran scared into the lodge. The elephant saw her bag and decided to do some mischief. He grabbed it with his trunk and raised it above his head. He swung it round and round and threw it high into a nearby tree. The bag burst open, littering the tree with its contents. All of her panties, bras, and personal items were strewn like Christmas ornaments in the tree outside the lodge entrance. It was a Victoria Secret moment, and all of us rangers tried to keep a straight face as we retrieved the delicate feminine items. She was so very embarrassed. What a way to make an entrance!

Now I am tasked to deal with this naughty character. I grab my rifle from the ranger room and head over to confront the nuisance elephant. In my mind, I examine my options. Now if I were Fraser, I would run fearlessly and chase him off, as I had seen Fraser do many times. I would have no fear, just make a lot of noise and run straight at the elephant, shouting and waving. But I didn't have it in me to face off like Fraser. I thought about aggressively running and shouting but just couldn't do it. I needed to find my own methods.

We trained extensively to anticipate these situations and learned tactics from the experienced rangers. We were taught to recognize an aroused animal, and the difference between a real charge and a mock charge. But I knew that a mock charge could turn deadly in an instant. I have my loaded rifle ready but hope to use my wits instead of a bullet. It is only when you are forced to deal with threats to your personal safety and the safety of others, that you discover what you are capable of, how far you are willing to go.

I head over to the pool on foot to confront the largest land mammal, one of the most dangerous when provoked. I see him lazily feeding in solitary grandeur, and his ears flap to acknowledge my approach. I decide to just stand my ground and see what he will do next. I am hoping that he will eventually move along and a confrontation will be avoided. But he doesn't budge. Just continues to lunch, all the time eyeing me warily with his hazel eyes, fringed by ridiculously long eyelashes. He senses my presence, my vigilance, and is equally on alert. I can tell he doesn't like me there.

After about twenty minutes, he ambles up to me on his pillar-like legs. He does not shift on his front feet or display any signs of aggression, but walks straight up to about fifty feet from me. It is clear there may be a challenge, an obstinate ten-thousand-pound elephant vs. a two-hundred-pound me, odds I'm not particularly impressed by at this current moment in time. I constantly check to make sure that there are no guests in the area as our standoff continues.

Another twenty minutes pass, and he waltzes closer. He is now within twenty feet of me, and he keeps slowly walking. I am forced to make a decision, whether to stand my ground or run away. I calmly chamber a round in my rifle, preparing for a confrontation.

The .375 Magnum is a deadly weapon, effective for both large and medium-size game. We were taught in ranger training how best to load the rifle in preparation for all situations. We carried two types of bullets—soft and solid, depending on the type of game. But it was equally important to know the physiology of the animal you are shooting. Killing an animal requires using the right bullet as well as having an accurate aim to fell it with one shot. You usually only have one chance, especially at close range.

The soft bullets break up in little pieces, creating a small entry and a large exit. They expand and destroy tissue and flesh, seriously damaging vital organs. Soft bullets are used to shoot antelopes and cats like lions and leopards. The solid bullets make a small entry and a small exit. These powerful bullets are needed to penetrate the thick skin and bone mass of large game, like an elephant's skull. To kill an elephant as it is charging, you need to hit the brain with one shot. An elephant brain is the size of a football, and you must know where it is at all times. Depending on the angle of the elephant's head, it can be difficult to hit. It was an extensive part of our ranger training, learning to discern where the animal's brain was positioned in any given elephant posture.

There are many theories regarding loading the weapon in preparation for an excursion into the bush. My strategy was to alternate solid and soft bullets, starting with the solid. So I usually loaded solid — soft — solid — soft — solid. In this way, I would be prepared for both big and small game. The solid bullet would enable me to shoot big game like elephants, rhino, and buffalo. I had one shot to penetrate the brain casing. If I was shooting cats, I could sacrifice the first solid shot as a warning.

There was no question what I would be facing that day. I loaded five solids into the magazine in preparation for my upcoming rendezvous.

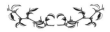

I raise the bead of my rifle at the oncoming elephant, hoping he will stop. I continually scream in my loudest voice.

"Get away. I don't want to shoot you."

I really do not want to shoot him. To shoot an animal on the reserve is very serious. There is a massive inquiry, and you do not want to go there. This is the last thing you want to do. Personally, my deep affinity and respect for elephants probably prevents me from acting too rashly. Perhaps I recognize my own rebellious youthful behavior in this adolescent of a different species.

He walks up to me with short, swinging steps and closes the gap until he is within six feet. He could reach out with his trunk and grab my rifle. Push me to the ground, roll over on me and gore me with his tusks. I am in a very dangerous situation. I don't know if it is fear or self-control, but time seems to stop and I experience remarkable clarity. I had heard about this phenomenon of time slowing down when faced with danger. There are no thoughts, just pure instinct and reflexes. I remember every fold of his skin, every saggy wrinkle. I will never forget that moment. I don't always recall names or faces, but I will always remember facing the elephant, his hazel eyes looking straight into mine.

I do not pull the trigger. My finger is twitching on the trigger, but I do not fire. I am gauging every aspect of the situation, anticipating whether he will take one step closer, then another one. Instinctively, the elephant knows that he is pushing me to the edge. Our eyes are still locked as he spreads his ears, those ears shaped like the continent of Africa, and challenges me. By now I am not shouting anymore. It really comes down to one shot. We stand there facing each other, for a brief moment or an eternity of moments. I don't remember.

Then, to the relief of both of us, he shakes his head and walks off. Turns toward the bush and makes his exit.

I lower my rifle and just watch him leave. I am visibly shaken. Now that the danger is passed, I grasp the immensity of the encounter I just witnessed. I return to the ranger room to place the rifle back in the safe. The other rangers are there and notice me shaking.

"*Jislaaik Bru*! You look like you just saw a ghost!" Fraser says.

I am speechless. My usual bravado is replaced by feelings of shock and an overwhelming sense of relief. I realize that this day has seen one lucky elephant and one lucky ranger.

I thought often of that lone elephant and our exchange. I did not relish facing him again, when he was older, smarter, and certainly a lot bigger. If he were prudent, he would join a herd of bachelors and become an *askari*, learning wisdom and manners from an old bull. If he remained a renegade, he would continue to roam solitary and cause trouble.

I'm afraid he made the latter choice. A few months after our confrontation, I heard that he had trespassed in the wrong place, at the wrong time, and picked the wrong person to challenge. Once again, the unfortunate task of dispatching the troublesome bull fell upon Karl and the wildlife conservation team. I was glad it wasn't me who pulled the trigger and ultimately felled this spirited animal.

ODE TO THE LONGNOSE AND ME

You, the true king of Africa
Magnificent Colossus
You, the Speaker of Silent Language
Whose pleas fall Unheard on lesser ears
You, the bearer of the Convoluted Brain
Unfathomed Intelligence
You, the Great Nomad of the Wild
Stifled Wanderings in a Diminishing prism

Me, the scourge of Africa
Unpunished Rapist
Me, the Speaker of many Tongues
But Listener to one Selfish Voice
Me, too, the Bearer of the Convoluted Brain
Stupid Intelligence
Me, the Great Nomad of the World
Suicidal Plague of Encroachment

OH, Sufferer!
Your fate is in the Hands of a Killer

JAMES ALEXANDER CURRIE

LEGS OF THUNDER

Voices come back again and hang on a dry pole
They walk aimlessly
They speak to each other as though from memory.
But the winds carry them away
And cover their footsteps with desert dust.
MAZISI KUNENE,
"The Fearful Ruins"

Akukho mful' ungenathunzi.
There is no river without a shade.
ZULU PROVERB

ROCKERMAN WAS MY CONFIDANTE, MY close friend, my partner... and my hairdresser. Although his real name in Zulu was Mavuso, meaning "one who has risen," he went by the entertaining name of Rockerman. He was with me when the fatal elephant attack occurred, and together we witnessed the aftermath of the controversial killing. But we were also to learn that the deadliest killers in Africa were those unseen by the human eye, invisible killers that robbed the continent of its best and brightest.

On a game reserve, a ranger is only as successful as his tracker. So a successful ranging team hinges on the relationship between the ranger and tracker. As a ranger, I tell stories, interpreting the bush and its inhabitants for the guests. It is the tracker's job to read the signs of the bush, find the wildlife, and give an insider's perspective into the traditional uses of plants and animals. The tracker shares the responsibility of the safety of the guests. But he shoulders the safety of the ranger too. When we leave the vehicle and track dangerous game on foot, the ranger relies on the tracker's acute senses and superior tracking skills.

The art of tracking is an integral part of everyday life in Zulu culture, handed down from one generation to the next. From a very young age, Zulu boys will watch the family's cattle. When they lose a cow, they will track that animal until they find it, sometimes spending nights alone in the bush. They know they cannot return home until they account for every animal in their care. In Zulu communities, cattle are a form of currency. Seven head of cattle might buy you an ordinary-looking wife. Ten head of cattle might buy you a particularly beautiful wife. And twenty head of cattle might buy you a chief's daughter. So tracking is a vital part of protecting wealth, and there is no room in Zulu communities for slack trackers.

Some Zulu trackers are fortunate to possess a keen intuition in addition to their tracking skills. When tracks are lost, they have a natural ability to get into the mind of the animal and know exactly where it's headed next. I had the privilege of working with two young men who possessed this uncanny gift. It was a very rare occasion when I managed to spot wildlife before these talented men.

Rockerman was especially good at locating the elusive leopard, the most sought-after Big Five sighting. I learned a great deal about animals from books and my mentors at Phinda. But Rockerman imparted to me a deep knowledge that seemed to come from some ancestral wisdom, some innate connection with the earth. He was always saving me from trouble, and his dedication to our friendship never wavered.

I am a newly minted game ranger when I receive the news. The top shareholder of the company is coming with his family for a game drive, and I am the lucky ranger selected to escort them. I want this day to be flawless.

Rockerman and I carefully prepare the Land Rover to ensure that we have everything we need for an evening in the bush. Setting out, I am very nervous guiding one of the principal people in the entire company.

"Where shall we start?" I ask Rockerman. "Shall it be lions, buffalo, or elephants?"

Before he has time to answer, the radio sparks to life.

"Stations. I've located a pride of lions on the north side of the Inkwazi flood plain. They are slowly mobile east."

I thank the fellow ranger for the tip, and my spirits soar as I spin the vehicle toward the open grasslands. I relax, knowing we'll be starting the drive on a high note.

From his seat up front, Rockerman looks for signs of movement in the tall grass. I watch him out of the corner of my eye as we drive into the bush, slowing down when he needs to look closer, speeding up when he indicates to go forward. Then he motions to stop, steps down from the exposed tracker seat, and climbs into the passenger seat next to me. His human outline is clearly visible from the perch, but masked once inside the vehicle. The lions are close, only about a hundred yards away, so we must take every precaution when approaching these great predators.

I position the vehicle so that we can view the savannah and the behavior of the lions without interfering. We can see that the lions are on a hunt, stalking a herd of zebra. This is an amazing sighting! I turn to the family and perch on the windshield, the lions visible off to the side of the vehicle. I do my best job as an interpretive guide explaining their feeding habits and history, knowing that I am being evaluated the whole time. The owner is watching my every move, listening to my every word to see how well a newly trained ranger functions with guests. A good ranger, after all, means happy guests, and happy guests mean repeat guests, and repeat guests mean a healthy and sustainable bottom line for the company. But I am in my element. It's not every day we see lions in pursuit, in their natural habitat, the predator and prey dynamic at work. The excitement creeps into my voice.

"Watch how the lionesses slink through the grass and the males stay behind. The females do most of the hunting. Notice those adolescent lions behind that dominant lioness. See how they stay behind the female, watching her every move. As cubs, they would have used the black ears and black-tipped tail of the lioness as visual marks so they did not lose sight of her in the long grass. Now they are developed enough to join in the hunt. But it will take many hunts before these youngsters are able to kill successfully. Much of what they learn over the next few months will not be instinctual but rather, taught to them by the adults. ..."

Facing the family, I launch into a detailed explanation about the danger of the hunt we are watching. I have the rapt attention of most of the family, except for the father. I notice his eyes wandering between the stalking lions and the front of the vehicle, looking directly behind me.

"Where is your rifle?" he interrupts.

Horrors! There is no rifle in the vehicle! The rifle rack is empty. I have totally forgotten it! This is a cardinal error, one that could have life and death consequences on the reserve. I know this mistake will cost me dearly, will probably be the end of my short-lived career as a game ranger. Here we are out in the bush, just a few yards from predatory lions, and I have no means of protecting my guests, should a situation arise.

I apologize and immediately speed back to the lodge to retrieve the rifle. I rush into the ranger's room, open the safe, load the rifle and dart back to the car park. We head out again to continue on our drive, but I can tell that the shareholder is upset. The atmosphere is heavy, and try as I might, I cannot restore the earlier jovial mood. I know I have to somehow salvage the situation. I turn to Rockerman.

"We have to do something extra special," I urge him for some comforting advice.

"*Sizothole ingwe,*" he replies with confidence.

We will find a leopard.

I know that the chance of spotting a leopard is remote. Leopards in the area have been heavily persecuted and are still getting used to vehicles and people. Many days can go by without spotting any trace of a leopard, not even the faintest tracks. The radio has not crackled with the report of a leopard sighting in weeks. But Rockerman senses that not only is my career on the line but the future of our newly formed partnership. He is determined to save both.

Unlike the other large predators, the leopards roam far and wide on the reserve and beyond. Fences cannot contain them; they tunnel under using escape routes dug by hyenas or cross over using highways created by overhanging trees. So it's difficult to tell how many leopards are actually on the reserve at any time. They are the masters of stealth, active after dusk, their rosette-patterned coats providing the perfect camouflage. The most difficult of the Big Five to track and a very prized sighting for every visitor to the reserve.

In spite of the odds, I know Rockerman will give his best effort to locate a leopard. We drive through the soft sand as evening descends. From his elevated seat, Rockerman identifies zebra tracks, warthog tracks, nyala tracks and baboon tracks crossing the road. He motions me to stop the vehicle to look closer at a new set of tracks.

"*Impisi,*" he says.

Hyena.

Hyena tracks closely resemble those of the leopard. They are a similar size, but the hyena tracks are distinguished by having visible claws. All cats, with the exception of the cheetah, have fully retractable claws that are invisible in their tracks, unlike the dog family.

Finding hyena prints can be a good sign, and we often track hyenas when looking for leopards. Hyenas follow some distance behind leopards, waiting for the cats to kill something, and then try to appropriate the meal. We continue following the hyena tracks but keep an eye out for solitary cat tracks, with four toe pads and a light tread.

Sure enough, Rockerman finds that the hyena tracks have now joined the telltale tracks of a female leopard in the soft dirt.

"*Ingwe.*" He smiles.

Leopard.

Tracking in a vehicle requires a different art than tracking on foot. The reserve is designed to help you find the tracks on and off the roads. The roads are laid out so they create blocks of wilderness, which are traversable by a vehicle on all sides. So if you follow tracks on a road and the tracks disappear into one of these blocks, all you need to do is drive around the block to find out where they come out. If the tracks do not come out, chances are high that you have isolated your quarry.

We follow in the Land Rover for about an hour and a half along the road, taking great care not to drive over the tracks and lose the trail. The hyena tracks eventually leave the road, and we are now following very fresh leopard tracks, which go off into a patch of beautiful sand forest. We traverse the perimeter of the block and see where the hyena tracks come out the other side but the leopard tracks do not. We've pinned it down. It's somewhere in the block amid the tall forest trees and croton undergrowth.

Rockerman's skills are put to the test. He must locate the leopard on foot and find the best approach to view the animal from the vehicle without disturbing it. Not an easy task. And dusk is fast approaching. The sky is turning from a muted orange to a darker purple, punctuated by a brilliant star. The planet Venus is now visible. We must act quickly before we lose the tracks in the dark.

Leaving the guests in the vehicle, I grab the rifle, and the James-Rockerman team heads off, taking advantage of the remaining daylight. As we follow the spoor into the brush, I watch Rockerman's every move, determined to learn as much as possible from the native expert. He stops to examine the impressions closely, obviously a female but with faint, smaller tracks next to hers. His eyes meet mine. We both know that a female leopard can be especially dangerous if she has cubs with her. But it is also one of the most coveted and rare sightings possible. My mind flashes back to the training course, how mindful I need to be. If the bush gets any thicker, we'll need to pull out and abandon the search.

We must be cautious if we are to nail this sighting for our disgruntled guest. I nod and check the rifle. No room for accidents. We would not venture into the block without the rifle, and it is actually fortunate that the shareholder noticed that I did not have it earlier. We would not be able to track the leopard in the brush without the guarantee of protection and would have had to give up on the chance of spotting the leopard.

Rockerman heads out silently and swiftly, using his every sense to intuit the animal's intent. I follow, imitating his stealthy walk in my soft rubber-soled shoes, rolling each step in, taking great care not to disturb any tracks or make any noise. I can tell he is in the mind of the leopard, thinking like the leopard. Where would she melt into the ground, her perfect camouflage blending with the scrub and lengthening shadows? If she had a cub with her, she would be especially secretive and protective. Taking advantage of every remaining ray of filtered light, Rockerman looks for anything even remotely out of place. Is that a gently overturned leaf? Has the earth been disturbed under that Lebombo wattle? He tilts his head slightly to obtain a different angle of view. Does that slight depression in the ground have two green eyes?

Her faint tracks disappeared when she entered the block, the sparse undergrowth masking her light tread. Rockerman's intuitive tracking skills are now in high gear, he is determined to find the elegant lady in the fashionable coat. His nostrils flare slightly, as he sniffs the air for any trace of the decaying scent of a kill. No, nothing. Is she on the hunt? There is no pan in this block, so she isn't looking for a water hole where she might nab one of her favorite delicacies, a red duiker or baby nyala. He glances behind to make sure she has not circled back. His eyes are constantly scanning the trees and grass for any sign of movement.

"*Yima!*" He whispers for me to stop.

Rockerman points out the female leopard, which is barely visible except for a brief movement of her face as she snarls defensively, her cover blown. Her tawny color with black rosettes blends perfectly into the evening shades under the reflective croton leaves. Normally, any leopard at Phinda would be long gone by now, especially a smaller female who would be unwilling to confront humans.

Rockerman holds up three fingers. His sharp eyes have picked out the two tiny gray cubs snuggled next her, barely distinguishable in the creeping shadows. We are simultaneously thrilled and appalled to see that it is indeed a mother leopard with cubs. Female leopards are particularly protective when with their young, and the rapidly fading light is now in her favor.

Time to go into action. We retreat carefully, mindful not to disturb the protective mum. The leopard is a silent killer, and does not often give off a warning growl like the lion. She could charge and be on us in a flash, all one hundred pounds of steely muscle and razor sharp claws ready to shred the khaki intruders to bits.

By now, the sun has set as we retrace our steps to the vehicle. The guests ask what took us so long and seem irritated that they were literally left in the dark.

"You guys are in for a special treat tonight. We found a leopard," I say. Being careful not to ruin the bigger surprise.

Rockerman plugs in the spotlight and attaches the red filter that we use for viewing animals after dusk. I drive carefully into the brush with our guests. Rockerman swings the light back and forth through the enchanted forest as we try to relocate the feline trio.

They are exactly where we left them, as if waiting for us. For some reason, these normally secretive wild animals are all totally relaxed. Perhaps the mother knew that she did not have the time to move her two tiny cubs before we got back. Perhaps this beautiful female is comfortable in our presence. The evening only gets better when the little cubs peel away from their mum. They tumble and take turns chasing each other, playing at stalking and pouncing.

Then, as if on cue, they advance closer to our vehicle. Curious and inquisitive, they climb a tree above the Land Rover to get a better view of us! With the red-filtered spotlight, we watch these tiny twin leopard cubs, about three months old, frolic fearlessly overhead. I sit silently and let the baby leopards work their magic.

It is an incredibly special sighting. I watch the owner's demeanor change as he views these little animals playfully scampering about, illuminated by the red glow. He has had the privilege of experiencing some of the best wildlife sightings across Africa, and it takes a lot to impress such a seasoned traveler.

This is one of my best sightings to date. Thanks to Rockerman's skill at finding those cute little cubs, my career as a game ranger is salvaged.

And I never forgot my rifle again.

At the end of a grueling day in the field, it was customary for ranger tracker teams to go their separate ways. The rangers either spent the evening entertaining guests or congregating back at their lodgings. The trackers disappeared to their shared quarters and reappeared the next morning to help prepare for the day's activities. I always found it somewhat strange that social mingling and interactions were usually limited to the shared game drives. Although there were white rangers who were color blind, the influences of the apartheid regime were still apparent in some of the white staff, even though the mantra of the company's leadership preached inclusivity and racial tolerance. Or perhaps it was more that apartheid had created such strong divisions between black and white that the resulting lack of cultural understanding on both sides created a natural reluctance to mingle freely.

Rockerman and I broke the mold and quickly formed a brotherly bond, which was highly unusual. Our relationship extended beyond work and was built on trust, mutual understanding, and respect—so much so that when I introduced Rockerman to our guests on safari, I would be careful not to use terminology that some of the other rangers used, like "This is my tracker." Which infers ownership.

One human cannot own another. The havoc of apartheid unfortunately still lingers in many interracial relationships in South Africa, hanging around like a bad smell. But at the same time, I believe that it's vital to truly understand the prejudices of many white people in South Africa. Inherently, apartheid was built on a deeply rooted fear, a fear of a people that the white minority did not understand. Years of religious and political propaganda at a young age shaped the attitudes of South Africa's white youth. In a Calvinist culture where freethinking was discouraged, it is easy to see how the bulk of South Africa's white minority grew up with some form of racial baggage, ideas and beliefs that were not easy to shed after the dismantling of apartheid in the early 1990s.

As a child, I was taught a painful lesson about human dignity on the streets of Cape Town. I grew up a sheltered youth and had little experience with the realities and atrocities of the oppressive political system and its effects on the majority of the population. In the 1970s, apartheid was something adults whispered about, the whispers of fear floating in the wind. It was just an abstraction, not something I could grasp concretely. Even though I spent quite a bit of my youth with my Auntie Jan, an anti-apartheid activist, her words about all people being created equal were just words. Words that didn't penetrate my young consciousness until one dreamy Sunday afternoon when I got a big wake-up call.

I would run freely back then with my fair-skinned buddies, with no thoughts or concerns about our safety. It was just taken for granted that, as whites, we were safe. The blacks and coloreds who came into our lives were there to provide for us as housekeepers, gardeners, and cooks. Under the apartheid system, they were required to have an identity card to enter our neighborhoods, and thus there were few incidents with strangers.

I remember playing in the streets with my buddy Carl. We would venture out from our neighborhood in the Doordrift Gardens in Plumstead, where I lived with my family in a modest maisonette. We would run and play and do the things that boys do when they are eight years old.

Carl was a Canadian living in South Africa, which I always thought was very strange. Most white South Africans were making plans to emigrate to Canada or Australia, to escape the encroaching black armies on our borders. I knew about these conflicts. My father was a Cape Town Highlander, called up to fight in the Angolan War. His frequent absences were a reminder of the Nationalist Party propaganda, warning us to be ever vigilant against the threat of black invasions.

Far from those borders, Carl and I knew we were safe under apartheid rule. Safe to pursue childish pastimes, unsupervised and free to explore. Typical boys, we enjoyed throwing rocks and sticks and stones at each other. It was on a quiet Sunday afternoon, in the midst of one of our imaginary battles, when we noticed a tall man with a beard walking alone down the street. He was black and we were white.

"Let's get this guy," I whispered to Carl.

We each picked up a stone and aimed. One of the small rocks made its mark, cruelly hitting him. His initial surprise changed immediately to anger, as he turned to face his attackers. It took a moment for us to realize that he was coming after us. And after us he ran, pursuing us down the streets of Plumstead. He was fast, faster than me.

My youthful burst was no match for his long legs as he quickly caught up to me. He seized me by the scruff of my neck and flat-handed me across the face in full view of all the white motorists. If a policeman had witnessed the scene, he would have been imprisoned and probably "disappeared."

I could feel his fury as he held my aching face close to his, his black eyes locked on mine. I will never forget his words.

"I may be black," he said. "But I am a Zulu. A proud Zulu, and I will never be treated like a dog."

That was the moment I knew that Auntie Jan was right. My son today bears the name of both a beloved dog and a Zulu friend. But not a Zulu dog.

That incident had a profound effect on my life. In school, I was one of only three white kids that studied isiXhosa. Our private school, unlike all other segregated schools, had "token" black kids and offered African languages as a subject in high school and in the last two years of primary school. I excelled at Xhosa and later went on to major in African languages at university.

Under apartheid in South Africa, very few whites made the effort to speak an African language. The propaganda spilled out by the nationalist government promoted an insular lifestyle. Learning an African language and being able to speak to the majority of the people in their mother tongue would force us to take the shell off, the shell of apartheid that encapsulated the white people. It protected us from things we did not understand and therefore perceived as threatening.

Everyone was required in school to learn Afrikaans, the language of the Nationalist Party. In addition to their native Zulu or Xhosa, the blacks had to learn both Afrikaans and English to survive in their roles as laborers under this tyrannical system. To be hired as a housekeeper, gardener, factory worker, even a sanitation worker, the blacks had to speak the language of their oppressors or risk starvation for themselves and their families.

Nelson Mandela said, "Speak to a man in his own language, and you speak to his heart."

He understood that language was the way to overcome the obstacles to reconciliation. And the major obstacle was fear. The Nats wanted to keep the barrier high between whites and blacks. They used religion, the educational system, and language to indoctrinate and control every facet of life.

Early on, I discovered I had a natural affinity for learning languages. So it was easy to learn Xhosa even though I was by no means fluent. Phonetically, Xhosa is a simple language, although it was a bitch to learn the fifteen different noun classes, each with different verbal prefixes. A tonal language, speaking it means learning the distinctive clicking sounds associated with consonants. It involves rolling your tongue and clicking the syllable while pronouncing the word, forming a distinctive speech pattern unique to the Xhosa language.

I noticed immediately that when I spoke Xhosa to an African person, at a petrol station or in the street, faces would light up. Speaking to a white person in their native language was very foreign to them. It broke the invisible barrier, shattering it straightaway through the power of speech. For me, it was an awakening to feel truly a part of South Africa. After all, how can you say that you are South African if you can't speak South African?

So it was only natural that when I came to Phinda, I found myself in my element. Here I was in the midst of native speakers, as the trackers and staff spoke Zulu, which is very similar to Xhosa. Working closely with Rockerman, I quickly learned basic Zulu, earning the respect of all the trackers. Just like the early African explorer Sir Richard Francis Burton, who mastered over two dozen languages, I found that the key to understanding and assimilating the culture is the ability to speak the native tongue.

My relationship with Rockerman escalated into a deep friendship, and we became *abafowethu*, like blood brothers. We were one of the first ranger tracker teams to spend our off time together, exploring each other's culture. Sharing special glimpses into each other's lives. I went to his home and experienced the daily life of the Zulus. Sleeping on the floor. Washing in a basin. The traditions and the food. I dreaded having to eat *sadza*, or *pap* as it is sometimes called, the staple local food that is a form of mashed maize. I had a strong dislike for the taste, but I always held my nose and asked for seconds, not wanting to offend. I recognized the warmth and hospitality of his family, sharing what little they had in the spirit of *ubuntu*.

Then Rockerman came with me to Cape Town, his very first experience with modern civilization away from the camp. We rode the cable cars up Table Mountain and visited Robben Island, where

Mandela was imprisoned. Even caught an opera at the Spier Wine Estate in box seats, gifted to us by the Phinda owner we had impressed with the leopard sighting. *Carmina Burana* explored "the fickleness of fortune and wealth, the ephemeral nature of life, the joy of the return of Spring, and the pleasures and perils of drinking, gluttony, gambling and lust." I remember laughing together that evening at these themes, these universal human attributes that transcended both time and cultural differences, themes that ran so intimately through our own lives and would soon define our future paths.

Through Rockerman, I saw the things I took for granted with fresh eyes. I still have the hand-written thank-you note from him acknowledging the impact of his visit.

> James:
>   It's been great pleasure to be with you on my visiting here in Cape Town. More to James, the time he speaks to me about Cape Town it was just like a dream, but I realised that the time he saying he confirmed the ticket for my flight, then I realized he's true. I would like to thank James to what he did to me because if I become a ranger I've got things to talk about to the guests like: Cape Point, Table Mount, the waterfront aquarium, Robben Island and IMAX, the biggest screen in Africa.
>   I will be silly if I forget the Spier with its beautiful Carmina Burana. Thank you again for traveling me a long journey, I got to see a lot of places. For me, this is something I won't forget even into my next generation, I will still be talking about what I've seen in Cape Town. Thank you.
>   All the best till next time,
>   Rockerman
>
> See you back at Phinda. Pass my regards to all the friends in Cape Town.

Back at Phinda, it was clear to everyone that we were a team—an equal team, and we split all of our tips down the middle. If you were to go on a game drive with us, you would be met by a tall, lanky ranger with dark hair, twinkling brown eyes, and a welcoming smile. Alongside would be a stocky, light-colored Zulu, attractive and muscular, with equally spirited black eyes and a lively grin.

Rockerman's Zulu nickname was Legs of Thunder. He had tree-trunk–size thighs and was an excellent soccer player, hence the nickname. But it was his complexion that stood out for me as unusual, the light color of his skin. That is the thing about Zulus. They can be tall, dark, light, fat, skinny. Unlike some other cultures, you can never say for sure if someone is a Zulu or not unless you hear the person speak. This is a throwback from the wars that the Zulus waged over the subcontinent, gobbling up smaller tribes and incorporating them into the Zulu nation. What this means is that, even today, some Zulus can trace back their ancestry to these smaller tribes and their distinctive features.

I met Rockerman at his prime, around age twenty-eight. One of the aspects of traditional Zulu culture is that a male's manhood is measured in part by how many wives and mistresses he has. Polygyny, even today, is still firmly entrenched in many parts of the countryside.

"*Hawu, uyindoda!*" People will say when learning you have multiple wives. "Wow! You are a man!"

And people in Zululand were dying like flies—more so than ever before—from common illnesses like tuberculosis, malaria, and even innocuous afflictions like the common cold. An unstoppable and silent killer had woven its way into the lives of this proud people.

Rockerman and I had been working together for about a year when he started getting sick more and more often. He always had a cough, which continued to grow worse. But now he would say that it was just the flu. I started getting concerned when I noticed him perspiring in the early morning when it was still cold. Yet he always showed up for work. He loved his job!

In late 1998 I left on one of my off-stints to go back to Cape Town. Before I departed, he'd given me my customary haircut at "Rockerman's Barbershop." I remember thinking on that particular day that he was looking better than he had these past few weeks.

We laughed and talked about his son, my travels, his love of soccer, my unruly thick hair. Words flowed easily that day, as we spoke in a combination of English and Zulu. My short time at Phinda so far had been nothing less than spectacular, and I felt lucky to be working with the best tracker, someone who read my mind like he read the spoor, someone so open about sharing his life.

Several weeks later, I returned from leave to learn that Rockerman was ill. For a few days, I was assigned another tracker and I carried on with my job, thinking he would return any day now. One of the other trackers finally broke the news that he was not coming back. I immediately went to see him at his home. He was sitting outside, in the late afternoon sunlight. I couldn't believe how someone could lose so much weight in the space of three weeks! It was hard for me to believe that this emaciated person was Legs of Thunder.

Rockerman didn't even say hello. Just looked up at me with sunken eyes.

"*Ngiyagula mfowethu,*" he said.

I am sick, my brother.

That was when the realization of what I already knew hit me like a punch in the face. AIDS is like an avalanche. It settles quietly, like powder snow. Unnoticeable. And then it piles up, gradually gaining critical mass until the body can't fight back anymore. A once strong, youthful body comes crashing down to earth.

Before the end of that six-week work cycle, Rockerman was dead. I remember sitting with him in a ward at Bethesda Hospital, angered by the way that they treated AIDS victims like lepers. His bed hadn't been changed in days. Urine all over the sheets. The stench unbearable. Left to die in his own piss and feces. Alone and ostracized from the world. I will never forget his last words to me.

"Promise me that you will take care of my son," he whispered.

It was a promise I never kept. I meant to, but I didn't want to be reminded of all the times I'd spent with Rockerman. I just couldn't look at his young boy and be reminded. Just couldn't face it at this time in my life. Hopefully, I said to myself, I will remedy this some day.

I spoke at his funeral and said my final good-byes. Just crying and crying, horrible. This would not be the only time that the scourge of AIDS and untimely death would make an unwelcome appearance. I found it hard to carry on. As difficult as it was to absorb the shock of Rockerman's death, it was clear I needed to accept that life in Africa continues at its own pace, and that death is a frequent visitor.

ROCK STAR TRACKER

And the hero is he who brings a total gift
Narrating a tale of danger through invincible love,
Bringing into the circle, a witness of endless wisdom.
MAZISI KUNENE,
"Secret Wisdom"

Iso lilodw' aliphumeleli.
One eye does not succeed.
ZULU PROVERB

"LOOK AT THOSE MONKEYS FUCKING over there!"
I cringe as I hear the words. This bright and sunny morning, my new tracker partner, Norman, is practicing his interpretive skills, trying his best to entertain the guests on our early game drive. He wants so badly to make the transition from tracker to ranger. But he has a lot to learn about guest etiquette. Norman has heard us rangers using such vulgarities when we talk among ourselves and assumes that this is the correct way to describe the activity he is pointing out.

"Watch carefully, as this will be very quick," he continues. "Notice the bright red penis and the blue balls next to the white stomach. Just like the American flag—red, white and blue!"

I almost cut in and put an end to his misplaced attempt at humor. Fortunately, our American guests all burst into laughter as they turn to photograph the aroused monkeys. We have been with this group of guests for several days, so they are used to our quirks and humor.

We are just finishing our midmorning drink stop of crispy biscuits and strong coffee spiked with amarula, a delightful creamy liquor made from the intoxicating fruits of the local marula tree. The primate chatter alerted us and betrayed the vervet monkeys, copulating overhead. A brief, colorful encounter that will likely result in a furry black infant with a pink face in less than six months.

Norman smiles at me, delighted that he has gotten a chuckle from the tickled guests. I just shake my head. What he's lacking in manners, he makes up for with wit and charm. I will have to have a little chat with him later about the facts of life and how to describe it in more appropriate terms. Humor and lewd expressions need to be tempered  with sensitivity when communicating animal behavior to guests. Since our livelihood depends on gratuities, we need to always be mindful of cultural differences and keep the conversations friendly but professional.

As Norman and I pack up the gear from the coffee break, the guests head off into the bush to do their business. We assigned them each a spot that was cleared of danger, but we keep a wary eye out nonetheless. We haven't lost anyone yet and plan to keep it that way. Everyone returns quickly—they don't want to miss a moment of our entertaining game drive.

Even though we've only been together a few months, Norman and I have gained a reputation as one of the best ranger/tracker teams at Phinda. In a short space of time we have concocted a guaranteed recipe to provide our guests with an unforgettable African safari experience: excellent tracking, spellbinding interpretive storytelling, and, most important, the collective determination to go the extra mile for our guests. If they wanted to go on game drive the entire day, we would do it. Nothing was too much trouble for our guests. We loved it. And the guests loved it too.

"Where shall we go next?" I consult with Norman.

"Ingulule?"

We still have an hour or so before we return to the lodge for breakfast. The cheetahs were reportedly out for a morning hunt several miles from here on the Mziki Marsh in the north. An impressive sight, to see cheetahs hunting at full speed. Maybe we would get lucky.

In their relaxed and jolly mood, the guests climb into the raised seats and agree that we should end the drive with a visit to see the cheetahs. Somehow our mixture of caffeine and alcohol at nine in the morning works its magic. Maybe because everyone has already been awake for hours and needs a bit of a pick-me-up combined with a hair of the dog from the previous night's indulgences. Our laughing Land Rover heads off to the marsh as we all enjoy the warmth of the morning sunlight.

The play of light and shadow through the spindly terminalia trees creates ripples on the sandy road, fashioning a leafy pattern over the tire tracks of previous vehicles. A pair of majestic bateleur eagles, with their characteristic rolling flight pattern, circle overhead in the cloudless sky. It's another perfect day at Phinda.

"Does anyone know what a bateleur is?" I ask.

No one usually does.

"Watch how the eagle uses its wings, how the bird dips and raises those wings to compensate and catch its balance, much like the outstretched arms of a bateleur, which is French for 'tightrope walker.'"

"*Yima!*" Norman interrupts, bringing our attention from the sky back to the earth. He holds up his hand, indicating that I should stop as he points to shallow indentations in the soft sand. I can see evidence of recent drag marks perpendicular to the tire treads. Even from the vehicle, it's obvious that something large has been hauled across the road into the neighboring block. The trail leads into a stand of thick acacia and scrub.

The trip to find cheetahs will have to wait. Any unusual activity is worth checking into, always an opportunity for our guests to see nature in action, always an opportunity to feed my inquisitive nature. I grab my rifle, and Norman instinctively reaches for his panga.

"Stay seated, guys. Someone's been working really hard this morning."

The tracks are those of a leopard, although leopards aren't normally out and about this time of the day. I am eager for a sighting, as the leopard is the only one of the Big Five they have not seen. This would be a rare daylight sighting if indeed there were a leopard nearby.

Leopards cannot hide from Norman. If there is a leopard nearby, he will find it. Weapons in hand, the two of us are off on foot into the stand of thick acacia bushes. Like Sherlock Holmes and Dr. Watson, we search for clues. This time, it's my turn to be the apprentice. What will we find at the end of the blood trail? I can tell it is still fresh, the red drops sticky, clinging to the blades of grass.

I observe Norman's every movement. He is stalking silently, following the drag marks into the bush. Stooping to examine the trail, intuiting the direction from the crushed grass where the animal had been put down for a moment, where the predator had shifted its grip on the heavy carcass. Not far from the road, Norman stops and points to a low shrub hugging the ground. Barely visible in the shade, I notice dark objects that turn out to be cloven hooves attached to legs. Norman's keen senses have led us to a pale, tawny body melding into the ochre grass. The mystery is solved. A large male leopard has stashed a freshly killed reedbuck under the tree.

Reedbucks are known for their quirky behavior, running about in short jerky movements, stopping frequently to emit a high-pitched whistle. This one must have picked the wrong location to be bouncing about on this bright morning, too close to a hungry predator. His shrill whistling probably gave away his whereabouts, cutting his dancing career short.

"*Ingwe!*"

Norman points out the unmistakable signs of a leopard kill. The reedbuck's neck is crushed, its stomach punctured by the cat's hind claws and then torn from its hindquarters. But where is the leopard?

Unlike in other areas of Africa, Maputaland leopards rarely hoist their kills up trees. I believe this is due to a combination of factors. First, the bush is very thick, allowing leopards to stash their prey in almost impenetrable thorny thickets that lions would have a tough time accessing. Second, there were relatively low densities of hyena and lion in the area. Since the 1940s, farmers and hunters had religiously kept the numbers down except for the odd straggler lion wandering from Mozambique every once in a while. Lastly, Maputaland leopards are some of the largest leopards in the world and have been known to successfully defend their kills from a lone hyena looking for an easy meal. So leopards had grown up being the top predator in this area.

However, this didn't stop them from being the victims of human persecution. Some of the local ranchers were always on the look-out for big game wandering through their adjacent properties. The large leopards that crossed in and out of Phinda and Mkuze game reserves were especially coveted. As rangers, we were often conflicted. We would spend many nights getting leopards accustomed to vehicles, only to hear of them getting shot when they crossed onto neighboring properties. Grooming leopards for almost certain death was heartbreaking.

One of the farmers in particular had gained a nasty reputation and was a thorn in our side. He would bait the leopards away from the reserve by attaching a fresh impala carcass or goat to his side of the fence. Then, to earn more money, he would use his legal destruction permit, easily obtained for "problem" leopards, to provide a foreign hunter the opportunity for a guaranteed trophy kill. One day, he proudly displayed the dead body of one of our favorite leopards, clearly visible to a group of guests on game drive, and we never drove down that adjacent road again. Something needed to be done to safeguard the cats.

Leopard management policies in the area began to change in 2005 as a result of an intense research program. The Mun-Ya-Wana Leopard Project monitored leopard activity and collected scientific data. The recommendations included revamping the way hunting permits are allocated, overhauling trophy hunting protocols, and working closely with the local farmers to increase tolerance. Guy Balme, one of the Mun-Ya-Wana project members, reported in *Africa Geographic* in 2010 that the number of illegal leopard kills had decreased significantly and leopards were now thriving.

But in the mid-1990s, the leopards at Phinda were very shy and secretive, wary of all humans. Norman and I needed to be very careful, treading near a recent kill.

I glance carefully at the partially eaten rump of the reedbuck. This once-prancing antelope is clearly now a leopard's interrupted breakfast. The kill is so recent that even the flies, the normal first responders, haven't found it yet. In fact, there are no buzzing insects, no bird sounds, nothing to be heard. Just dead quiet.

Norman and I look at each other, sensing that we aren't alone. The hair on the back of my neck starts to crawl with that feeling you get when you're being watched. I become keenly aware how exposed we are.

"*Qaphela*," Norman whispers in warning as we turn to retrace our steps.

Be careful.

He immediately motions me to stop. My gaze follows his. There, in the scrub that we just passed, is a large male leopard. We literally passed within eight feet of this dangerous predator! There he is, crouching under a bush, melting into a shallow indentation in the ground, his spotted fur blending with the yellow acacia.

On hearing our approach, this stealthy animal had doubled back on his tracks and hid within easy view of the kill. His cold green eyes had been riveted on us the whole time. Tricky bastard. Unlike lions, leopards will hardly ever growl to reveal their presence, preferring instead to rely on their camouflage. If you see one, it's best never to stop and look it in the eye. In my experience, if he thinks you have not seen him, he will be content to watch you walk past until he feels it's safe enough to return to the kill.

We immediately fall into retreat mode. I face the leopard but turn my head so I am never looking at him directly, just watching out of the corner of my eye. Norman grabs my belt and guides me slowly step by step back to the vehicle.

The leopard doesn't move, doesn't charge, satisfied that his prize is safe from the two-legged intruders. He is somewhat acclimated to humans and vehicles, but one always needs to exercise the utmost caution when facing large cats on foot. No matter how familiar you are with a wild animal, you never know what might set it off, how hungry it is, what it's protecting, or whether it's just plain having a rotten day. That could easily be one of us under the tree, our boots in the air, our youthful dancing days curtailed.

I am dripping with sweat as we make our way back to the vehicle. Maybe because the day has heated up. Or maybe because I have never been that close to a leopard on foot before. Or maybe I am just so excited to show this amazing sighting to our guests! A leopard and his victim in broad daylight. I drive the Land Rover into the block, positioning it far enough away so that the leopard won't feel threatened but close enough so that everyone has a view. This is an extremely rare sighting, and the guests are thrilled. So thrilled, in fact, that I know I have a problem.

"Too bad the Smiths missed the morning drive," I hear one of the guests say. "This is their last day and I can't wait to tell them about this. Just amazing! James and Norman — you guys rock!"

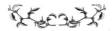

As I expected, the guests shared their experience at breakfast with the others, and the disappointment was palpable. Sharing sightings, logging them in the lodge book, bragging about adventures, this was all part of the experience. This was what people paid for, and the pressure to repeat a great sighting was often intense. I knew I was going to have to somehow repeat the experience for the disappointed guests before they left.

There was also healthy competition between the ranger-tracker teams. Who would find leopards that night? Norman and I specialized at locating this shy and nocturnal animal. More often than not, it was our names entered into the guest book next to the leopard sightings. I remember that, after one particularly successful six-week work cycle, Norman made enough money in tips to buy himself a decent secondhand car.

Norman was the closest thing to a rock star that a tracker could be, and damn, were we a good team! But it was no accident that Norman and I were able to wow our guests, blowing them away with a combination of interpretive stories and exceptional tracking. Because Norman had a checkered past. Like some of the best trackers on the reserve, he was a reformed poacher.

We were the same age, now in our mid-twenties, but while I spent my youth birding with my aunt on Table Mountain, living a privileged life and reading stories of great explorers, Norman was tending the family's cattle and learning the art of tracking from his father. While I was attending an elite high school in Cape Town and running with a fast gang of friends, Norman and his buddies were supplementing their education with a side business of poaching.

Tracking and killing animals to survive, the young Zulus were well versed in the art of "tangle, dangle, strangle, or mangle." They would use snares made of wire to capture game for feeding their families, and also to sell in the local black market. But it wasn't just the antelope, warthogs, and other edible small game that got caught in the cruel traps.

Sometimes the snares would maim or kill animals that weren't considered edible, like zebras, cheetahs, and rhinos. The young boys did not think of consequences, leaving scores of animals to suffer and die. That was just the way it was in Africa—they had been brought up to deal so casually with death.

I learned all of this sitting with Norman in the Land Rover in the evenings as dusk turned to dark. We would often spend all night near a leopard, getting it habituated to vehicles. Norman would make a nasal sound, mimicking the sound of a dying impala. Then we would wait for the leopard to emerge out of the darkness, a lithe figure changing from shadow to solid form in the dusky moonlight.

Once Norman even called a young female right up to the vehicle, his calling was that good. Mostly, we just rested quietly in the moonlight, chatting softly while we watched the leopards in the distance, every once in a while maneuvering the vehicle closer.

It was through Norman that I gained a deeper understanding of how the communities viewed poaching and the neighboring reserves. Another perspective on how the past one hundred years of colonialism and conquest had shaped the Zulu youths who were now my closest friends. Norman grew up in the rural and impoverished area west of Mkuze Game Reserve, not far from Phinda. He lived in a mountainous village called KwaNgwenya, near a traditional Zulu community called KwaJobe, meaning "place of Jobe." Jobe are the line of chiefs who run this particular community. You couldn't do that in America, as your city name would change every four years. But in Africa, chieftainship is a constant. The Zulu have an unwavering loyalty to their traditional leader, their *inkosi*.

Growing up, the local population considered the nearby game parks and reserves the domain of the rich. Decades ago, these reserves had been carved out of their traditional communities by the colonial government and the inhabitants relocated to less desirable areas. Even worse, they no longer had open access to travel back to their neighboring communities to visit family and friends. They now had to trespass through the reserves or take long and circuitous routes around the fenced parks. There was even a sacred burial site of chiefs of the KwaJobe clan located in the nearby Mkuze Game Reserve, and only clan members could go there and commune with their ancestors.

Consequently, the reserves became symbols of the intruders depriving the local communities of their legitimate right to live off the land. Because the locals were viewed as outsiders and not allowed on the reserves, this fed the perception of game parks as the enemy. So Norman and his friends never considered it a serious crime to trespass and hunt on the reserve property. They were poaching for survival, just enough to fill their pots and a little extra to sell. The reserve was like a candy store, with free food for the taking. Kind of like Robin Hood and his Merry Men, stealing from the rich to give to the poor.

All they needed to do was use their well-honed bush skills to set snares while avoiding the field rangers. Sound easy? Poaching is a precarious way of life, requiring great skill and endurance. You must know how to read the spoor and game trails, have a keen eye for the surrounding environment, understand how scent travels in the wind, have deep knowledge of the animal's behavior, and know how to avoid the sharp teeth and hooves when removing an animal from the trap if it is still alive, injured and frightened. All in the dark while living in a state of constant vigilance, learning to avoid snakes, lions, elephants, spiders, buffalo, leopards … and the arm of the law.

It's interesting that there is no equivalent word for "poaching" or "trespass" in Zulu. Probably because the words imply something illegal, and hunting to feed the family, just enough to fill the pot, has never been an illegal activity in the eyes of a rural Zulu.

So how did Norman end up at Phinda? How did he graduate from hardened poacher to rock star tracker, wannabe ranger, and raunchy comedian? A man named Jabulani came to his school and spoke about the need for conservation, the interrelationship between wildlife, the game reserves, tourism, and jobs for the community.

The lights went on for Norman once he realized he could make an honest living using his bush skills. Instead of living day to day, not knowing where the next meal was coming from, he could earn a steady income and still be near the wildlife he had come to know so well. "The hands wash each other" was a Zulu proverb that now made sense to him. Being a rehabilitated poacher, his tracking skills were almost unmatched, so he could work in the reserve, supporting his young family while now preserving the game that made his job possible. Yes, Norman had been snared by the conservation bug.

But tracking for Norman wasn't just a job, a source of income. It was his life, and he wanted to take it one step further. He confided to me that someday he wanted to be a ranger, like me. I noticed how intently Norman listened to everything I said to guests. The stories told, the niceties, the hospitality.

When I first started working with Norman, he was pretty green when it came to guest etiquette. He would blurt out the most inappropriate things. But he was a quick learner, and soon Norman and I were sharing the ranger responsibilities. I remember one particular day when we had private guests. I was so hung over from the night before that we switched roles. I took the tracker seat and Norman drove the guests. Norman and I had our fights, our disagreements, but he was one of the most loyal friends one could wish for. We spent so much time together, once again like brothers. An unlikely pair, the tall *umlungu* and the short dark Zulu.

During those long nights habituating the leopards, we shared intimate details of our personal lives. The issue of AIDS came up often. I was still reeling from the pain of Rockerman's death and did not ever want to lose another companion to that dreaded disease. I pleaded with Norman to use protection and be faithful to his wife. All the while I was philandering around with lots of different girls. He always told me, reassured me that everything was fine. That he did not mess around. But with his charm and good looks, and his newfound success, deep down I knew that there was probably more than one woman in his life.

Norman and I worked together for two years. Sometimes I would travel with him on our breaks to visit his family in KwaNgwenya, his home on the outskirts of a cluster of small villages and clan groups. We would navigate the badly corrugated dirt roads, keeping an eye out for wandering cattle on the way. It was strange that they lived just a few miles south of South Africa's fifth largest dam yet had such limited access to water. The Jozini Dam was built in 1974 to provide irrigation to sugarcane and cotton farmers established along the fertile flood plains of the Makatini Flats. More recently, the dam has been celebrated as a biosphere that attracts a large diversity of birds and is renowned among leisure seekers for its sailing and fishing. But the people of KwaNgwenya are reliant on a few communal water points scattered around in the community. Adding to the cruelty of the village's location, KwaNgwenya falls on the rain-shadow side of the Lebombo Mountains, shielding it from the summer rains that fall on the east coast of KwaZulu Natal, and making it difficult to harvest significant rainwater.

After the hot, dusty drive along the primitive roads, I was greeted with a big welcome from Norman's family and neighbors. I became close to his family and I loved his two little boys. The older one took after Fakazile, his beautiful mother. The younger was a spitting image of Norman. In spite of their limited resources and lack of electricity, they always made room for one extra. The Zulu people are warm and hospitable, and they are truly the "people of heaven."

Once again, I found myself immersed in a deep friendship that went beyond cultural boundaries. Like brothers, we liked to laugh and joke and dance. We loved wildlife and beautiful women. We took risks and actively courted danger. Our youthful friendship was forged under the African stars, in the shadow of the leopard.

There is only one way to improve the odds for another leopard sighting that evening for the disappointed guests. Norman and I jump in the Land Rover and head back, hoping the reedbuck carcass is still there. The leopard is extremely fluid and unpredictable and could easily drag the remnants deeper into the impenetrable bush, usually where there is no vehicle access. Its goal is to keep the morsel out of sight. Leopards can be quite secretive, hiding their prey in the shade and away from vultures and other pesky undertakers. Or inquisitive onlookers like us.

Norman and I arrive back at the scene and retrace our path on foot into the block, this time with extra caution. The carcass has not been moved. But where is the leopard? We feel its presence before we actually see its muted outline in the hollow under the tree. He has not felt the need to stir in the midday sun and so is lying there very discreetly. If we hadn't seen him earlier, we would have had a difficult time detecting his black and yellowish form in the long grass.

We keep our eye on the leopard as we discuss strategies for keeping it in the area. Norman's skills as a former poacher bubble up; he knows how to bait for leopard. We need to secure the carcass to the tree, as a leopard will not usually leave its own kill until it has sated its hunger, feasting under the cover of darkness.

"Did you bring any rope?" I ask.

Norman shakes his head. In our haste, we have not come prepared. We don't have much time, so we need to improvise.

"Use your shoe strings," Norman says. "They're longer and stronger than mine."

I stoop to untie my boots, hoping I won't have to explain my lack of laces when I return to the lodge. Approaching the carcass, I see it's now covered in flies. The smell of the congealed blood is overwhelming in the hot sun. I gag at the sight of the torn flesh, the bones and sinew exposed. And there's that awful smell that only comes when the entrails have been ripped apart and are left to rot in the African heat. I need to act quickly before I lose my cookies. Grasping the hooves, I knot the laces with two half hitches, securing what is left of the buck to a thick branch, making sure that enough of it is still hidden so that the leopard will be comfortable approaching it but still visible for our upcoming evening game drive. All the while, Norman keeps an eye on the male leopard, whose amber stare is fixed on us.

Mission accomplished and we retreat. Would the shoelaces hold up against the incredible strength and determination of the large leopard? Or would our impulsive and reckless attempt to contain the sleek spotted cat's supper with a few pieces of string be for naught?

What we did was very frowned upon. We weren't supposed to interfere with nature and the hunting process. But that evening, the guests were happy. They saw a leopard that night only forty yards away.

Norman and I upheld our reputation as one of the best leopard teams at Phinda. The rogue ranger and the rock star tracker.

Abafowethu.

Blood brothers.

ROGUE RANGERS

We wandered through the savannahs and the tree-shades
We sat together at the gatherings and sang our song.
They were those who came to listen;
They were those who came to see the wound;
They were those who came for the dance
Yet others sent their hunting dogs after us.
MAZISI KUNENE,
"Myeza and His Musical Instrument"

Uyindab' egudwini.
He is a topic for discussion over smoking pipes.
ZULU PROVERB

A RATHER LARGE AFRIKAANS LADY FINALLY answers our banging on the door to the inn. She is one of those fine specimens of humanity that make you struggle to discern whether it's male or female or something in between. We can tell she is not pleased, as it is very late at night, too late to entertain a couple of drunken game rangers.

Richard and I are trying to prolong our evening out on the town. We have left our rifles behind and taken off our khaki uniforms. Any chance we have to distance ourselves from the reserve, we see how fast we can get drunk as cheaply as possible. We started at a restaurant on the outskirts of town, ordering burgers and gin and tonics. But to make it fun, we have established the "Ice Out G&T Twist" ritual. This is an elaborate ceremony where, in tandem, we dump the ice out on the floor with our fingers. Then we drop down on one knee, link our arms, and knock back the gin and tonic in one gulp. Smash the glass on the table and order another. When drinking beer, it's called a "Drop Knee," and it's celebrated in bars as far afield as Lake Worth, Florida. After a dozen or so downed gin and tonics, the bartender at this restaurant kicked us out.

Undaunted, we proceeded to look for another place to carry on, and the lights of the inn beckoned us. But now the proprietor becomes even more annoyed when we demand not only entry but to be served her finest wines. We want them here and we want them now. She wisely refuses our drunken demands, but not before I brazenly tell her that on our way over, we'd seen a whole pride of lions walking up the Sodwana Bay Road toward the center of town.

"Die leeus kom. Sluit jou deure. Hou die kinders veilig," I say wickedly.

The lions are coming. You'd better lock your doors. Keep the children safe.

Her eyes widen as she slams the door in our faces.

By now it is very late, and we are disappointed that all the bars are closed to us. With our fun for the evening over, we head back to Phinda. We have no worries about driving drunk, as it is rare to see another car or any pedestrians on the deserted roads. The greatest danger is hitting an animal, which could emerge suddenly from the side of the road. Or something could be lounging on the still warm tarmac, too low for our headlights to detect.

We arrive safely and tumble into bed. This is a typical evening for us, Richard and I sharing good food, good drink, and good company to pass the time.

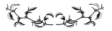

I was always getting into trouble with my fellow ranger Richard. Mix together our youth, brashness, and sense of mischief with a bit of alcohol and the resulting chemistry proved dangerous. Our days alternated between the excitement of locating wild game, the boredom of menial chores, long days serving as both revered guide and glorified butler for picky guests. All this for six weeks straight followed by two weeks of leave back to civilization. No wonder we needed an outlet for our pent-up energy whenever and wherever we could find it. Throwing darts in our small quarters at pictures of lodge managers on the back of the door was just one of the ways we relieved our boredom. Sometimes we just needed to get away, if only to the nearest village for a change of scenery.

The closest town to Phinda was Hluhluwe, which served as a funnel for tourists traveling through northern KwaZulu-Natal to the various game parks in the area. It was a six-hour drive from Johannesburg, or a three-hour drive from Durban, on good roads in a two-wheel drive vehicle. Or a thirty-minute drive from Phinda in whatever vehicle we managed to muster for the evening.

Although a hub for visitors, Hluhluwe was more like a village than a town — really just a frontier settlement full of local Afrikaners and other "wild frontier" types. The small local watering holes evoked untamed spirits of the past, some even adorned with bullet holes in the walls from previous miscreants. The residents eked out livings catering to the local populations as well as the tourists who passed through on their way to the surrounding game parks and the occasional naughty safari rangers out for some fun. Hluhluwe was difficult to pronounce if you weren't a local or familiar with the Zulu dialect. The "hl" sound of the name is vocalized with a strange hissing sound at the back of the throat and can generally only be pronounced by locals. When talking with foreigners, we used to call the town "Huey Lewey" so that they could understand.

The road to Hluhluwe passed through the local Zulu communities, still largely segregated from the white farms, a relic of the recent apartheid era. Richard and I had headed out earlier that evening, passing by small villages of colorful houses, corrugated tin structures, and wandering animals. We were full of energy and glad to enjoy some well-needed venting. When we weren't talking about girls, guns, guests, or the staff and management, we turned to our favorite subjects, birds and botany.

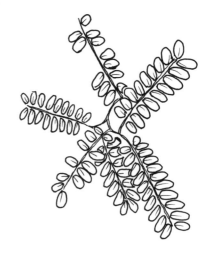

"Did you know that the town is named for the thorny monkey bush, the Hluhluwe creeper?" Richard asked me as we drove along the Sodwana Bay Road. He was always proud to show off his knowledge of botany as he pointed to a thick stand of the monkey rope, its thorny spines hooking onto adjacent trees, climbing to reach the sun. I knew that the thorny-rope flat bean found in this area was often confused with the acacia, since they both have leaves, thorns, and pods. But the precise difference had something to do with the once-compound vs. twice-compound leaf arrangement.

"The village boys would use the branches to make a muzzle for the cows. They also used to make love charms from parts of the tree. Maybe we should stop and pick up some charms for all the chicks we're gonna come across tonight," he teased.

I shrugged off his suggestion, knowing that the chances of any nubile young women visiting Hluhluwe were about as guaranteed as a group of nuns visiting a strip club.

We continued on our way, heading through the pineapple plantations managed by the predominantly white Afrikaans farmers. The Queen Victoria pineapple was a profitable crop and grew well in this region of hot summers and cool, frost-free winters. In fact, it was about the only crop that survived in the harsh conditions and sandy soils of Maputaland. Sunburn during the scorching summer months was the only hazard, if you didn't count the loss to hungry primates and other game pilfering the tempting ripe fruit.

This sweet fruit, actually a perennial herb, originated in South America. It made its way around the world on sailing ships as a known preventative for scurvy, first from the islands in the West Indies to Europe, then to South Africa in 1655 and finally to the eastern coast of KwaZulu-Natal in the 1860's. Here, European entrepreneurs, determined to turn the land into farms, found that growing pineapple was much more lucrative than growing sugarcane. The feathery plumage of many of the sugarcane fields was soon replaced with the thorny leaves of sweet pineapple. Today Hluhluwe produces ninety percent of all edible pineapples for the South African market.

Richard kept on trying to impress me with his botanical smarts. "Did you know that pineapples contain bromelain, which is used to remove body hair? Maybe rubbing your face with pineapple juice every day would save you some time shaving." Richard was referring to my noticeable five o'clock shadow.

We continued on our way to Hluhluwe in good spirits. Entering the town, we passed the supermarkets and automotive repair shops, the farm supply and hardware stores, where both the Zulu communities and the local farmers purchased their provisions. We headed straight for the local hotel, the gathering place for white farmers and rogue rangers.

Richard and I had hatched a plan to pass ourselves off as construction workers for the company that was tarring the road from Hluhluwe to Sodwana Bay. Soddies, as we fondly called it, is a popular tourist destination that offers excellent deep-sea diving and fishing, surrounded by the southern-most coral reefs in Africa. In the name of development, the scenic gravel Sodwana Bay Road would be no more as the laborers indiscriminately destroyed the rare balanites trees and Lebombo wattles along the way. The perfect cover, we ditched our khaki clothes that might give us away as game rangers and posed as construction workers, not wanting our behavior to reflect badly on Phinda.

Our evening out on the town was about to begin with a round of heavy drinking. Who knew it would culminate in a crisis with recriminations? Like the Hluhluwe creeper threading its way through the bush, my actions that night would have far-reaching effects, far beyond the town, the pineapple farms, and Phinda Private Game Reserve.

The next morning, Richard and I are rudely shaken awake. There is a massive emergency meeting of all the rangers on the reserve. Still hung over, with no memories of the previous evening, we join the rest of the staff. We are not prepared for the news that sends a chill of foreboding down every ranger's spine. There is a report that one of the prides of lions has escaped from Phinda. How has this happened? Is there a break in the fence? An escape facilitated by poachers? The lions are in danger, the people in the communities are panicked, and everything at Phinda comes to a standstill while many of the staff search for the escapees.

Everyone is required to do what is necessary to find and contain the pride before anyone is hurt. This means checking all the fence boundaries and engaging all the patrols both on land and in the air via helicopter. This was so serious that the head of Phinda was flying down from Johannesburg to evaluate the situation and do damage control.

Now, it's important to understand the innate fear that the local people had about the introduction of predators into the nearby game reserves. When starting Phinda, there had been much contention between the community and the reserve. The biggest fear was that the lions and other predators would escape and kill cattle or, more disturbingly, attack people. This was a very sensitive issue.

Richard and I look at each other. Even in our foggy state, we realize that my casual remark to the disgruntled innkeeper the evening before had caused serious damage. Rolling out a massive search for a fictitious pride of lions would cost the reserve dearly. I have a decision to make—do I own up and save the company a ton of money at the risk of losing my job, or go with the flow and join in the imaginary search?

My decision is a no-brainer. I confess to Morty the head ranger that the cause for the alarm was my own drunken behavior during our wild night on the town. He immediately calls off the whole search and saves the reserve from a major expense. Upper management never did find out that the source of the panic was one of their very own rogue rangers. Morty just told them that it was a misunderstanding. Of course, I am given a written warning. And I am glad that we had somehow survived another round of mischief and miraculously kept our jobs.

Careless words, serious consequences. Another lesson. Later in my time working as a ranger at Phinda, I instigated another senseless act.

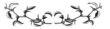

It is midafternoon, and I am on standby with my good mate Gavin Foster. Being on standby means that we are responsible for helping other rangers when needed or transferring guests. Mostly we just have some free time as long as we keep our radios on. Calls tend to be infrequent, so this is down time for us, away from the demands of driving guests.

Gavin and I decide to head down to Nobonobo Pan, a well-visited water hole for game when it heats up during the day. This is an almost guaranteed place to view herds of elephants coming and going during the winter months.

Sure enough, we see quite a few elephants in the area. I

desperately want to get a closer look. A real close look. I have a crazy idea. What if we conceal ourselves in the water when they come down to drink? How cool would it be to stand right next to an elephant in the pan? Now Gavin is not easily persuaded to do stupid things. This is dangerous, risky, he says. Of course, he is right. But I am not easily dissuaded.

Fraser had taught me a trick, how to mask the smell of humans. I rationalize with Gavin that we could reduce any risk of the elephants detecting us by covering our heads and faces with fresh elephant dung. It takes some convincing but I can be persuasive. Gavin's restraint is no match for my contagious enthusiasm. Once he comes around and catches my excitement for adventure, he agrees this will be great fun.

Although I am repulsed by the smell of shit to the point of throwing up, I am determined to see how close I can get to the elephants. We find some dung near the pan and mix it with mud to make it pastier, since the dried up dung consists of mostly fiber and grasses. We joke about working like dung beetles, forming the shit into round balls with our hands. The pungent smell is  overwhelming, and I use every ounce of control to keep from hurling as we cover every inch of our faces and heads with the dark, thick mixture.

"We really shouldn't be doing this," are Gavin's last words, as we strip to our boxer shorts and descend into the tepid water, maybe about the size of a large swimming pool. Our reflections blend into the shallow mud as we walk over to a patch of reeds on one side. The perfect place to hide chest deep and wait for the elephants to arrive.

It isn't long before a herd of bull elephants come down to drink. For the first time, we realize how foolish this is. It was okay to view these large animals from a vehicle, where we always had an escape route and plenty of acceleration to get away quickly should things become dicey. But here we are just a few feet away, completely unprotected, knowing we can be trampled any second. Gavin and I look at each other, simultaneously crouching down until we are up to our necks in the water, then deeper until only our eyes and noses stick out. There is no escape. We are standing just a few feet from the elephants. How cool is this!

The elephants approach the pan and look up and down. Elephants have a very keen sense of smell. Contrary to popular belief, their eyesight is also quite good. Not as sharp as the predators on the reserve, but certainly good enough to see two grown men close by. It is so important to stay camouflaged. We don't want to provoke any curious or aggressive behavior. So when they look our way, we go under and hold our breath, completely submerged and invisible in the murky water. Silently and without making ripples, we exercise tremendous self-control to stay still and quiet, not wanting to draw attention to our presence.

This is a small herd of about seven males. Unlike female elephants, who stay with their matriarch and birth family, a male adolescent gradually leaves the birth clan over a period of several years and joins up with a group of other males. This bachelor herd roams freely until mating season, when each individual breaks off to seek out a desirable female. He will court her for several days. If he is lucky and she accepts his overtures, there will be a new calf in about twenty-two months.

We spend the next half hour observing the bulls enjoying their midday drink. The elephant's trunk is an incredibly useful appendage, one of those peculiarities in nature that makes a lot of sense. The super-sensitive trunk functions as an instrument for grasping food as small as a peanut, reaching high into a tree for fruit or lifting things as heavy as a golf cart. It's used for communication, as they frequently touch affectionately, entwine trunks on greeting, discipline their young. Today they are using the trunk as a giant straw, sucking up water gallons at a time and hosing it into their mouths. A large bull elephant can drink up to sixty gallons a day, downing over twenty-five gallons at a drink stop. We know we will be here a while.

Finally, all the bulls leave except for one. He stays behind and ventures farther into the water, moving toward the patch of reeds where we are hiding. I wonder if he suspects the two intruders in his pool and is preparing to roll his tons of bulk right over us. He slowly shuffles over as Gavin and I go down once again. As he ambles nearer, he fortuitously turns to face the other direction. I hear the sound of water being sucked up in an endless stream, then a loud hiss as he sprays it over his backside to cool off.

Just eight feet from me, I can see his saggy elephant butt up close and personal. Always pushing the limits, I can't resist the temptation. Gavin watches silently in horror as I pick up a clump of mud, fashion a mud cake and throw it hard. It stings the large bull squarely on the butt cheek.

The elephant is totally surprised. Who would dare mess with me when I'm having my drink? He looks all around, smelling the air and using all his senses to determine if there is any further danger. We once again hold our breath and descend beneath the surface. Eventually he decides there is nothing to be concerned about, finishes his drink, and moves off.

Wordlessly, Gavin and I emerged from the water and got dressed. After the reckless encounter with the bull elephants, we were both badly in need of a stiff drink, so we headed over to the Stikit Inn, a crudely named makeshift bar at one of the rangers' digs. This adventure called for copious amounts of Mainstay and Coke, a particularly strong concoction endemic to Zululand. Mainstay is made from fermented sugarcane, not to be confused with rum. It is known to disrupt the stomach and give the partaker the squirts, but we didn't care. We were not driving the next morning, and we had a story to brag about.

But we didn't brag for long. Our escapade had been incredibly foolish and dangerous. We had put our lives and the lives of the elephants at risk. We knew the seriousness of toying with nature and had even witnessed the aftermath caused by the power of an enraged elephant. What had we been thinking?

Most likely, we hadn't been thinking at all.

TOO EARLY FOR THE SKY

Shadows of ourselves dissolve into space
And come out again seething like smoke in circles
Like this we dance to the limits of the universe ...
MAZISI KUNENE,
"Son of the Beautiful Ones"

Kusa kusa.
It never dawns the same way.
ZULU PROVERB

AFRICA TEACHES US TO ALWAYS be on alert. You never know when or where a heap of pebbles, a leafy branch, or a termite mound can come alive with teeth and claws and kill you. This is never more evident than after dusk, when the nocturnal predators come out hunting.

Oh halala, I'm home, looks like I made it,
Oh halalo
Oh halala, oh halala, ngasinda,
Oh halalo

I sing along with Johnny Clegg as I drive through the Makasa community on the outskirts of Phinda. I love making my way through the rural communities that surround the reserve. The main road is normally bustling with people—mamas buying goods at makeshift stands, kids walking home with dusty bare feet, men sitting under trees drinking ilala palm wine and discussing important business, young girls carrying drums of water on their heads, and workers going to or returning from work. Dogs, goats, and Nguni cattle periodically wander onto the road, oblivious to the occasional speeding car.

But this night the streets are quiet, not a soul in sight. It is midnight, and everyone is fast asleep inside their huts on reed mats or mattresses, depending on their level of affluence. It has been a long drive back from Cape Town, twenty-two hours without stopping. All for two weeks of civilization sandwiched between six-week shifts of game drives. I pull into the reserve where Vigilant, the gate guard, sleepily makes his way toward my vehicle.

"*Kunjani mfowethu!*" I greet him.

He shakes his head and wipes the latest dream from his eyes.

"*Hawu! Kunjani Usicelo,*" he returns my greeting, addressing me by my Zulu name, Usicelo.

I often mused about how cool and descriptive some of the Zulu names and nicknames were, and surprisingly fitting. Like Maingate, one of the other guards at the entrance. Or Lucky, a tracker whose name reflected his uncanny ability to find game even when there were no tracks. Or Lettuce, who worked in the kitchen. So it was not unusual for this night watchman to be named Vigilant.

We exchange some pleasantries, and I apologize for coming in so late, explaining—in perhaps too much detail—how difficult it is to drive for a full day without sleep. As Vigilant opens the gate, I wonder how long it will take before he becomes a tracker. I have been helping him from time to time with old textbooks on wildlife. He studies the books when on duty in his kiosk and hopes one day to pass the interview as a tracker. Zulu rangers often begin their work at the reserve as game guards or security personnel, later becoming trackers and ultimately serving as rangers.

I wave good-bye to Vigilant and make a mental note to give him my old copy of *Sasol Birds of Southern Africa*, as I have just purchased the updated version in Cape Town. The roads of the reserve are pitch dark on this moonless night, but Johnny Clegg keeps me awake for the last ten minutes. I am happy to be returning to the reserve, where life has settled into a comfortable routine of predictable unpredictability. No two days are ever the same; I never know what tomorrow will bring. By now, I can hardly keep my eyes open. In only five hours, I will be meeting my guests to take them on game drive.

I park the bakkie under the carport, relieved that I made it back safely and have not fallen asleep at the wheel. Dead tired, I swear that I can actually hear my bed calling my name. I pop the cassette out of the radio and grab my worn backpack. Typically, I do not lock the vehicle when I am on the reserve, as there is no need to worry about petty crime. But on this particular night, still in the habit from my holiday in the big city, I press the button on the key ring as I make my way to my humble dwelling.

Bleep. Bleep.

The doors lock, and the orange indicator lights from the truck illuminate the front of my little house. In that brief instant, I see it. Waiting for me in the cover of darkness, disguised as my doormat, a huge male leopard lies sprawled less than twenty feet away.

I stop mid stride, and as the adrenaline courses through my veins, my mind immediately switches from a sleepy state into high gear, evaluating the situation. Leopards are normally shy creatures that avoid human contact. But at night, they emerge from invisible hiding places to embrace their nocturnal world. This is prime time for marking territories, finding mates, and hunting. It is extremely rare to see a leopard up close like this, posed so casually on the steps of human lodgings, with little regard for the inhabitants.

Leopards are recognizable by their whisker patterns, a unique "fingerprinting" method for identifying individuals. This massive male leopard is easy to identify, even in the brief flash of my orange indicator lights. I know this leopard well. He is the one Norman and I track all the time, following his footsteps through the brush. This evening the roles are switched, and the leopard known as One-One is waiting for me.

Bleep. Bleep.

I click the button again and notice that he is now sitting upright on my doorstep. Aided by the double flash of light, I can easily see one dark whisker spot on each side of this leopard's face, standing out from his yellowish coat. Yes, this is definitely One-One. Other leopards were Three-Four, or Six-One, depending on the arrangement of their whisker spot patterns. We came to know most of them on the reserve.

For some reason, One-One had dropped by to welcome me home, gracing my doorstep with his fashionable rosette cover. I guess he hasn't come for a party, as leopards are solitary hunters, driven by instinct, very opportunistic. I am completely unarmed and vulnerable. My rifle is in the gun safe in the ranger room, as I never carry it when traveling off the reserve. I have no access to a weapon, not even a Zulu panga. Only my wits. So I steel myself. There is no need to panic. He will either attack or not. He is either hungry or not.

He is three or four lengths from me but I know that in one fluid bound he can easily hurtle himself through the dark, closing the distance. Before I am able to say "brandy-and-Coke," he can sink his long fangs into my neck, crush my vertebrae, and suffocate me. All muscle, bone, and sinew, leopards are effective killing machines, built with powerful jaws to tear through fur, with tongues rougher than the coarsest sandpaper to peel back flesh. His one hundred eighty pounds of pure, raw strength would have no problem dragging my limp body through the bush, away from the camp where he could munch on me in peace. Gruesome thoughts indeed.

I hastily hatch a survival plan.

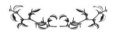

Leopards do not normally view humans as prey, preferring impalas, warthogs, and nyalas. They may also hunt monkeys, rodents, and birds, even insects. Instances of man-eating leopards are rare. However, it is a leopard that holds the macabre record of killing more humans than any other single cat.

Several notorious man-eating leopards ravaged the countryside of parts of rural India in the early part of the twentieth century. The Leopard of the Central Provinces, also known by the descriptive name of the Devilish Cunning Panther, was a male leopard that killed over one hundred fifty women and children in the Central Provinces of India. Apparently, this leopard was so brazen in its attacks that villagers were reluctant to leave their homes. Even still, the cat managed to take a victim every two to three days over several years.

Another Indian leopard, known as the Leopard of Rudraprayag, terrorized residents of villages between two Hindu shrines. Villagers feared walking the road between the shrines for fear of meeting the male cat. Over the course of eight years, this legendary killer accounted for the lives of at least one hundred twenty-five people, although some estimates put it much higher. Eventually, the man-eater was tracked down and shot by the legendary big cat hunter, Jim Corbett, in 1926. Corbett later wrote that the cat had such a fondness for human flesh that it ignored other, easy prey, once killing a fourteen-year-old boy in preference to the forty goats that were with him at the time. But by far the most destructive leopard of all time was the Panar Leopard, which reportedly killed over four hundred people before Corbett killed it in 1910.

Instances of man-eating leopards in Africa are far rarer than those of their Indian counterparts, but there have nonetheless been quite a few disturbing cases, some very recent. In August 1998, a young game ranger called Charles Swart had been guiding his guests in Kruger National Park when he stopped for a rest at the Matsulwane Bridge. He had his rifle in his lap and was smoking a cigarette when an emaciated female leopard crept up behind him and killed him with a swift bite to the back of the neck. The tourists were unsuccessful in chasing the cat off his body by shining lights and shouting at it. They went for help at a nearby lodge, and rangers finally tracked down the leopardess and shot and killed her.

More recently, in 2001, also in Kruger, a ten-year old boy, Mothusi Nobela, escaped an attacking leopard by running into his house. An hour later, the wife of the park manager was making her way between the nursery and the staff village when she was attacked and killed by the same leopard. Rangers tracked and killed the big cat, reporting back that it had been sick. But then, in 2003, another leopard made an appearance at this location. Bizarrely, and in a strange twist of fate, nine-year-old Tshikani Nobela, the brother of Mothusi, who had escaped death two years earlier, was walking in the very same village in broad daylight when he too was attacked, and this time killed, by a marauding leopard. Rangers responded and shot the animal as it was dragging the boy into the bush. Sadly, the child was said to have been besotted with wildlife and particularly loved hippos and lions.

But the above instances can be misleading, as leopards will usually avoid encounters with people, although they do have a partiality for man's best friend, known as "meat on four feet." It's often the dog that tempts a leopard into man's abode, and a leopard may attack, maul, and even kill a human when their paths intersect. Like all cats, leopards are armed with long fangs and sharp claws. Before antibiotics, anyone who survived a leopard attack and escaped the dagger-like teeth would often die later from their slashing wounds. The deep injuries inflicted by those razor-sharp claws, which harbored decaying flesh from prior kills, were a source of serious infections from deadly bacteria.

The leopard is built to ambush, pounce, carry, and lift up to three times its own weight. It can drag its kill deep into the bush, and often up a tree, out of reach from opportunists like the hyena. Known as the "purifier," the hyena has a reputation for stealing carcasses, fresh or rotting, and cleanly disposing of the remains. These "piranhas of the bush" are drawn to the smell of blood, relentless scavengers always on the lookout for a free meal.

When Phinda was established, leopards were present but seldom seen. They would disappear into the forest as soon as a human approached, behavior learned from years of being shot at by farmers or baited by hunters. However, their ability to adapt and thrive in diversified habitats and consume any type of protein, from ungulates to beetles, ensured their survival.

For the Zulu and other cultures that live close to nature, the dividing line between the human and animal world is very fine, especially around the creatures of the night. Superstitions surround those animals with uncanny night vision and hunting prowess, animals like the owls, aardvarks, hyenas, and leopards. The hyena is often associated with evil and witchcraft, its unnerving howl at night resembling wild human laughter. Many Zulus believe that witches and their familiars, especially baboons, ditch the proverbial broomstick and ride around on hyenas to conduct their mischief. The *tokoloshe* is the Zulu version of the "boogie man," a mischievous character who plays tricks on people after dark, and is sometimes described as a baboon without a tail.

The mysterious and unpredictable nature of the stealthy leopard is recognized in cultures throughout Africa.

> *Gentle hunter*
> *his tail plays on the ground*
> *while he crushes the skull.*
>
> *Beautiful death*
> *who puts on a spotted robe*
> *when he goes to his victim.*
>
> *Playful killer*
> *whose loving embrace*
> *splits the antelope's heart.*
> YORUBA PRAISE POEM

The leopard has always been a symbol of power. The ultimate shape-shifter, with its cloak of invisibility. The nightwalker, man morphing into leopard and leopard into man. Its beautiful coat, whiskers, claws, and tail were coveted and worn as signs of authority. To take on the qualities of a leopard signified everything that was noble and strong.

According to Allen F. Roberts, author of *Animals in African Art: From the Familiar to the Marvelous*:

> Leopards are one of the most commonly portrayed animals in African art. Throughout Africa, the leopard is symbolically associated with political authority. As extraordinarily intelligent and courageous animals, leopards readily lend themselves to the production of politically useful metaphors. As predators of humans, leopards are associated with individuals and organiza-

tions that have the authority to take human life. Leopards are often considered the animal-others of chiefs, kings, and members of the governing bodies charged with maintaining law and order.

King Shaka's legendary prowess was enhanced with the story of how at age nineteen, he single-handedly killed a leopard that was attacking livestock. A gifted military commander, Shaka was surrounded by heroic myths, and stories of his unusual training methods were handed down through the oral tradition. It was said that before battle Zulu warriors were required to touch the head of a living leopard for courage. No wonder Shaka is credited with creating the most powerful warrior nation in southern Africa.

If the elephant is the poem in my story, then the leopard is the silken thread that silently weaves its way through. The many hours spent tracking the *ingwe* with Norman and Rockerman cemented our friendships, binding us together in pursuit of the solitary hunter. I never tired of sharing in the joy of a sighting with guests, if only for a momentary glimpse in the darkness, fascinating and mesmerizing us. Appearing and disappearing, sometimes elusive and sometimes strangely present, the leopard slunk in and out of my nights at Phinda.

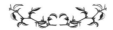

This evening, on my return home after a long drive, it's just the leopard and me in the inky darkness. My survival plan has been rapidly put together.

There is only one way out of this situation. I need to return to the safety of the vehicle as calmly and confidently as possible while illuminating the big cat constantly, clicking the button on my vehicle immobilizer. The dark night envelops me, and I strain to listen for any cat movements although I know it is futile. Leopards move like smoke, in complete silence on their heavily padded feet, their movements often described as "the moving past of a phantom." I press the button again.

Bleep-bleep.

The leopard is still there, his cold green eyes staring right through me.

Huhu. Huhuhu. Huhu.

A wood owl, another creature that haunts the night, greets me and provides me with some comfort that I am not alone and that there will be at least one witness to my death should the leopard attack. Like the leopard, the wood owl is a master of disguise. An incredibly difficult bird to locate by day or night, it has the ability to remain undetected in the thick tree canopy, hidden by its finely horizontal barring.

I am on high alert, and in between my brief illuminations, I sense the leopard's presence, still melting into the doormat. If I show any panic, the attack instincts of the large, invisible cat could be ignited, and I am not quite ready for my remains to be shipped back to Cape Town in a FedEx envelope. I glance over my shoulder to see that the bakkie is only about six feet away, just out of arm's reach.

Step by cautious step, I retreat backward. I feel his cold, calculating eyes watching my every movement, and the darkness prevents me from locking eyes with him. A good thing, since he is innately programmed to respond to this visual cue. Step. Listen. *Bleep-bleep.* Step. Listen. *Bleep-bleep.* Step.

Bleep-bleep.

I reach behind me and quickly open the door. I swing my tall frame back into the security of the cab and slam the door shut. The lights flash on again briefly, revealing an empty doormat. He has vanished in a streak, slipping silently back into the bush.

One moment death waits for me on the threshold. Then it is gone in a twinkling, and I am granted a welcome reprieve. That's the way it is in Africa, one never knows. I pop the cassette back in the player and settle back in the seat. The light of dawn is only a few hours away.

> *Oh halala, I'm home, looks like I made it,*
> *Oh halalo*
> *Oh halala, oh halala, ngasinda,*
> *Oh halalo*
> *I'm too early for the sky*
> *Wenkunkulu wami wangisindisa mina*
> *(Oh my Lord, you spared me)*
> JOHNNY CLEGG,
> "Too Early for the Sky"

SPOTTED SPHYNX

He that seeks the power of the lion's heart and
the speed of the cheetah
must also suffer the burden of feeding that heart and
the blisters on the soles of the runner.
AFRICAN PROVERB

Though the cheetah is fierce, it does not eat its cubs.
ETHIOPIAN PROVERB

*K*WEH. *KWEHHHHHH.*
Go Away. Go Away.
A grey lourie, a bird not often seen on the reserve, calls from a nearby tree. These large birds are renowned for foiling the hunting attempts of predators by uttering their distinctive call. Antelope and many other prey animals have learnt to heed this warning.

Kweh. Kwehhhhhh.

The "go away" bird's incessant calling is compromising our chances of viewing a hunt on this game drive. Nearby, three male cheetahs are grooming each other, a means of strengthening the bonds between them. These cheetahs are in the prime of their lives and well known to all of us rangers as the dominant cheetahs on the reserve. Coalitions of more than two male cheetahs are very unusual, as these cooperative groups are nearly always comprised of brothers. Since the mortality rate of young cheetahs in most areas of Africa is over seventy percent, it is highly unlikely that more than one brother from the same litter survives to adulthood. So this is a very special sighting – three brothers, lords of their domain.

An Australian couple looks on in awe, hoping for some action. These three males often provide amazing sightings for our guests. They are the ultimate speedsters, and if they decide to hunt, chances are very high that their coordinated missile attack will bring something down. I can see from their sunken bellies that they have not eaten for a few days.

"Do you guys want to wait and see if these boys decide to hunt? I have a sneaky suspicion that they are craving some fast food."

My guests nod enthusiastically, their eyes still firmly locked on the spotted cats draped languidly on top of a nearby termite mound. Norman and I prefer taking it slow on game drives, instead of rushing around the reserve and trying to see as much as possible as quickly as possible. We have found that the very best sightings occur when we act on a hunch and wait to see nature unfold before our eyes.

Kweh. Kwehhhhhh.

Go Away. Go Away.

The grey lourie continues to spew its warning, then takes off unexpectedly, leaving us in silent anticipation. The cheetahs are stretching, a sure sign that they want to start moving. Our patience is rewarded. Norman signals that an impala herd is making its way onto the open areas from the south. I follow his gaze to a long arm of woodland that reaches out into the grassland about two hundred yards away. I can just discern the tawny shapes making their way between the trees and out onto the open grass.

"This could get very interesting," I whisper to my guests.

Ever alert, the cheetah brothers spy the approaching herd and are quick to seize this opportunity. Intuitively, they slink low to the ground and fan out in a three-pronged formation downwind of their potential breakfast. They proceed slowly and determinately in the direction of the oblivious impalas.

Tututu. Tututu.

A new sound breaks our silent concentration, and we struggle to identify the source. It's definitely not a sound found in nature.

The drone of a motorized vehicle is coming from Zinave, a main road that fringes the open area. Under my breath, I curse that this awesome sighting is once again about to be rudely interrupted. First, the pesky grey lourie, now a vehicle. I can hardly believe my eyes when I see that the approaching commotion is a motorbike being ridden by none other than Jimson, one of the land management staff, completely unmindful of the drama playing out around him.

Tututu. Tututu.

The three male cheetahs are now distracted from their hunt,

their attention diverted to the rapidly approaching motorized human. I turn to my guests.

"A cheetah chase is triggered by a fleeing prey item. Cheetahs will typically stalk an antelope and get as close as they can before being noticed. As soon as their cover is blown, they will take off after the fleeing animal and quickly catch up to it in a short, high-speed chase. So this is what we would expect to happen if that motorbike wasn't around!"

We were hoping to see the cheetah in full stride, displaying their legendary speed. Now I find myself salvaging the sighting, imparting interpretive information.

"In rare instances where the prey item does not take off but stands its ground, the feline hunters often seem confused and abandon the hunt altogether. The prey's flight response alone triggers the attack. Whereas lions and leopards will often attack an animal that stands its ground, cheetahs are reluctant to do so. The risk of injury to their fragile bodies from a well-aimed horn, hoof or tusk far outweighs the benefit of a satisfying meal."

As if on cue, the three male cheetahs ignore the largely immobile herd of impalas. They abandon the hunt as their focus is shifted to the fast moving object racing right through the middle of their planned path of attack. Unable to resist the challenge, they break away after the motorcycle, exposing themselves to the impalas. The herd explodes off in the opposite direction, away from the cheetah, as an amazing spectacle of stealth and speed unfolds before our eyes.

Jimson notices the cats coming at him from behind and to one side of him, in a diagonal approach. The whites of his eyes are clearly visible as he opens the accelerator and tries to outrun them. Even though their rubberband-like bodies are surging forward with each stride, their heads appear remarkably motionless and fixed intently on the wheels of the bike.

Tutututututututututu.

The cheetahs catch up to the motorbike effortlessly. Two of the brothers flank Jimson on either side whilst one tries to tackle the back wheel from behind. A last minute hesitation forces the rear cheetah to pull out and avoid serious injury to its front paw from the spokes of the back wheel. But the other cats continue their pursuit, albeit now with less serious intent.

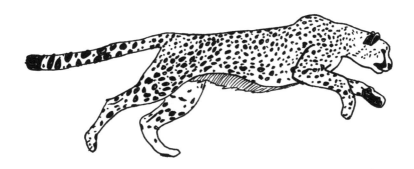

Tutututututututututu. Tutututututututututu.

Jimson opens up the bike's throttle to its maximum now but even at top-speed, the off-road motorbike is no match for the striding cats. The Australians remark how the cheetahs appear so fast that their feet don't seem to touch the ground. The speedy cats continue to toy with Jimson for a hundred yards or so, until their brief burst of stamina gives out. They've had their fun, as if the entire encounter is simply an experiment to prove beyond all doubt that cheetahs can outrun humans even if we have motorized assistance!

Meeting up with Jimson several days later at a staff party I asked him about the incident.

"Those *ingulule* were faster than my *isithuthuthu*," he replied laughing. The word *isithuthuthu* for "motorbike" is a great example of Zulu onomatopoeia.

"Maybe *isithuthuthu* should refer to the pounding of your rapidly beating heart after outrunning the *ingulule*," I replied.

On many prior game drives, I have borne witness to a successful cheetah hunt, one of the most exciting and mind-numbing spectacle that one can witness in nature. No other land mammal is as well designed for pure, breakneck speed. Tall and elegant, the cheetah has the ability to accelerate from zero to sixty miles per hour in just three seconds. As it takes off after its intended prey, a finely tuned body kicks into gear like a high performance racing car. A flexible spine alternately concaves and convexes as the back legs are pulled between the front legs, briefly touching the ground every twenty feet. The illusion is that of an airborne missile. The cheetah opens its mouth as it runs, inhaling air into its enlarged lungs, much like a V-8 engine sucks gas for propulsion. It flattens its ears to remain as aerodynamic as possible and uses its laterally compressed tail as a rudder to adjust as it twists and turns in response to an evading prey animal. The tough pads on its paws, with semi-retractable claws for grip, provide the immediate traction needed for rapid bursts of speed and quick changes of direction. As the cheetah closes in on its intended quarry, it extends its forepaw, armed with a razor-sharp dewclaw, a specially modified hook that comes complete with an extremely strong tendon. The dewclaw grips into the rump of the animal like a barbless fishhook. This allows the cheetah to close in on the throat with its vise-like jaws, which clamp down tightly, cutting off the air-supply to the hyperventilating victim. To experience a cheetah hunt is to observe arguably the finest natural demonstration of a body built specifically for the high-speed chase.

In many ways, the cheetah is very uncat-like. Whilst most other cat species prefer the cover of darkness for an opportunistic ambush, the cheetah works for its meal during the daylight hours, especially the cooler hours of dusk and dawn. In some ways, its body design is more reminiscent of a greyhound or a whippet. Unlike lions and leopards, a cheetah can also be trained to hunt with people and the ancient Egyptians readily kept cheetahs as pets for this very reason.

There are five large predators in Africa. Ranked by dominance, the order is lion, spotted hyena, leopard, wild dog, and cheetah. But there are various factors that can turn the dominance tables in one direction or another. During a species-on-species encounter, the advantage almost always goes to the species with the numbers. For example, four or five hyenas can kill a single lioness. A pack of wild dogs can easily chase a leopard off a kill.

Another factor is the sex of the big cats versus the other carnivores. A large male leopard can often hold his own against a single hyena, whereas a female leopard is more likely to give way. A lioness would likely struggle against a group of hyenas, whereas a large male lion would usually prevail. In most cases cheetah will give way to the other four predators, although there have been instances of male cheetah coalitions defending their kills from a single leopard or hyena.

Once the cheetah has made its kill, it does not rest for long. Although its super-charged body is still overheated from the quick sprint during the chase and needs time to recuperate, the cheetah intuitively knows that it sits right at the bottom of the totem pole of super-predators. It bolts its food, sometimes finishing a small antelope in forty-five minutes. Even though it is blessed with mind-boggling pace and a very successful kill-to-hunt ratio, the shy cheetah must often relinquish its meal to lions, hyenas, leopards and even groups of smaller jackals and vultures. These animals all take advantage of the easy pickings and move in, stealing the prize, a behavior called *kleptoparasitism*. Because a cheetah relies so heavily on its flawless body design, even as part of a coalition, it most often cannot afford to stand its ground as even a small cut or scrape that turns septic becomes an ill-afforded risk.

While leopards flourish in spite of significant human threats, cheetahs are far less adaptable. They are sometimes confused with leopards, as both cats have dark spots on a light coat. The easiest way for a novice naturalist to identify a cheetah is by the tearstains. These black marks run from the corner of the eye down to the jawline, a distinctive marking absent in leopards. Cheetahs possess spots rather than rosettes and they are longer-legged and slighter in build than their nocturnal cousins.

When Phinda was established, there were initially no cheetahs to be found, although the occasional animal was spotted on the neighboring Mkuze Game Reserve. Cheetahs were one of the first of the predators to be reintroduced to the Phinda grasslands. Because they live on a very specialized diet, preferring fleet-footed antelope and their relatives, they pose little danger to man and livestock. The reintroduction of cheetah was perceived to be of minimal risk to the surrounding communities. However, cheetahs do require large home ranges, so cars and people add to the long list of perils for individuals that travel under a hole in the fence and enter communal lands.

The reintroduced cheetahs thrive on Phinda. Elsewhere in Africa where cheetah mortality rates are high—Namibia and the Serengeti, for example—there is limited thick bush for a mother cheetah to conceal her babies. But on Phinda, there is ample cover where mothers can hide their cubs during the most vulnerable first months. This has given Phinda the reputation of being the best place in Africa to view cheetahs and it is not uncommon for guests to leave Phinda with multiple sightings of mothers and cubs.

Even in this ideal environment, surviving to adulthood can be challenging as mother cheetahs unfortunately have their fair share of disastrous encounters with larger predators on the reserve.

A few months after the motorbike incident, a mother and her four young cubs melted my heart. In my opinion, there is nothing more adorable than a group of young cheetah cubs tackling and falling over each other, entirely ignorant of the "oohs" and "aahs" from an attentive Land Rover full of guests. For weeks, this family provided us with unbelievable sightings. These youngsters were just beginning to lose the distinctive black mantles on their backs that make young cheetah cubs look remarkably similar to honey badgers, creatures with notoriously bad tempers and brazen fearlessness. Even lions tend to give honey badgers a wide berth and some zoologists believe that cheetahs have developed these markings over time to dissuade would-be predators from attacks - a form of evolutionary mimicry. I personally think that the black mantles on young cubs create a very effective camouflage when they lie up in the shade during the heat of the day. Whatever the reason, the four youngsters were growing up fast and losing their cub characteristics quickly.

Cheetah cubs stay with their mother for over a year, so tracking this family became a ritual on my game drives. It was sheer joy watching them grow up, pointing out the subtle changes in behavior and appearance, from day to day and week to week. Until one disturbing morning, when I felt for the first time a strong compulsion to rebel against Phinda's strict hands-off policy of humans not interfering with nature.

"Nantsi amasondo wengulule," I say proudly.

There are the cheetah tracks.

This is one of the rare occasions where I have spotted tracks on the road before Norman. I cannot resist the opportunity to banter with him.

"Ngicabanga kuba uphuz' ibhiya kakhulu izolo ebusuku!"

You must have drunk too much beer last night!

He laughs loudly in response as he jumps off the tracker seat and examines the tracks more closely.

"Umama nezingane ezine."

Mother and four cubs.

We have hit the jackpot! Now we just need to find them. The good news is that the tracks are super-fresh. The road is wet from the morning dew and dry, white sand is visible under each pawprint, an indication that the group has recently passed through. We climb back in the vehicle and follow the trail.

From the tracker seat, Norman signals for me to stop every so often to get a closer look. At one stage, he points out to our guests the flattened patches of sand and the deep, crisscrossed indentations where the cubs have been playfully chasing each other and rolling around. We trail the tracks for some time until Norman suddenly holds up his hand for me to halt. He is shaking his head and examining the road carefully.

"Hawu. Hawu ..." Norman mutters his surprise.

The cheetah tracks have been joined by the distinctive pugmarks of several lions. This is bad news. They are well beyond the age where a mother will conceal them carefully while she goes off hunting. They are vulnerable, having lost most of their camouflage while not yet having developed the speed to outrun lions.

Our apprehension grows when we find both the lion and cheetah tracks veering off the track into a patch of open woodland. We stop and pause to listen. Nothing. Except for a bird chirping in the distance.

Swip ... swip ... swip ...

The urgent chirping continues.

Almost simultaneously, Norman and I recognize the chirruping of a young cheetah in distress. Something terrible has happened. The disturbed earth and bits of bloodied fur confirm the telltale signs of a cat-on-cat encounter. And then Norman points out one of the most heart-rending things I have ever seen – the miserable, stiff body of a young cheetah. Its eyes are wide open, its fur still wet from the morning dew, just lying next to the road a few feet from our open vehicle.

Norman hops off the tracker seat and delicately picks up the cub, showing how its neck has been cruelly broken by a violent shake from a much larger cat. My heart sinks as I have grown close to these youngsters over the past weeks and enjoyed searching for them on a near daily basis. I can barely speak to my guests and the hushed mutterings on my Land Rover reinforce the sadness and gravity of this situation.

The lions are nowhere to be seen and neither is the mother cheetah and her remaining three cubs. Without saying a word, Norman places the carcass of the cub softly on the ground exactly as he found it and we continue towards the high-pitched chirping.

I am startled by the radio sizzling to life.

"James. James Currie. Come in."

I grab the mike and respond.

"Go ahead, Greg."

"Ja James, I've just found one of those cubs you were looking for. This poor thing is stone dead. We're about two hundred meters to your east." My fellow ranger has found another body and I wonder if the predatory lions have exterminated the entire group.

I don't even acknowledge the other ranger who has been helping us look for the cheetahs. Without uttering a word, I turn the radio down and focus on locating the remaining two cubs and their mother, hopeful that the pitiful cries will lead us to them. And sure enough, as we round a thick copse of guarri trees, a cheetah cub stands up in a small clearing. But the youngster is desperately alone.

"Swip ... swip ... swip ... swip ..."

Every couple of seconds, the cub utters the chirruping contact call that cheetahs use to communicate with their mothers. But its cries are answered with silence.

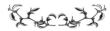

I have no doubt that we could easily have captured the little soul and reared him to adulthood but the strict reserve policy forbade us from interfering. Only in cases where an animal was suffering as a direct result of humans were we allowed to become involved.

Had poachers killed the little one's mother, we would have been allowed to capture it and save its life. But because this was a natural scenario, we had to let nature take its course. As hard as it might have seemed at the time, this was the right policy. Lions will take any opportunity to kill a competitor, be it a cheetah, leopard or hyena. Unfortunately, the young of lesser predators are not spared their wrath.

That particular cheetah cub was not seen again after that fateful morning. But there was a small glimmer of good news. Later that day the distressed female and her one remaining cub were located several miles from the site of the killings.

This disturbing scenario had a huge impact on Norman and me. We both loved animals and it was hard to absorb the gravity of how nature can be so red in tooth and claw. This was the only time that I witnessed the aftermath of a cheetah/lion interaction and thankfully, it was not every day that the brutal side of nature tugged at my emotions.

Cheetahs have proven so successful on Phinda—even with the high densities of lions, leopards, and other predators—that the reserve is now an important source for cheetah restocking programs across Africa. Every few years, surplus animals are relocated to areas in Africa where they historically occurred but were exterminated, thereby aiding significantly in cheetah conservation.

The lives of the three siblings that died so cruelly at the paws of the lions were not in vain, as their deaths gave the mother precious time to escape with a single offspring. As cold as it sounds, sometimes a few must die for one to live. The surviving cub was a female and she lived on to rear litters of her own. I take comfort that the genes of those three dead cubs still live on in the athletic bodies of the remaining cub's offspring, forging new boundaries in cheetah conservation throughout the African continent.

RESCUE ON THE RANGE

The lone bird perches on the once favourite stone
She sings and blows away the afternoon
Everything falls suddenly into a fearful night.
MAZISI KUNENE,
"The Fearful Ruins"

Isilo siyawafinyez' amazipho.
The lion pulls in his claws.
ZULU PROVERB

IBHUBESI. IMBUBE. INGONYAMA. ISILO. THE Zulus have many names for the lion but *isilo*, the Zulu praise name for "His Majesty the King," best describes the place this magnificent beast holds in the Medieval Chain of Being. In this classic hierarchical structure of all matter and life proposed by the early philosophers Aristotle and Plato, the lion and elephant share the highest esteem in the animal world, just a notch below man and far removed from mouse.

But on the occasions when human flesh becomes part of the lion's diet, there are darker names. *uSathane.* Devil. *Osama.* Terrorist. *Umoya.* Spirit. *Isipokwe.* Ghost. *Ukuhlwa.* Darkness. They are spirit lions, not real animals but *amabubi*, evil shades embodied in the shapes of lions. Angry spirits with supernatural powers that come to take revenge.

When a lion becomes a man-eater it assumes qualities above and beyond an earthly creature, fueling superstition and instilling intense fear in future victims. It's in the way they move, the uncanny way they appear out of nowhere in spite of their size. It's their ability to sense and avoid traps, eluding pursuers by heading to rocky ground, where their tracks disappear into thin air. And at other times the pugmarks seem, creepily, to morph into human footprints.

They are keen on only one goal. To satisfy their cravings with the taste of fresh human flesh and blood. Once a lion becomes a man-eater, its days are numbered. It is a lose-lose situation for everyone. For the human victims … for each lion that must be killed … for the conservation official who must order the execution. For Africa herself, losing another precious resource.

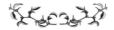

We are watching the North pride near Mziki Marsh, when the lioness perks up. She is looking intently into the distance from the convenient elevation of a termite mound. This dominant lioness is one of the biggest ever recorded, weighing in at about three hundred seventy-five pounds. She is heavier than some adult male lions and hugely powerful. Like most prides, the North pride consists of the matriarch's daughters and their offspring.

It's a picture-perfect sighting, the late afternoon sun illuminating the tawny coats of the lionesses, the head of the majestic matriarch displaying a flawless profile against the hard earth of the dirt castle. Now her black-tufted ears are twitching and her tail is swaying. We watch as she slinks down off the termite mound and out into the grass, the other lionesses in tow.

From the safety of the vehicle, my guests and I see that she is earnestly stalking something. I glass the area, looking for the obvious prey—her favorite dinner, wildebeest. The Mziki Marsh, an extension of the Mkuze River floodplain, attracts herds of wildebeest to the open grasslands where they can easily see predators approach. I scan for the telltale, sloping silhouettes of the slate-gray animals. Wildebeests can be identified from a distance by their broad shoulders, which angle downward to smaller hindquarters, a physical characteristic not unlike the hyena's.

Then, across the marsh, I spot her quarry. A head just visible over the softly waving grass, bobbing up and down. I focus in on the moving object. The bobbing head is followed by another round, bobbing object, larger than the first. My mind races as I struggle to comprehend the unfamiliar spectacle in my field of view. Then both objects stop and I see the hind object rise into the air, suspended on something that looks like a stick or a pole.

"Cheese-and-Rice!"

I gasp.

The severity of the situation hits me the moment my mind assembles the visual puzzle into an intelligible picture. A man is walking through the reserve directly toward the lions, carrying his belongings wrapped in a blanket suspended on a long stick.

I drop the binoculars and reach for the radio. I know we have a rescue operation to contend with, or our guests will have a gruesome story to tell when they return to the campfire tonight. The lionesses are hunting, their prey in sight. But the target is not their favored prey and is apparently unaware of his impending sticky situation. This will be a double tragedy if they attack him, as all man-eaters must be destroyed. Not just the lion that pounces and kills, but the entire pride. Once the young cubs see how easy it is to physically bring down a man and taste the human flesh, they also become unwitting accomplices and a grave danger.

By now, I have lost sight of the lions in the tall grass. I know they will be deathly quiet, their soft bellies pressed against the black cotton-soil. They are hunting as a coordinated team, encircling their victim in wing formation, the largest lioness lying low in the center. The other lionesses will carefully maneuver their quarry directly toward her. With one quick, powerful bound, she will emerge from the thick grass and grasp lunch in her strong jaws.

The wind carries a droning sound across the marsh and I can just see Richard's vehicle with Bheki and guests approaching from the other side. He is much closer to the wanderer than we are, but he will need to act quickly. Lions are very businesslike on a hunt. I desperately need his help, relieved that he is on the other side of the boggy marsh. I call out to Richard on channel one and tell him to go to our line-of-sight channel, channel six.

"Richard, there's an *oke* walking directly into the path of the North pride. It's gonna be curtains for him unless you get there quick, bro." I give him some landmarks and hear the sound of his engine roar to life.

"Put your foot down and go as fast as you can. Get that guy before the lions do."

Richard speeds off with his vehicle full of guests, heading toward the hapless wanderer. They stop and pull him inside, just as the lions appear out of the grass, ready to pounce.

"Don't you see the lions?" Richard asks the wanderer.

"Ja, I saw them but I thought they were *izinja*," he replies.

Dogs.

What kind of dogs roam in his neighborhood? We all wonder at his ignorance and folly. These are very large lions! Yet from a distance, and silhouetted by the setting sun as they sat perched on the termite mound, I could perhaps appreciate how he had arrived at this potentially disastrous conclusion.

The wanderer told his story, and how he came to be crossing through the reserve illegally. How he had walked down from Mozambique to visit his family in Mnqobokazi and was now returning.

In colonial times, there had been a border dispute between Mozambique and South Africa. The reigning French monarch arbitrarily drew a line on a map. The pen and ink on paper provided an immediate solution for the remote rulers but created serious consequences for the local Tembe community, which was split in two. Now some family members still live in Mozambique and some in South Africa.

The residents don't respect the border, since they had not been consulted in times gone by. So to visit their different clans in the area, they often just walk in a straight line. If there is a fence, they climb over it. If there is a river, they wade through it. If they come face to face with wild animals ... well, that's all part of the risk of the journey to visit their loved ones. This young man was lucky that the staff at Phinda was able to help him find his way back to safety, but many others are not so fortunate.

The socioeconomic situation in Mozambique prompts many refugees to seek a better life in South Africa, braving the dangers in Kruger National Park farther to the northwest of Phinda. The borders are not heavily patrolled because there are natural deterrents. The lions in Kruger National Park have developed a taste for human flesh. So every year, sad piles of clothing and remains are found, all that is left of these poor people risking everything for a better life in South Africa. These refugees from Mozambique are keenly aware of the dangers, but every year they take their chances, crossing through the park at night. No one knows exactly how many succumb to this cruel fate, ambushed in silence by the ultimate carnivore, paying dearly with their lives for a chance at freedom.

There are many theories as to why lions become man-eaters, the most popular giving credence to the deleterious effects of old age. In his early work *Missionary Travels and Researches in South Africa*, David Livingstone wrote:

> When a lion becomes too old to catch game, he frequently takes to killing goats in the villages; a woman or child happening to go out at night falls a prey too; and as this is his only source of subsistence now, he continues it. From this circumstance has arisen the idea that the lion, when he has once tasted human flesh, loves it better than any other. A man-eater is invariably an old lion; and when he overcomes his fear of man so far as to come to villages for goats, the people remark, "His teeth are worn, he will soon kill men."

But in reality, old age accounts for an incredibly small percentage of documented cases. In research for his popular hunting book *Death in the Long Grass,* Peter Capstick points to statistics compiled by a well-known South African game ranger and author, Peter Turnbull-Kemp. A survey of the conditions of eighty-nine man-eating lions revealed that a stunning ninety-one percent of the killers were in good or fair condition at the time of their demise and less than five percent were aged and injured. So while a few lions do become man-eaters when beyond their prime, this is not the norm.

I believe it is their very nature that causes them to develop a taste for human flesh. In my opinion, too much emphasis has been placed on the adage that lions are the ultimate opportunists, feeding on anything that happens to cross their paths. While it is true that their expanded menu can include anything from tsamma melons to elephants, most lions become specialized consumers. A pride develops highly unique strategies for hunting a specific prey species, whether it's wildebeest, zebra, buffalo, or even elephant and man. This learned behavior can be a remarkably strong driver. I have personally witnessed, on numerous occasions, lions ignoring easier prey to hunt their preferred prey species.

I firmly believe that this internal propensity for specialization is the primary motivator behind lions becoming man-eaters, rather than the traditional explanations of old age and ill health. Lions have a natural fear of man and, thus, a tendency to avoid chance encounters. It takes a combination of factors to fall into place and convince a lion that it's time to turn the tables on tradition. Like any new behavior, a catalyst is needed to set off the grisly chain of events that ultimately leads to specialization in habitual man-eating.

That spark can be a natural occurrence, such as a drought, a seasonal change or a disease that depletes a lion's usual prey item. As a result, the lion's default instinct of opportunism kicks in, and driven by hunger, it kills anything that crosses its path. The unlucky victim could, given the right conditions, be a human—the classic example being a single unarmed person walking through thick bush on a dark night without a torch.

Human encroachment on a lion's territory can be another trigger. By attracting the cats with cattle and other livestock, man unwittingly provides easy pickings. Sooner or later, clashes will become inevitable, leading to an interaction between lion and human. Depending on the outcome of that conflict, humans may be on the menu the next time a lion wanders into a village.

Another factor relates to the maternal instinct of a mother lioness. One should never underestimate the strength of a lioness' instinct to defend her youngsters. A mother with young cubs, disturbed by a human, will usually give a warning. But sometimes her maternal instincts will override her natural fear of man, prompting her to attack and kill. Once this lioness establishes that humans are actually easy prey, she will try this again when driven by another trigger—hunger. Similarly, a lion that feels trapped by a human will be driven to attack, and this event may spark the habit.

Learned behaviors play a major role in the development of eating habits. Lion prides are closely knit groups, and cubs watch closely, picking up the necessary survival skills from their parents. Including a fondness for the taste of certain species. A cub that watches its elders hunt people and then feasts on human flesh is likely to develop a preference for that tasty morsel.

So I believe that, while it's opportunity that triggers the first kill, specialization is what drives lions to become serial killers. After the initial success, they will seek out the taste of human flesh, and no other will do.

Like most people who work in conservation in Africa, I have always been aware of the history of man-eaters, the stories and legends. I know that while actual documented cases of man-eating lions are rather uncommon and isolated, the practice occurs more often than one realizes. Actual numbers are difficult to obtain because Africa has a unique way of erasing its dead without a trace. In some of Africa's rural communities, deaths are not always reported to government authorities due to remoteness, indifference, or reluctance.

The most famous man-eating story, the one that is quoted most often and provides the greatest insights, was told by the engineer who came to Kenya in 1898 to build a railroad bridge. His classic book *The Man-Eaters of Tsavo and Other East African Adventures* tells the true tale of a pair of male lions that terrorized the workers building the railroad in Kenya and the officer who made it his dedicated ambition to kill them. Lt. Col. John Henry Patterson wrote:

> In the whole of my life I have never experienced anything more nerve-shaking than to hear the deep roars of these dreadful monsters growing gradually nearer and nearer, and to know that some one or other of us was doomed to be their victim before morning dawned. Once they reached the vicinity of the camps, the roars completely ceased, and we knew they were stalking their prey. Shouts would then pass from camp to camp, *"Khabar dar, bhaieon, shaitan ata"* ("Beware, brothers, the devil is coming"), but the warning would prove of no avail, and sooner or later agonizing shrieks would break the silence and another man would be missing from roll-call next morning.

Patterson goes on to describe how the brutish lions would brazenly walk into camp, boldly enter a tent, and seize a victim. Dragging it off just beyond the ring of firelight, the panicked screams of the victim could be heard emerging from the darkness, followed by the sound of smothering as the lion seized its victim's head in its mouth. It closed its long canine teeth through the thinnest part of his head at the temples until they met again in the brain. Then silence. Until the sound of bones crushing, flesh being torn in huge chunks and swallowed whole. A sickening sound for those remaining huddled and shivering in their tents.

This would be disturbing enough if the victim were an antelope or zebra. I have witnessed and heard the sounds of a kill being devoured, and I can't imagine what it would be like, listening and knowing it was one of your companions. And that this could possibly be your fate in the very near future.

It's been estimated that the Tsavo lions killed dozens of Indian workers and even more unfortunate Africans, with some accounts stating that there were a total of one hundred thirty-five victims. Patterson eventually shot both lions, known as The Ghost and The Darkness. The skins are preserved and still on display at the Field Museum in Chicago, where their story continues to both horrify and mesmerize people. Theories abound regarding what motivated their behaviors. As in the case of most man-eaters, it was probably a combination of factors culminating in easy opportunity and solidified by the instinct to specialize.

Scarily, the Tsavo lions were to be radically outscored by even more dedicated and more bloodthirsty cats. In the early 1940s, the notorious Ubena pride in Tanzania carried out their dedicated hunting of humans for ten years before a certain game officer named George Rushby put an end to their antics. It took two full years for him to hunt down each member of the large pride, but during those two years alone, they were responsible for two hundred forty-nine gruesome deaths. Who knows how many they killed during the terrifying decade before Rushby afforded the locals some meager sense of solace.

Around the same time, also in Tanzania, there existed one of the most feared man-eating lion prides. This gut-wrenching collection of felines killed as many as one hundred humans a year during their fifteen-year reign from 1932 to 1947. The Njombe pride is considered to hold the "all-Africa record" with over fifteen hundred victims, far exceeding the reign of terror created by the Tsavo lions. Rushby, the same man who had spent two years knocking off the Ubena lions, was once again called in to end the relentless killing spree. "The renowned man-eaters of Tsavo were very small fry compared to what these proved to be," said Rushby, who obviously knew his lions.

What's interesting about the Njombe lions was the set of circumstances that led up to their unprecedented ruthless behavior. Everything had been peaceful in the area until the colonial government decided to eliminate all antelope and prey animals in a concerted effort to control and cease the rinderpest outbreak that was threatening cattle stocks.

Hunger drove the lions to conquer their natural fear and pursue humans as a substitute. And boy, did they overcome their natural fear! To top it off, they developed totally un-catlike hunting behavior. They would hunt humans in the afternoons, killing by daylight. And then use the dark hours to move, traveling undetected over distances of up to twenty miles, where they would then settle in to watch the next village on their hit list. Definitely not the typical behavior of a nocturnal predator. This pride of up to fifteen lions was believed to be unusually sophisticated and calculating during their murder sprees. According to Rushby, they even used a relay system to carry dead victims between the village and the bush.

Man-eating is by no means a thing of the past, and notorious man-eaters have come and gone right up to today. Recent examples of this exclusive club are Osama, a single lion who killed more than fifty people near Rufiji between 2002 and 2004, and the Mfuwe lion, the single male from Zambia who killed six people before parading the laundry of one of his victims right through the center of the village in 1991. And of course, there are all those stories about the lions of the world-famous Kruger National Park in South Africa who still prey on desperate Mozambicans in search of a better life down south.

Most of the known man-eaters are named after the territory where they take up residence and satisfy their cravings. But the infamous "paper lion" of Tanzania, Simba Karatasi, was named for his ability to drift like a piece of paper in the wind, traveling vast distances, appearing out of nowhere, randomly selecting victims, defying everything we know about lions' hunting techniques. That is the nature of a man-eater and what makes it so terrifying. When it hunts humans, when we become the prey, the spotlight shines and magnifies our deepest fears.

Phinda itself is not immune to man-eating behavior. The reintroduction of lions into the reserve in the early '90s had its own risks and rewards.

Lion prides were largely exterminated from the region of KwaZulu-Natal by the late 1930s. An individual lion would occasionally make its way south from Mozambique, running the gauntlet through populated areas of armed and wary locals. There are several substantiated reports of lions, mostly males, showing up in areas where they had previously not been seen for many years. A notable example was a huge male that suddenly appeared in Hluhluwe-Umfolozi Game Reserve, a little farther south of Phinda, in 1958. Another male lion was reportedly shot by a farmer in the early 1990s on a farm that now forms part of Phinda. It is ironic that it was around the time of this senseless killing that lions were formally reintroduced to the Phinda area.

Throughout history, lions roamed the savannas and forests of Africa. Nature herself controlled the constant shifting and rebalancing of the predator-prey dynamics. It was only when man's hand began shaping the landscape through intensive farming and hunting that the biodiversity of the area began to decline drastically. The first to suffer were the predators, who were perceived to be unwanted competition for the hunters, and, later, large trophy game like elephants and rhino, valued for their ivory and horns.

When the big game had been all but annihilated and the grasslands largely replaced by pineapple, cattle, and cashew nut farms, a new dynamic was in play. Not all animals suffered from the drastic changes, and certain species clung to the islands of natural bush that remained and some even thrived. So when Phinda was founded in 1990, it was the domain of hyenas, leopards, and one of the largest populations of nyala antelope in the world. Bringing a new predator species into this area, which for decades had an established lion-free predator/prey dynamic, was no easy matter.

The large cats, cheetah and lion, were reintroduced in a carefully orchestrated order. But it was not without controversy and tragedy. The local human populations had to be convinced that the reserve would be a benefit and not a risk to their families and livelihoods. A predator-proof fence was erected to keep the newly introduced cats from escaping, from returning to their place of birth or from seeking prey outside the carefully crafted world of the reserve. But a fence can also create a false sense of safety. For both those inside and outside.

A lion is capable of creeping and sneaking through any opening in an enclosure to get a meal. If cornered, it will almost always jump over the barrier in its hurry to escape. But more important, the lure of cattle and livestock on the other side of the fence sometimes proves too great a temptation, and lions invariably find a way under or over the barrier. In the early years, Phinda had to recapture lions that had escaped into the local communities on several occasions, simultaneously reimbursing the local community members for their livestock losses. Thankfully, there was no loss of human life outside the reserve. But this was not to be the case inside the confines of the reserve's boundaries.

Just a few months after the second successful lion release on the reserve, one of these pioneer lionesses and two unrelated sub-adult females made their way into the area around Phinda Mountain Lodge where they waited until nightfall. Guests had just returned from game drive and were gathering in the boma to have dinner. A lady decided to make her way back to her room to retrieve an item or change her clothes. She left the boma alone, unescorted by a security guard.

When she did not return for dinner, her husband went to look for her, perhaps worried that she had fallen asleep. On the way to their room, between the boma and the swimming pool, the three lions attacked him. The staff heard his terrified screams and they instantly rushed to the scene and chased the lions off. Their actions came just in time for the husband, but his wife had not been so lucky. She had been killed just a few minutes earlier, the victim of a silent, lethal attack. Circumstances, the dark night, hungry lions, all contributed to the horrific event. All three of the lions that participated in the attack were immediately dispatched.

Places like Phinda are wild. It's not Disney here. While I was at Phinda, lions came through the unfenced camps fairly often, sometimes just passing through, sometimes hunting the relaxed animals that took sanctuary among the human residences. At any reserve, there is a constant need for caution, and visitors are frequently reminded that the camps are open to wild animals. Vigilance is especially required when the diurnal creatures retire and the lions come out to play under those starry African nights.

Back at the Mziki Marsh after the lion episode, I breathed a huge sigh of relief, not just for the lucky Mozambican, but also for the future of the North pride. This beautiful lioness was among the first settler lions to be reintroduced, and it would have been a great shame to lose such an enigmatic and large matriarch, especially now that she was the leader of a new generation of lions born on Phinda soil. For our guests, it was a huge coup to sight this lioness, so I always made a special effort to locate her. Sitting on the steering wheel, facing the guests, I loved to tell the story of my experiences, up close and personal with this lioness. I, like many of the other rangers at the Forest and Vlei lodges, felt I had a personal connection with her. One story in particular, I now told to my wide-eyed guests. ...

When I was fresh off the selection course, Morty, the head ranger, assigned me to accompany a very special guest. He was a certain well-known international actor, who wanted to walk through the reserve to view big game on foot. Wisely, Morty wanted to take no chances allowing a celebrity to walk deliberately close to big game with a rookie like me. So Morty also assigned Benson, my close Zulu colleague and one of the most experienced rangers, to escort us.

The protocol for walking big game was to drive until you either picked up fresh tracks or saw your quarry from the vehicle. You would then carefully assess the conditions — the wind direction, the terrain, the thickness of the bush — before making your approach on foot. We had just enjoyed an excellent stalking of two white rhinos, a mother and older calf, and were driving back to the lodge when Benson picked up fresh lion tracks on the road. Our guest was keen to see them and he eagerly said yes to getting a closer look.

We followed the tracks in the Land Rover until they headed off the road and into a block of combretum trees. Benson grabbed his rifle, and leaving the guest in the vehicle, we proceeded to scout the area. We inched forward on the tracks as they side-winded through the open bush between the thickets. And then they disappeared right into one of the larger thickets in the middle of the block. We circled the block, looking for exit tracks. None. The lions had to be less than twenty yards away and we could not see them, they were so carefully concealed in the shadows of the velvet bushwillow.

But Benson touched his nose to indicate that he had picked up the slightly acrid smell that can only be sensed by humans when at close quarters. As Benson signaled me to retreat back to the vehicle, I heard the telltale low growl that normally precedes a charge. And then, as sure as the Springboks beating England at rugby, the thicket erupted as two lionesses from the North pride made it clear that this was a lions' only neighborhood. With his right hand, Benson pulled me behind him as he raised the rifle with his left.

There is a Malagasy saying when two men enter a forest. "He is my confidence and I am his."

I instinctively felt for Benson's belt, more through fear than protocol. We were together in this adventure, he facing the lions and I pulling him back, groping our way to safety. I watched as the split second of the charge slowed down tenfold. I heard Benson yell something in Zulu about the cats' mother, and they stopped. Over Benson's shoulder, I could see one of them halt only a lion's length from us, before she retreated into the thicket.

Slowly, slowly, we made our way back to the vehicle. I guided Benson while he faced the bush, but there were no further charges. For some reason, we were warned away, told in no uncertain terms that we were not welcome. Back at the Land Rover, our guest was disappointed. But Benson's experience told him that there was no way we were going to experience a lion sighting that afternoon, especially not on foot!

My guests were enthralled with the tale of my close encounter with the females of the North pride. I could see their eyes widen, imagining what it would be like coming cheek to jowl with those tawny, muscled bodies, looking deep into those cold amber eyes.

By now, the lionesses at Mziki were retreating into the cover of the long grass, and thanks to Richard's quick maneuvering, the Mozambican was on his way. This day's adventure was over, and it was time to head back to the lodge. There would be much to talk about that evening.

My experiences with lions have thankfully not always been so precariously balanced between life and death. Most visitors leave the continent with the perception that lions are lazy pussycats with little more to do than doze away their lives, half-waking occasionally to swat at the odd irritating fly or discipline a pesky cub. And for the most part, this is true. Lions will sleep for up to eighteen hours a day and sometimes more. But those who have the chance to spend much time with these large cats know that there is nothing that grabs your attention more than a roaring lion.

There are certain sounds of the bush that epitomize Africa's wild places — the haunting call of the African fish eagle, the hideous whooping of the spotted hyena and the froglike chirping of the African scops owl. But the sound of a lion in full roar at close range truly captures the essence of Africa. Deeper in bass than an African drum, a lion's roar has the ability to silence all things.

My favorite memories of lions are close-range roars. On several occasions, I have been within ten feet of a lion executing a full-blooded roar. Lion vocalizations can be heard by humans over four miles away and, one would have to surmise, many more miles away by lions themselves. So when you are sitting in an open Land Rover in the dead of the night and a lion is advertising its presence but a few feet away, the sound literally goes right through you.

Roaring is quite a process, and to watch — and hear and feel — it unfold is unforgettable. The roar starts unimpressively enough — with a few low moans, interspaced by a few seconds. And then the moans gradually increase in crescendo until the sound comes from deep within. A deep, rumbling roar. I'm no expert on the vocal chords of large cats, but I can tell you that the sound seems to come not from the throat region but from the stomach area.

The amount of effort expended cannot be overstated. Every muscle in the cat tenses and contracts with each roar. The sound seems to be driven from the cat's very core — from the stomach up through the lungs, past the vocal chords, and through the outstretched neck as the lion points its head as far out horizontally as he can. The sound is finally ejected in a teeth-rattling boom from the trumpet-like lips of the lion.

And then, similar to the beginning of the whole affair, the roars gradually become shorter and softer, until they are gobbled up by the stillness of the night. And after a lion's deafening roar, everything is pin-drop quiet, as if all living things are seriously contemplating whether they will see the light of dawn.

Lions roar when they are patrolling their territory, using the audio signals to signify dominance. Rather than being an aggressive display, roaring is a passive form, an effective communication to reduce conflict between dominant pride males. The roaring of a dominant lion or coalition of lions will often be answered by the dominant male or males from the surrounding territory. And, over-whelmingly, territorial boundaries will be respected and conflict will be avoided.

Roaring is generally reserved for male lions, but on two occasions, I have witnessed lionesses roaring with as much gusto and volume as their male counterparts. In both instances, male lions were not present with the pride, and I would surmise that either the females were taking over the territorial duties of the males in their absence or they were communicating with their dominant males, who were answering their calls, unheard to human ears, some-where off in the distance.

But conflict between lions is not always averted, and rare occasions exist when prides engage in full-blooded feline warfare, the short-range effects of which are enough to make you dictate your final will and testament into the microphone of your shaking video camera.

The large swath of land that comprises the northern area around Forest Lodge was strictly controlled by the North pride, a coalition between the dominant lioness and her two daughters and their young. Due to the relatively small fenced-in area that is Phinda, conflicts erupt over territorial boundaries when prides ex-pand. Lions multiply rapidly when conditions are perfect and there is plenty of food. But when territorial expansion is impossible, the lions are forced to self-regulate their numbers. I witnessed one such battle on a game drive with guests, when the North pride lioness was forced to defend her territory and the lives of her offspring against her very own blood sister.

"*La mabhuzesi ashesha kakhulu*," Norman shouts from his perch, the specially modified seat on the front of the Land Rover's bull-bar.

These lions are really moving it.

Norman and I left the lodge especially early this morning with our Land Rover full of American guests, a family of four and a young couple on honeymoon. Within five minutes of the Forest Lodge car park, after leaving the confines of the magical sand for-est, Norman's keen eyesight picked up the fresh tracks of an entire pride of lions. Their pugmarks are quite distinct in the headlights, as the blackness of night is just morphing into the dark navy-blue of predawn. I follow the tracks using Norman's signals as a guide, driving carefully so as not to disturb the trail with the vehicle treads.

We know that there is a good chance we will be able to show our guests the uncommon sight of lions on the move, possibly on the hunt. After following the tracks for a good twenty minutes, Norman indicates to me that the lions have not stopped to rest, scent mark, or stalk anything. These lions are moving with pace, obviously on a mission.

It is just then that I suggest we switch off the Land Rover to listen. This was something we often do when we are on very fresh tracks. Nyala antelope, impalas, monkeys, baboons, and even birds will all frantically alarm-call when they see predators. The warning calls enable us to leapfrog the tracking process somewhat and head straight toward the action. As the hum of the V-8 Land Rover abruptly stops, I hear the craziest commotion imaginable in the distance, as if a large gathering of beasts were executing some other living thing.

As if this were an everyday occurrence, Norman states matter-of-factly, "*Amabhubesi ayashayana.*"

The lions are fighting one another.

My heart leaps at the chance to see the clash firsthand, and I ask Norman in Zulu why the North pride would be fighting among themselves.

"*Mhlawumbe nkomazi ithethisa izingane zakhe ngoba azibulanga wena izolo,*" Norman says with a straight face, ever the comedian.

Perhaps the Queen is disciplining her daughters for not killing you yesterday when you and Benson were tracking them on foot.

I start the vehicle and bounce toward the scene of the spine-chilling vocalizations.

"Lions!" one of the guests shouts and points.

Directly in front of us, in a small clearing surrounded by monkey-apple trees, three lionesses are snarling viciously and pacing in a perfect circle around a massive lioness crouched down on her haunches. Immediately, we recognize the North pride's dominant female, an intimidating female held in awe by the Zulu trackers for her tendency to sometimes eat animals alive.

But the cats surrounding her are not her daughters. These

intruders are the females of the South pride and they are out for blood. Interestingly, the dominant female of the South pride is the full-blooded sister of the North pride female, and they had once been part of the same pride.

They had separated several years earlier and formed their own prides comprising their now adult daughters and their young. Today it is obvious that any previous sibling alliances are clearly forgotten as one by one the South pride females take turns charging the cornered queen. Strangely, the North pride female's own adult daughters are nowhere to be seen, and she is entirely on her lonesome. But she is not about to submit to her old pride-mate and surrender the heart of her territory.

Every time one of the snarling South pride females moves in, the defending matriarch bravely counters with fur-flying swats of her massive paws. When she bites the neck of her assailant and pins her down, the other invading females lunge in and attack her vulnerable rear. The North pride lioness is now bleeding profusely from several large lacerations down her flanks.

We watch in awe as the massive North pride lioness starts gaining the upper hand in the protracted conflict, each attack sounding as if four lions had been placed momentarily into a giant blender. The effects of her determination have taken their toll on the younger South pride females, both of which have several crimson rivulets trickling from their noses and clear puncture wounds around their necks.

Perhaps thinking that discretion was the better part of valor, the two youngsters back off several yards to lick their wounds, leaving the two dominant sisters to compete in a one-sided showdown. While the North pride female, in stark contrast to her sister, is relatively relaxed toward humans, she does not afford the same liberties to any animals, especially other lions.

In an instant, realizing that she is now in a one-on-one showdown, the queen of the North surges forward in a blur of claws and teeth. Using her extreme weight advantage, she latches onto her sister's back and mounts her in a show of dominance, simultaneously sinking her long fangs into the neck of her incapacitated sister. She holds her grip as her sister twists and roars, trying desperately to escape.

I glance back at my guests and notice that they are becoming emotionally unstable as the dramatic event looks as if it is leading to a particularly grisly end. For what seems like eons, the large lioness maintains her death grip, with little to no movement from the smaller cat. And then, in what can only be described as an uncharacteristic act of altruism, she releases her grip. Her sister runs off at pace, followed closely by her sidekicks, and seemingly none the worse for wear. The victorious lioness then chases all three vanquished cats until they cross over their territorial border. We follow at a distance until she returns, limping but victorious, back to her domain.

She disappears into an unnegotiable patch of sand forest, probably to lick her wounds and rest up from the fight. This incredible sighting is over and we prepare to leave the scene, all of us a bit amazed and still in awe of what we just witnessed. And then the most amazing thing happens.

The North pride lioness emerges from the other side of the forest with something in her mouth. We drive closer to see what she is eating, only to discover a tiny cub, umbilical chord still attached. Very few people have had the privilege of viewing a cub so young because lionesses do not show their cubs to anyone, not even other pride members, until they are at least six weeks of age. She had been alone, protecting her cubs in the thick nursery of the monkey-apple trees. This certainly now explained why her daughters were not present with her during the clash with the South pride.

How proud she is of her newborn! She walks right up to our vehicle, carrying the little cub in her mouth, the remnants of recent birth still evident. I am delighted; she is showing it off just to us! My admiration and respect grows for this spectacular lioness and the close bonds she has with her pride. Now I understand why her female pride mates had taken such a forceful stand when Benson and I invaded their territory the previous day. Her older, adult daughters were protecting the birth of their young siblings with their lives.

After stashing her cub in a fresh hiding spot, she does not return, presumably nursing her only surviving youngster. Lionesses typically give birth to three to five cubs. Whether the marauding South pride lionesses killed her other cubs we never knew, but one thing was for certain. Never, ever test the will of a mother lion, especially one of the largest ever to walk the planet.

MOUNTAIN OF MUSCLE

For all creatures have their way of finding a home
Like the hunting dog, like the stampeding elephant,
Like us who have found a moving mountain.
MAZISI KUNENE,
"Vision of Zosukuma"

Ayihlabi ngakumisa.
It does not stab according to the shape of its horns.
ZULU PROVERB

T HE WOUNDED CAPE BUFFALO IS one of the most dangerous animals to walk the earth, arguably the most lethal of all the Big
Five.

Very few people survive an attack by an enraged buff.

Historically, the Big Five were the animals the great white hunters of the past deemed most difficult and dangerous to hunt on foot.
And each came with a trophy symbolic of the beauty and grace of
the animal. The smooth ivory tusks of the elephant, the precious
horns of the rhino, the sleek spotted pelt of the leopard, the luxurious black mane of the lion.

But to these early hunters, there was nothing more valuable
than the polished horns of an old Cape buffalo bull. Back then, to
bag a "dugga boy," as the old bulls were known because of their
affinity to cover themselves with mud, or *dugga*, was to prove your
manhood. But even more important, attached to the trophy horns
was a priceless reward. A story to tell over and over. How one came
face to face with this most short-tempered and cunning beast and
lived to tell about it. If these great hunters of the past could only tell
us their stories in person. If we could only gather them all in a pub,
fill them with drink, and let the adrenaline flow. Then the African
buffalo would be tops on the list of their closest encounters with

death. It was this very danger, this adrenaline-infused encounter that worked like a drug drawing them to hunt the buffalo.

One of these early hunters, Frederick Patterson—a different Patterson from the famous man-eating lion killer—documented in great detail his safari in Africa in the early 1900s with the well-known and respected big game hunter, Denys Finch Hatton. Patterson's description of the Cape buffalo in his book *African Adventures* whetted the appetites of future hunters:

> I would class the African buffalo as a different brand. In the first place, he is a deliberate first-degree murderer. His reasoning powers are prodigious, probably second only to those of the elephant. Usually he attacks when wounded, which enables him to plead self-defense; but occasionally he makes unprovoked charges that are unparalleled in their deadly determination. He pursues an enemy as relentlessly as death itself; and has been known, when wounded, to turn on his pursuers and hunt them through tangled thickets like a terrier hunting rats.

Patterson was fortunate to have Finch Hatton, Karen Blixen's dashing lover in *Out of Africa* as his guide, because Patterson's attempt to shoot a buffalo almost got him killed:

> [The wounded buffalo] charged with a bellow that sounded louder than the horn of Gabriel. My impression of him, before a lucky shot brought him down, was one of blood and horn and foam and speed all confusedly mingled in one black bulk.

The "lucky shot" that saved him from the "black death" was not from his gun, as he faced the deadly charge, but from Finch Hatton's. If you are going to hunt a buff, you had better rack up some serious hunting hours first. And even then, every time you do, you had better be ready for an early retirement package.

The early hunters would tell you that a buffalo seldom bluffs. Unlike an elephant, there is no such thing as a mock charge. White rhinos will charge blindly, mostly without knowing exactly where they are going. Lions are the masters of the straight-faced poker bluff. Even leopards, although less likely than lions, will feign an attack in preference to the real deal. A buffalo, however, means business and will not be thwarted. This is a major distinction that separates the buffalo from the other Big Five animals.

To hunt a buffalo on foot was a test of marksmanship, courage, and the ability to stay calm under pressure. The early hunter, without the luxury of today's innovations in optics, needed to advance within a hundred yards to look straight into the face of the buffalo in order to determine whether it was an old bull with a thick, heavy set of trophy horns. But by then he might be too close.

In his 1908 book *African Nature Notes and Remembrances*, the famous big game hunter and explorer Frederick Selous observed:

> Once however, a buffalo is actually charging, no bullet will turn or stop it, unless its brain is pierced or its neck or one of its legs broken. A charging buffalo comes on grunting loudly, with outstretched nose and horns laid back on its neck, and does not lower its head to strike until close up to its enemy.

The early hunters knew you needed to sink a heavy bullet on the first shot. But not into the impenetrable boss, the horn covering which only serves to protect the hollow skull underneath. You must shoot for the brain, right between the eyes. Anything else will only injure and infuriate the animal. If you shoot the horns, you may only stun him and make him forget that he is a vegetarian. It has been said that if your first shot on *inyathi*, as the Zulus call him, is a bad one, the next fourteen will only serve to further annoy him.

"The buffalo is inquired about from those ahead," the Zulus say. Because if the injured animal is not seen on the path before you, it's probably behind you quietly circling back for an ambush. The hunter is now the hunted.

While the Zulu revered the leopard for its power, the buffalo was admired for its cunning and strength, symbolized by those menacing horns. Buffalo horns are measured by their size, width, shape, and hardness. Known as the drop, curl, boss and spread.

The curved shape of the horns surrounding an impenetrable dome inspired Shaka, the great Zulu king, to devise a very simple yet effective battle tactic known as the "horns of the buffalo." His warriors would encircle their enemy, close ranks, and force the opponents toward the center where the main fighting took place. Rows of replacements waited just beyond the safety of the center, ready to join in the battle. This famous maneuver, surrounding the enemy by the "horns of the buffalo" and forcing an attack at the reinforced "dome," worked time and again to build and protect Shaka's empire.

Observing the Cape buffalo from the safety of the Land Rover, most people see a cousin of the domesticated cow, grazing placidly. It's hard to imagine that this vegetarian is responsible for several hundred deaths a year, many without provocation. Only encounters with hippos and crocodiles have proven deadlier, but since these two animals are not considered "big game" or trophy animals, they are not held in the same esteem as the buffalo.

The precept for finding buffalo seems fairly simple. Just look for surface water, grass, and shady forest. Follow the messy trail of increasingly wet patties, throw in a few oxpeckers, and you've located the buffalo. Sounds easy, but they are capable of concealing themselves for hours in the thickest thickets, in  the impenetrable acacia, or in the buffalo's namesake — the prickly buffalo thorn. Their hides are thick, up to an inch, protecting them during battles but also providing a shield from the thorny scrub of the shady forest.

When there is plenty of water and grass, buffalo thrive and multiply. During a drought, the numbers shrink. They are efficient grazers, using their tongues to pull up the grass while they continue walking. Often a twig will poke out their eye, and visually impaired buffalos are not an uncommon sight. The clever ones, those capable of avoiding or outsmarting their enemies, grow old, and a smart buffalo can live up to thirty-five years.

"Beware the widow maker," the early hunters would warn. Because this is an animal made for violence. From the fierce flared nostrils to the curve of those rapier-like horns to the split hooves.

Combine that weaponry on its head with the sharp, heavy weaponry on its feet. Add to that lethal mix a ton of mass and speed up to thirty-five miles an hour and you have a hurtling blur of supercharged energy. It will grab you with the horns and fling you into the air. Before you can rise to your feet, those same horns will gore you, exposing your innards. But it's not done yet. The hooves, sharp as giant axe blades, trample what's left of you beyond recognition.

Yes, stories told by those early hunters made it clear that one doesn't trifle with buff. Unless of course you are looking for an easy way to get out of your marriage. My friends Kathy and Kevin, who worked with me at Phinda discovered the hard way just how menacing a creature the African buffalo can be ...

Kathy bids goodnight to the last of her guests at around eleven o'clock and leaves the main lodge area with her fiancé, Kevin. It is a beautiful evening and the silver light from a full moon dances off the path as the couple return to their tented accommodation. Kathy is about to find out that the widow maker, contrary to its nickname, does not discriminate between genders.

The two of them talk softly about the twin US embassy bombings that have just taken place in Dar es Salaam and Nairobi as the plaintive calling of a water *dikkop* echoes loudly in the still air. They come to a small open area adjacent to their tent and see two large male buffalo, one lying down and one standing, illuminated eerily by the bright moonlight. The previous night they had passed these very same buff with Fraser and a few visiting friends from Phinda. The bulls are accustomed to people and are the resident dugga boys of &Beyond's Grumeti Tented Camp, situated along the Grumeti River in the iconic Serengeti of East Africa.

In sharp contrast to Phinda, which is easily accessible by vehicle from Johannesburg or Durban or Richards Bay, this camp in Tanzania is quite remote. It's an eight-hour drive from Arusha, where flights funnel in from Dar es Salaam, and Nairobi in Kenya. Most people choose to charter a plane to the small airstrip near the camp. The Serengeti gets its name from the Maasai language, meaning "endless plains" and is best known for the annual Great Migration of large herbivores. &Beyond's Grumeti camp is the most luxurious tented camp in the Serengeti, and also one of the most famous crossing points for viewing the wildebeest and zebra migration. Situated directly on the Grumeti River, it is home to some of Africa's biggest crocodiles and well known for its resident hippos. This evening, the danger does not come from the hippos, which emerge from the river to forage at night, or the crocs looking for a convenient meal. This evening, the lodge grounds perched above the riverbed harbor two massive Cape buffalo, clearly visible in the moonlight.

The closest buffalo stands up as Kathy and Kevin are about to reach their tent. The massive animal stares straight at them with its nose extended, smelling the air suspiciously. The management couple stops and faces the impending danger. Both Kevin and Kathy have extensive experience in the African bush. In his early days, Kev had been an excellent ranger at Phinda, with plenty of hours under his belt walking big game on foot. At well over six feet tall and with a large frame, Kevin is an imposing figure. Kathy is tall, with blond hair and blue eyes, and the two experienced lodge managers have certainly had their fair share of close wildlife encounters. But something about the way the bull got up and is now staring them down has Kathy a little unsettled.

"Let's turn around and walk back," she whispers to Kevin. Even though they are just a few steps from their tent, her intuition kicks in, warning her that something is amiss. The "big stinky cow," as she likes to refer to the buff, is looming large, the distinctive curve of the horns reflecting in the moonlight.

"Let's just wait," says Kevin. "He'll relax in a few minutes."

Kevin, with his many years experience, knows that at this close range, any movement, including a retreat can trigger a charge. The words have hardly come out of his mouth as the unpredictable buff storms forward. There is no time to think or react; so unbelievably swift is the monster bovine's attack. Kathy feels herself tripping backward as the bull effortlessly shakes its head and tosses her ten feet into the air like a rag doll. Her face crashes into the dirt some distance away as her fiancé watches in disbelief. Kevin screams and shouts at the enraged animal as it comes back to finish the job.

Kathy is fully conscious and shouting epithets as she hears the buffalo approaching. It walks right up to her as Kevin charges around swearing. She can smell its musky scent as the beast sniffs her with wet, dribbling nostrils. Perhaps either satisfied that she is dead or tired of the shouting, the huge bull turns around and disappears behind some thick bush. Kathy, infused with adrenalin, jumps to her feet, unaware she has been seriously injured.

"Kev, I'm so tired," she says. "Let's go to bed."

They walk the remaining few steps, and as she tries to step up into their tent, she realizes that she cannot move her right leg. Kevin looks down with horror at what remains of her thigh. One of the buff's colossal horns had met their mark in her upper leg, entering the top of her thigh and exiting just above her knee. Kathy had been impaled like a skewered kebab, then pitched like a bale of hay. She was fortunate that the razor-sharp horn had come out the same way it had gone in.

"You've been hurt," Kev understates, urging Kathy not to look down as he carries her into the tent. He lays her down on the bed before bolting out to get help.

"Please don't leave," she screams. "That bloody buff is still there. It will kill you!"

But Kevin is already gone into the night, sprinting past the now docile buffalo to wake up Hugh and Julie, fellow employees. Julie returns to the tent to sit with Kathy while Kevin and Hugh desperately try to contact the flying doctors on the satellite phone.

Kevin returns to their tent with the limited medical supplies available. He cuts off Kathy's jeans and does everything he can to try to stem the profuse bleeding from the entry and exit wounds, using every available bandage to fill the gaping hole. There are, however, no painkillers, and Kathy bravely fights off the pain as the adrenalin subsides, replaced by a searing ache.

In the meantime, after much convincing and several phone calls, Hugh makes sure that the flying doctors will come and that the small grass airstrip will be well lit by torch and flame to guide them in. At around two in the morning, Kathy is airlifted to Nairobi hospital, which is still reeling from the aftermath of the embassy bombings. She spends four nights in hospital in the Kenyan capital before being flown to Johannesburg, where she spends a further month in hospital undergoing skin grafts and sterilization treatment of her wounds. She is fortunate it is only a flesh wound, no bones are broken, no nerves damaged. Kathy lives to tell the tale of "the girl who survived the buffalo attack in the moonlight."

As horrifying as Kathy's experience was, she can consider herself extremely lucky that the bull did not attempt a second attack. Very, very few people survive an attack from a buffalo. Kathy went on to make a full recovery and is now left with a renewed respect for the power and unpredictability of this, one of Africa's most short-tempered animals. Not long after the attack, the same old buffalo that gored Kathy came face to face with a group of lions. It fought bravely for an extended period of time before succumbing to the coordinated attack of the pride.

Lions are the buffalo's archenemy. But even with their superior speed and agility, lions require significant numbers to bring down an adult Cape buffalo. Best to go after an old or injured buffalo if a lion is to get a meal and live to eat it.

Lions normally smother their smaller prey, clasping the head within their jaws. But that doesn't work for an animal as large and tough as the buffalo. The lions have learned that the most successful way to hunt a Cape buffalo is to wear it down over time, gradually weakening the animal until it can no longer rise up, its huge bulk rendering it immobile on the ground. Death seldom comes quickly and the bellows of dying buffalo are one of the most heart-wrenching of Africa's wild sounds.

However, the buffalo is fully capable of defending itself against lions and can be a formidable foe. There is strength in numbers, and when threatened, the adult herd will bunch together to protect the young by surrounding the calves. If a lion does single out a calf, the herd will answer the distress call and mob the unfortunate predator. It is not uncommon to see a lion treed, or even tossed, gored, and trampled.

For hundreds of years, the only insights into the behavior of the buffalo were the seemingly exaggerated reports of the big game hunters. But that all changed with the advent of photographic safaris, inexpensive high-quality cameras, and the Internet. One amateur caught an amazing sighting and posted the video on YouTube. If you have any doubts about the strength, resilience, and protective nature of the buff or the tenacity of the lion, the "Battle at Kruger" is guaranteed to change your perception.

A herd of buffalo with their young is slowly making its way down to a dam to drink. Three buffalo—a massive bull, a smaller bull, and a calf—proceed ahead of the rest of the herd, which is spread out behind them like a string of beads. They are blissfully unaware of the danger awaiting them as they plod toward the water, oblivious to the lion-colored mounds resting on the side of the earthen dam amidst the dried grasses. The three buffalo continue along the dam wall, the large bull buffalo taking the lead.

The yellowish-brown mass shifts as two lions, a female and a young male, emerge, inching their way forward along the wall. They crouch low so as not to reveal their outlines. Lions are most effective when hunting in teams of two or three, so the rest of the pride melts out of sight.

The big bull stops within twenty yards of the cats and suddenly raises his head, sniffing the air suspiciously. While buffalo have very good vision and hearing, the equal of any of the other Big Five, their sense of smell is astounding. He picks up the strong feline odor through his well-developed nasal scent glands. He flicks his head up and down as if irritated by the realization that cats are disturbing his afternoon drink.

The leader's next step down the bank triggers an explosive charge from the lions. Instinctively, the two large buffalo and calf turn on their heels, fleeing back toward the safety of the herd. It's too late, as one of the lionesses spots an advantage. She peels off, goes for the young calf running parallel to the water, and tackles it. Her timing is perfect. Entwined in a vicious embrace, the calf and the cat flip twice in the air, landing in the water.

The young male lion joins the lioness in the water, clamping down on the young buffalo's muzzle. The rest of the pride now joins the hunters on the bank. It is just a matter of time before the young buffalo succumbs. He is still on his feet in the water, still alive as the team of lions attempts to drag him out of the dam. Initially, they make progress.

The young calf uses all its remaining strength to resist, the commotion stirring the water. But his efforts to pull free from the lions summon another predator, one with even more menacing and powerful jaws. From the murky depths of the dam, a crocodile clamps onto one of the young buffalo's thrashing legs.

A tug of war ensues as the large croc pulls from one end and the lions pull tenaciously from the other. Finally, the croc releases its death grip, reluctant to take the fight onto land, where the lions clearly have the advantage.

The lions continue their teamwork and drag the poor calf, still alive, a little farther up the bank. Pausing to catch their breath, several lions look up intently along the water's edge only to see the entire herd of around sixty buffalo advancing in one massive tightly knit group, intent on saving their baby.

When the herd is within thirty yards, the leading bulls stop suddenly, waiting for the rest of the herd to catch up and gather for the final approach. En masse, they canter ahead with their tails raised erect, challenging the lions, who are getting ready to feed on the baby. The battle ensues as the entire herd closes ranks on the remaining pride-mates and a series of buffalo charges attempts to send the lions scattering.

Eventually, the horns meet their mark. A large buff hooks the defensive lioness under the shoulder and tosses her ten feet into the air. The bewildered cat lands directly on one of its pride-mates, and the two shocked lions run away in opposite directions, dodging buffalo as they make their escape. Most of the herd chases one of the retreating lions, as the other lion makes its way back to reinforce the remaining two who are still on the calf.

But the lions realize that they are outnumbered and have lost the battle. The herd approaches again, bellowing and bellowing. Emboldened by the cries, the young calf struggles to its feet and out of the lions' grip. It approaches the herd, only a couple of feet away, and though one of the lions makes a feeble attempt to get the calf back, it's too late. The calf disappears into the cauldron of seething, bulky black bodies.

The buffalo are not done. Infuriated and with murder on their minds, they relentlessly attempt to kill the remaining lions, eventually driving off all of them. And reclaim not just their calf but also the temporary rights to the title King of the Jungle.

Encounters as dramatic as this occur infrequently, which makes this an especially insightful event to witness. The lions are consummate hunters, confident of their speed and agility, trusting in their pride-mates to execute and dispatch their quarry. When stalking the buffalo, they risk being tossed like rag dolls, gored by those sharp horns, and stamped by the cutting hooves. It's a risk they are willing to take; the tasty flesh and protein of even a small buffalo will provide sustenance for the entire pride.

As one observes the details in the scene, it's interesting to note the cold efficiency in their brief encounter. This herd of buff and this pride of lions may well be familiar with one another, even aware of the reptilian dangers in the dam. All the characters act and react as if the scene were choreographed. Advancing, retreating, advancing, retreating. The buff gambling their lives every time they go for a drink of water, the lions willing to risk severe injury and even death to feed their pride, the wily crocodile always ready for an opportune meal.

The early hunters were the first to observe that the animals they hunted so passionately were on the path to extinction. Frederick Selous was a rare individual, a legendary explorer, hunter, and conservationist. His keen observations and experience as a naturalist earned him the respect of President Theodore Roosevelt. They became fast friends, sharing their enthusiasm for big game hunting and conservation. In the foreword to Selous's previously mentioned book, Roosevelt wrote in 1908:

> Big game exists only in the remote wilderness. Throughout historic time it has receded steadily before the advance of civilized man, and now the retrogression — or to be more accurate, the extermination — is going on with appalling rapidity.

Yet today, over one hundred years later, we see the Cape buffalo thriving. It's the only member of Africa's Big Five that is not listed as threatened, vulnerable, or endangered on the IUCN (International Union for the Conservation of Nature) Red List. The black rhino is considered "critically endangered," the lion and elephant are "vulnerable," the leopard and white rhino are "near threatened," but the buffalo status is "least concern."

My own thoughts on hunting are somewhat controversial. While I personally do not hunt, I strongly believe that hunting, if conducted in a responsible and sustainable manner, can actually contribute positively to conservation. We are, after all, part of the environment, and we interact with it in many different ways. Humans have hunted for survival for many thousands of years. It is an unavoidable part of our heritage and history.

As long as hunting is controlled and adds value to conservation, I don't see why many environmentalists are so dead against it. The key phrase is "adds value to conservation." I feel that there is a tendency to lump all forms of hunting under one detestable banner. Poaching, trophy hunting, subsistence hunting. It's all the same to some environmentalists.

While I do not have a problem with sustainable hunting, where the animal is killed for its meat, I find it harder to support trophy hunting, where an animal is slaughtered simply for its horns, tusks, or hide. I personally could never shoot a lion or a leopard; these animals are useless as a food source. I could also never bring myself to shoot an elephant for sport, even though the meat can be used to feed an entire village. Shooting an elephant must be like shooting a person. But even trophy hunting contributes significantly to conservation if done correctly and fairly.

Canned lion hunts, where lions are raised and released into large enclosures as easy targets for bloodthirsty killers, disgust me. Where is the sport in that? So I feel that animal rights activists need to distinguish between the different forms of hunting while evaluating at the same time the positive conservation effects of a particular type of hunting. I find it particularly irritating when non-vegetarians criticize hunting, and I often wonder how they can eat a slice of cow with a clean conscience but find it disgusting if someone shoots a deer or duck for food.

The USA has arguably one of the strongest hunting traditions of any nation in the world, and hunting has had a profoundly positive effect on the conservation of America's endangered species and wild habitat. More land by far is under conservation today in North America as a result of the financial funding of hunters and anglers than is due to all the conservation bodies put together. It always amazes me how critical some environmentalists can be of hunting. It would be interesting to do a survey and ask both hunters and self-described environmentalists when they last dug into their pockets. The results might surprise some. Duck hunters in America are required to buy a "duck stamp" license each year. The funds from the duck stamp initiative have conserved over thirteen million acres of waterfowl habitat since 1937. Not just the duck, but all the bird, mammal, fish, reptile, and amphibian species that rely on wetlands have prospered.

By the same token, North American birders are not required to pay anything when they "bag" a new species for their life list. In fact, birders as a group contribute relatively minuscule amounts to conservation when compared with hunters, who are enjoying their birds in similar, albeit more violent, ways. All this is not to say that I'm blind to the devastating effects of unsustainable hunting practices. The passenger pigeon, once the most abundant bird in North America, numbering in the billions, died out as a direct result of hunting. The American bison nearly met the same fate. All I'm saying is, let's not be so quick to judge.

During the past one hundred and fifty years, buffalo in Africa have undergone immense challenges and pressures, not the least of which has been human pressure from unsustainable hunting practices. Unlike the other Big Five, the buffalo has not been a target of poaching for high-value trophy artifacts. The horns have little value compared to rhino horn or elephant tusk. Even ivory from warthog tusk is considered more valuable.

No, the buffalo is the only one of the Big Five that has historically been hunted for its protein. Buffalo meat is quite tasty, and their immense bulk means that they can provide quite a number of steaks for a hungry village. The early white hunters were also taken with the taste of buffalo flesh, and as they embarked on their hunting forays farther north from the Cape, buffalo were a frequent target.

Most people have never heard of a *quagga*, a species of zebra, or a *blaauwbok*, also known as the blue antelope. Both of these animals disappeared from the South African landscape forever, due to extensive hunting in the early years of colonization on the Cape. Somehow, the buffalo avoided a similar fate, showing remarkable powers of recovery and adaptability. Although they were hunted extensively throughout southern Africa, buffalo still managed to thrive in some of the more inaccessible areas—wild places that were known for the twin dragons of malaria and tsetse fly. Rampant hunting, although it had a devastating effect on all game — including buffalo — up until the late 1800s, did not bring about the near extinction of the African buffalo as much as a more sinister, yet invisible killer.

In the late 1890s, a devastating disease rampaged through the African continent, wiping out millions of buffalo, giraffe, and wildebeest, as well as cattle and other livestock. The dreaded rinderpest had arrived in Africa — more than likely from India or Arabia — and it spread like a runaway fire through the landscape.

Around ninety percent of all cattle in southern Africa were wiped out, contributing to massive financial losses. Countless people from Ethiopia to South Africa died from starvation as a result, and it took many years for Africa to recover. Rinderpest was a very contagious viral disease that today has been officially eradicated across the globe. But in the 1890 outbreak, buffalo herds were systematically wiped out. The disease was easily transmitted through infected water and could even be transmitted through the air. The closely knit groups of African buffalo were especially susceptible.

As far back as 1908, Frederick Selous doubted the ability of the Cape buffalo to survive:

> As was to be expected, the rhinoceroses were the first to go, but the buffaloes, in spite of their prodigious numbers in many parts of South Africa only a generation ago, did not survive them, for wherever the epidemic of rinderpest penetrated in 1896 it almost completely destroyed all the buffaloes which up until then had escaped the native hunters. It is very difficult to say with exactitude how many buffaloes still exist in South Africa today.

Despite the prediction of its demise, the buffalo numbers bounced back only to become silent carriers of other diseases. Over the millennia, they had built up resistance to these infections, but domesticated cattle, with their reduced resilience, succumbed readily.

The tsetse fly is the carrier of a nasty parasite called *brucei rhodesiense* that causes sleeping sickness in humans and the deadly nagana in cattle. The buffalo were asymptomatic carriers. Nagana struck fear into the hearts of governments across southern Africa. It was clear that cattle could not exist in areas where Nagana existed, and the expansion of cattle farming was severely limited as a result. Fearing a repeat of the rinderpest epidemic, the government of South Africa began a disastrous eradication campaign in 1917. Instead of trying to eliminate the tsetse fly, they opened up the country's wilderness areas to indiscriminate hunting of the tsetse fly's suspected carriers. In Maputaland, all animals were instantaneously declared vermin, and the wholesale slaughter of game began. Only the rhino, hippopotamus, and nyala were spared.

Because buffalo were the favored host of the tsetse fly, they were first in the rifle sights. The herds that had begun to slowly recover from the rinderpest outbreak twenty years earlier were systematically wiped out. Some short-sighted officials even called for the deproclamation of Maputaland's game reserves, and several years later, when the guns had fallen silent and rotting carcasses had been picked clean by vultures, nearly all buffalo and other game had been wiped out ... while the tsetse fly still existed, ready to prey on the cattle waiting their turn to occupy massive graveyards, thanks to the impatience of the human settlers.

By the 1920s, buffalo had seemingly been eliminated from the Cape and from almost all of KwaZulu-Natal and the rest of South Africa. But somehow, this resilient species managed to survive the indiscriminate killing, and slowly their numbers began to increase yet again, only to become carriers of other diseases that would wreak havoc among southern Africa's cattle herds. The buffalo were once again singled out as the villains, being the largely asymptomatic and unwilling carriers of diseases like foot-and-mouth disease, corridor disease (which only affects herds in KwaZulu-Natal), bovine tuberculosis, and brucellosis. All are devastating to domesticated bovine populations.

Thankfully, today conservationists have learned from the past, and most buffalo in Africa are now confined to game reserves, where they are strictly separated from cattle. From being hunted extensively in the 1700s and 1800s to becoming nearly extinct in the rinderpest epidemic of the 1890s to again being almost eliminated in the Nagana campaigns of the early 1900s, buffalo have rebounded and now exist in excellent numbers in Africa's protected areas. But after all they've gone through at the hands of humankind, it's not surprising that they have, to put it mildly, developed bad tempers.

The term "Big Five" is an overused safari term that describes collectively the likes of lions, elephants, rhinos, leopards, and buffalo. Personally, I don't care for the term much because it places too much emphasis on a select group of animals at the expense of all the rest. The Big Five animals are the celebrities of the African bush — the stars that draw paying guests to our wild places. In this book, I have devoted at least one chapter to each of these celebrities, but it's important to remember that the most interesting aspects of the African bush, at least to me, come from all of its animals as a whole, not just the Big Five.

Today Cape buffalo are more often hunted with cameras than guns. For the most part, they ignore and indeed tolerate the daily human comings and goings. But who knows what can set off a death charge, even in a seemingly healthy animal if they feel vulnerable? It's always a risky proposition to come face to face with a Cape buffalo.

My personal experiences with the black death, widow maker, or *inyathi*, are thankfully limited to peaceful encounters. This is not altogether surprising, as many fatalities are a direct result of the malicious intent of wounded buff. All the buffalo that I have ever encountered were healthy animals that I mostly viewed from the relative safety of a Land Rover.

However, there was one time when I experienced how small a human feels confronted by a buffalo when on foot. I was at Victoria Falls in Zimbabwe, fishing for tigerfish in the Zambezi River. I had caught several nice tigers and a few robustus bream, both excellent fighting fish, when a large thunderstorm rolled in. Wisely deciding, as lightning crashed all around me, that fishing with a graphite rod was a bad idea, I started walking back to my campsite in the rain.

I got to within twenty feet of the bull buff before I heard him. I had inadvertently disturbed the large dugga boy in the shady forest, probably waking him from a late afternoon nap. He stood up quickly, emerging from out of nowhere, with a loud snort that frightened the crap out of me. His great bulk hovered just a few yards in front of me, blocking the trail. I could see the scarred hide covered with mud and insects, the sharp points of the horns, turned in my direction, on either side of the smooth and worn boss. The heat and humidity magnified the pungent smell drifting my way.

We stood facing each other for what seemed an eternity, and I was sure he was going to charge. There was no escape. If it were one of the other Big Five, I might have had a fighting chance by facing down a lion's bluff, standing up to an elephant's mock charge, avoiding a rhino's myopic stampede or even attempting to back off discreetly from a leopard's feigned attack.

But the buff was in control; the next move was his. There was no choice but to stand quietly and wait, fishing rod in hand. I guess he must have thought that I was not worth a raise in blood pressure, because he started calmly toward me without any malicious intent.

I stepped off the little game path as nearly two thousand pounds of black muscle walked right past. I watched in awe as the dung-caked rump disappeared down to the river for its daily wallow. Having heard of my friends' encounter in the Serengeti, I was incredibly grateful that this particular bull was having a good day.

I was very fortunate while at Phinda to witness the reintroduction of disease-free buffalo into the reserve, where they had not roamed for over a hundred years. They were important, not just because of their tourism value as the final member of the reserve's Big Five, but also for their ecological value. Buffalo are bulk grazers that feed on tall grass, thereby opening up the landscape to the zebra and wildebeest, which prefer the shorter shoots left behind. The weighty buffalo constantly till the soil, recycling important nutrients and improving the land's carrying capacity. It had taken five long and expensive years to release the initial twenty buffalo on Phinda, a place where they had once roamed in the thousands.

The addition of the dangerous and unpredictable buff was the final piece of the puzzle, transforming Phinda into a sustainable wildlife paradise. Each ranger was keenly aware that walks on foot were about to become a lot more interesting … now that the widow maker had returned.

DO NOT SPEAK OF RHINOCEROS

If by chance we come across those who are old,
Who have seen into the heart of the night,
We must not flee in terror of their secrets
But watch their eyes slowly reveal the chameleon.
MAZISI KUNENE,
"Encounter with the Ancestors"

Ungakhulumi ngobhejane kungheko sihlahla eduze.
Do not speak of rhinoceros if there is no tree nearby.
ZULU PROVERB

MANY PEOPLE COME TO PHINDA to celebrate life-changing events and milestones. Special occasions like birthdays, anniversaries, and honeymoons. The intimate settings of the lodges, with individual chalets built of glass and natural materials like thatch and teak, provide privacy and an escape from big cities and busy lives. From the air, arriving guests see spectacular views of the surrounding Lebombo Mountains and the coastal plains. On the ground, the bush mysteries come alive whether it's on a game drive or under the clear starlit sky with the sounds of the night creatures nearby. Risk-taking guests often test their mettle with something as simple as a walk through the bush, which can sometimes morph into an adrenaline-packed adventure.

Attracted by Phinda's beautiful setting, a young couple asks to go on a trip farther afield from the lodge. They have their heart set on seeing the black rhino, and the best way to locate the rare animal is to walk through the neighboring Mkuze Game Reserve where we can also do a little birding. Even though our days as game rangers are action filled, I perk up at the opportunity to lead one of the many alternate activities that Phinda provides to see more of the beauty of Maputaland. We offer deep-sea diving on the coral reefs off Sodwana Bay, day trips to the unspoiled beaches where the highest coastal vegetated dunes in the world watch over leatherback turtles laying their eggs on deserted sands. There are fishing excursions targeting sailfish and kingfish. For those who want a birds eye view, Phinda offers a light aircraft outing aboard the *Flight of the Fish Eagle* that flies over the Indian Ocean to spot whale sharks, and skims low over the crystal-clear waters of Lake Sibaya, where hippos gesture at the plane overhead. And yes, trips to see black rhinos in our neighboring reserve.

"Absolutely! I know just the place and I know just the man to take us," I say.

A walking safari through Mkuze Game Reserve is quite popular with wildlife enthusiasts who want to experience the thrill of seeing black rhinos. It is also a prolific birding destination with over four hundred and fifty species of birds recorded in the reserve. Since the black rhino has a reputation for being extremely aggressive, I enlist the help of one of the best rhino trackers and birders at Mkuze, a Zulu named MandlaNkosi, whose name means "strength of the king." Although he is about seventy years old, this wiry, spindly little guy can run faster than I can, and I am privileged to know him. In the early African dawn, at just before 5:00 a.m., we meet MandlaNkosi at the gate to Mkuze.

The bird that we are after is the shy and elusive pink-throated twinspot, named for the unique white spots on the coal- black breast. The Latin name *Hypargos margaritatus* loosely translates to "one hundred eyes below, adorned with pearls." These beautiful round spots are paired heart-shaped white marks on each feather hence "twinspot." A  stunning bird, it is endemic to northern Natal and Mozambique. Even though these birds are also fairly common at Phinda, at Mkuze they're pretty much guaranteed. Tiny and inconspicuous, they inhabit the same territory as the black rhino, deep in the thorny scrub. I have a rifle, of course, as we will be walking in the bush. And MandlaNkosi also carries a rifle. We begin with the usual safety briefing.

"If anything unusual should happen, whatever you do — do not run. Look at us and we'll tell you exactly what to do."

The couple nods in agreement, and the four of us leave the Land Rover for our walk. MandlaNkosi leads us through the thick bushes, all the while listening for the insect-like trilling that will direct us to where the birds reside. Yes, there they are, just a few yards from us, inconspicuous in spite of their bright colors. The males sport perfect mauve plumage on their heads and necks, in contrast to the black and white patterning on their bodies. They are darting in close to the bushes, while a martial eagle, one of the largest eagles in Africa, circles overhead. A perfect day. It's like the gods are shining on us, and it only gets better.

Under the fading remnant of a crescent moon, we ascend a ridge. MandlaNkosi brings the group to a halt and points out a dark shape down the other side of the valley. Even from a distance, the solitary rhino seems out of place, a prehistoric creature emerging from the predawn mists. It would take a great deal of imagination to conjure up such a strange being. Every aspect of its appearance is bizarre.

Through our binoculars, we see the scarred and wrinkled skin, hanging loose as if it is designed to fit a larger animal. The turtle-like head appears almost too heavy for the massive body supported by tiny feet, completely out of proportion. The myopic and lizard-like eyes set low on the cheeks seem too close to the triangular muzzle with its prehensile lips. But the bizarre horn growing out of the center of the head immediately draws the eye. That horn, with the distinctive upward curve and sharply pointed tip, has been the source of its downfall.

Unless you believe in unicorns, the narwhal whale is the only other mammal with an appendage growing out of this totally unexpected place. The whale's tusk is actually a long spiraled tooth that grows from its upper jaw. Like the rhino horn, it was once harvested and sold as a unicorn horn, and both the rhino and the narwhal are credited as being the source of the unicorn legend. There couldn't be three more dissimilar animals, the awkward-looking rhino, the majestic Arctic whale, and the creature of legend, the graceful and elegant unicorn.

In the mid-1990s black rhino numbers are at an all-time low, making this a particularly valuable sighting. We stand there for a bit behind the acacia trees, watching and listening. These megaherbivores eat extraordinary amounts of food to sustain their massive weight. The animal seems content just noisily browsing the leguminous trees and shrubs. Our guests want to get a better look, but MandlaNkosi and I know we need to use caution, as you never want to intrude too close. If the black rhinos hear us or smell us, they will turn on a dime and charge, quickly gaining speed up to thirty miles an hour. "Do not speak of rhinoceros if there is no tree nearby," the Zulus say. In other words, don't disturb a rhino unless you have an escape route.

Even a whisper will set it off. The calm and placid scene could instantly turn ugly. The guests take a few photos, and then it is time to return to the vehicle.

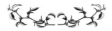

The terms "black" and "white" can be quite confusing since rhinos are not distinguished by the color of their hides. Both animals actually derive their color from the mud they wallow in and the dust they bathe in, and to an untrained eye, can appear similar from a distance. A close look at the muzzle reveals the difference. The white rhino has a square-shaped one for grazing grasslands, while the black rhino has a triangular one for browsing. In fact, the white rhino derived its name from a mistranslation of the Dutch word *wijd*, which actually refers to the "wide" mouth of the white rhino. A tracker on foot will always look for the strange three-toed footprints and the huge piles of dung, which leave clues as to the rhino's identity. A white rhino's dung pile will only contain grasses, while the black rhino's will also contain twigs and bark.

The book *Phinda: The Return* leaves little doubt as to what one should do when facing a rhino:

> Black rhino may be less than half the size of their
> cousins, but they more than make up the difference with
> their aggression. White rhino are the gentle grazers of

the grasslands. Black rhino are the tough bullies of the forests. When tracking black rhino it is essential to have the rhino in one eye and your escape route mapped out with the other. If there is not a nearby tree, then you have to be prepared to stand your ground. Another safety rule is to keep as quiet as a mouse. Rhino do not have good eyesight but they have acute hearing, and even a whisper will have a rhino spinning around with remarkable agility. Some people thrive on the excitement. … Many people prefer to watch the black rhino from a hide or from the security of a Land Rover.

That was how we got to know Bumper, a young white rhino. As rangers, we rarely named animals on the reserve, but Bumper became a familiar sight on game drives and earned our respect. Without warning, this naughty, aggressive little rhino would sometimes emerge from the grasslands and approach at full speed.

It became a childhood game of his, terrorizing the rangers and guests at Phinda. But he was never alone. Following in quick pursuit would be his protective mother. It was a common sight to see three vehicles racing off, followed by Bumper and concerned Mum.

Usually it was the black rhino that had a reputation for behaving like an out-of-control tank, blindly charging elephants, trucks, tractors, and trains, as well as unfortunate humans who happened to be walking nearby. For some reason Bumper, who was about the size of a warthog, played out this childhood game, chasing our Land Rovers. As Bumper grew into a mature adult, he thankfully gave up his sport and started acting more like his even-tempered mum.

At the turn of the twentieth century, as few as sixty white rhinos could be found in the world. The last of these survived in the neighboring reserves of Umfolozi and Hluhluwe. The reintroduction of white rhinos to Phinda in the early 1990s and later black rhinos in 2004 was one of the most amazing conservation success stories of its time. Maputaland is one of the last strongholds of black and white rhinos in Africa, one of the few places left where one can see the gentle grazers of the grasslands and the tough bullies of the forest.

Over our early morning tea, MandlaNkosi reenacts the story I heard many times, the story of how the bush can change lives in an instant. The old and wizened tracker speaks in his native tongue, his melodic voice rising and falling, pausing frequently as I translate and add interpretations for our guests.

MandlaNkosi begins with the traditional words, the Nguni version of "once upon a time."

"*Kwathi ke kaloku ngantsomi ... *"

And now for a story ...

"It is a beautiful day, not unlike today. A perfect day to look for the black rhino. I am walking a couple, newly married, and their ranger through the bush. Just like you. "

MandlaNkosi gestures with his hands to include us in the story.

"Not far from here, a mother rhino and her baby are also out for a stroll, browsing the sweet acacia across that same valley. This is a favorite spot for the rhinos. They return to the same places to browse, bathe ... and even defecate in large and growing piles."

He indicates how large such a pile might be. Rhinos consume tons of vegetation, which pass through them rather quickly.

"Like you, the guests are very excited to see a black rhino and her calf across the valley from the safety of the bushveld. But suddenly the wind changes."

MandlaNkosi sweeps his hand rapidly through the air, gathering the imaginary gust and releasing it.

"The wind carries our smell across the valley, directly to the wary mother. She raises her head high, dilates her nostrils, and inhales our telltale human scent."

MandlaNkosi pauses as we all take a deep breath, imagining what the mother rhino sensed in the breeze.

"Perhaps she remembers the scent of others of our kind, others who came before us, who spelled destruction not only for her but for her entire species. In any case, her curiosity and maternal instincts kick in. I know immediately that she senses us, perceives a threat to her small charge. She turns on her heels and starts toward us."

He stretches out his fingers and spins them quickly, once for the mother and again for the calf.

"We are in big trouble if she comes much closer to investigate. Black rhino are incredibly inquisitive and aggressive. But their poor eyesight makes them unpredictable."

MandlaNkosi entwines his fingers latticelike over his eyes and inhales deeply, showing how a myopic rhino might view this beautiful day, driven mostly by the sense of smell.

"She does not hesitate, does not run or shy away, but lets out a loud snort as she keeps coming down the valley and up the other side of the hill. I need to act quickly."

MandlaNkosi speaks to us from within his trance, as if we are the trio on that fateful day. He expertly weaves us into his colorful narrative.

"'Listen. If this rhino comes closer, I need you to run for the nearest tree. Climb up and sit at the top. Don't delay. When I say go, you go! You run to the top of the tree.'

"And the couple nods, looking a bit concerned. They are newlyweds, so it is kind of an awkward situation to be on your honeymoon and facing a potentially life-threatening situation. They are a little bit nervous, as the wife asks the ranger, 'Should we leave?'"

MandlaNkosi pauses, and we all laugh. "'Well, it's a little bit late now,' the ranger replies.

"Because out of nowhere, the female rhino obtains a fix on exactly the location of our group. She thuds toward us at full speed, calf in tow, all the while emitting a high-pitched squeal. It is a beautiful day with no clouds in sight, but the ground is shaking as if the heavens are thundering from deep within the earth.

MandlaNkosi demonstrates a pumping action with his hands, as he gestures the action of the rhino duo making a beeline through the scrub.

"'Get up tree! Get up tree!' I shout."

"Confusion and terror follow, the young guests run in circles, looking for a tree to climb. The wife goes to the nicest, biggest tree, and is about to climb up. With precious few large trees to choose from among the scrubby acacia, the husband panics. He chooses a tree a little closer and a little bit smaller. Now the ranger is also looking around to find a tree.

"But the trees are only so high, about shoulder height, and the ranger is tall, like James here—" He points to me.

"What is the ranger going to do with that short tree he is heading for, I'm thinking? He does his best to climb to the top of it. Out of the corner of my eye, I see that the rhino is very, very close, only about twenty yards away. And the husband suddenly has a change of heart. He realizes his tree is just not high enough and makes a quick, fateful decision. In a split second, he crosses to his wife, takes one step on her back and climbs to the top of her tree. Leaving her stranded on the shaking ground."

The story is punctuated with MandlaNkosi's whole body showing how the husband uses his wife as a ladder.

"And the rhino, she just keeps coming. I need to distract her, draw her away from the poor lady. So I start running around an acacia tree. That rhino keeps chasing me, round and round the tree, trying to jab me up the butt."

MandlaNkosi comically mimes how the rhino tries to use its horn to assault him on the backside.

"But I am very fast, I just keep running until she loses interest and wanders away, her calf trailing behind. Meanwhile, the whole time, this poor woman is stranded at the bottom of her tree with nowhere to go, scared witless."

MandlaNkosi pauses as we imagine the scene, which took place not far from where we are sitting.

"It was a beautiful day, not unlike today ... "

"*Phela phela ngantsomi ...* "

"And that is the end of the story," says MandlaNkosi.

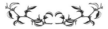

Needless to say, I'm sure that wasn't the end of the story. Africa has a way of bringing out the best and the worst in people. It was probably the end of their honeymoon as the new bride took her T-shirt *and* her new husband to the cleaners. She must have been absolutely livid.

The legend of the honeymoon couple facing the charging rhino always brought smiles and chuckles, as everyone who heard it imagined what they would have done in that situation. But the true story of the rhino is anything but funny.

Africa's rhinos are in trouble. And unlike most other threatened species, their woes are directly caused by human hunting. Few animals go extinct because of hunting alone. In most cases there are other contributing factors—habitat loss; invasive species like rats, rabbits, pigs, or cats; natural disasters. But rhinos do not suffer significantly from any of these other causes. They die because people shoot them, hack off their horns and leave the carcass to rot in the savannas and thornveld of Africa's wildest places. It's as simple and as gory as that.

Throughout history, wild animals were hunted because of their unusual appearance or legendary ferocity. To possess a piece of that animal, whether it was the claws, teeth, horns, tusks, or feathers, was to take on the qualities of that animal. In Elizabethan times, in a famous scene from Shakespeare, Macbeth challenged the ghost to assume the form of an exotic and feared animal:

> *What man dare, I dare.*
> *Approach thou like the rugged Russian bear,*
> *The armed rhinoceros, or th' Hyrcan tiger;*
> *Take any shape but that, and my firm nerves*
> *Shall never tremble. ...*

Shakespeare was quite prescient when he cited these three species, all very different yet currently facing severe decline, if not total extinction. In traditional Chinese medicine (TCM), the bear is desired for its gallbladder, the tiger for its bones, and the rhinoceros for its horn.

While you may have seen bizarre things like rhino feet made into umbrella stands in the trophy rooms of the early safari hunters, the horn was the most coveted part of the animal. This organic outgrowth is not, like elephant ivory, formed from dentin but is composed of keratin, the same protein found in hair and nails, hooves and quills, with the ability to regenerate. Although completely different from ivory, rhino horn also lent itself to intricate and detailed carving for decorative cups, statues, buttons, hairpins, combs, and weapon handles.

Yemen imported rhino horn from Africa for their elaborately carved daggers called *jambiyas*, symbols of wealth and power. A dagger with a handle made of horn was particularly coveted for its ability to take a high polish and improve with age. As the oil business grew in the 1970s, so did the per capita income. Now the newly rich could also afford the jambiyas, once a status symbol reserved only for the wealthy. The demand for carved daggers escalated until the 1990s, when the oil economy took a downturn.

But Africa's rhinos were not granted a reprieve, because the Chinese medicinal market was now booming with the rising middle class. For thousands of years, TCM had touted its claims for rhino horn as a cure-all for many illnesses, from fevers and headaches to rheumatism and snakebites. Contrary to popular belief, it was not used as an aphrodisiac.

The Sumatran (or hairy) rhino, the Javan rhino from Indonesia and Vietnam, and the Indian (or greater one-horned) rhino were all targeted for their horns. As the Asian species were decimated, the growing TCM market turned its eyes, money, and guns toward Africa. TCM wasn't particular where the powdered horn came from, as long as it was rhino horn.

The western black rhino, a subspecies of the black rhino, was last seen in Cameroon in 2006. From hundreds of animals in the 1980s, the struggling population could not withstand the unrelenting poaching in west-central Africa. In 2011, it was declared extinct by the IUCN (International Union for Conservation of Nature). Similarly, the northern white rhino is all but gone. This subspecies of the white rhino declined from an estimated two thousand animals in 1960 to just four in the wild by 2005, and it is highly unlikely that any remain alive in the wild today.

Farther south, where the vast majority of Africa's rhinos reside, the tremendous gains made in the 1970s, '80s and '90s are being rapidly eroded. The last white rhinos disappeared from Mozambique in 2013, due to poaching, and conservationists are now scrambling to save the remaining black and white rhinos in reserves across South Africa, where over seventy-five percent of all Africa's rhinos reside. After both species were saved from the brink of extinction, poaching has increased exponentially since 2008, when the country lost eighty-three rhinos to poachers, to 2013, when a staggering one thousand four rhinos were slaughtered.

Until 2008, few rhinos were lost to poachers in South Africa, and the conservation efforts were celebrated worldwide as numbers of both black and white rhino blossomed. But the conservation success years were, like our afore-mentioned young couple's vacation, just a brief honeymoon period. As rhinos were eliminated from the more approachable, less vigilant countries, so poachers began to turn their attentions to the more robust, conservation-oriented environment of South Africa.

Due to the rise in demand and the increased difficulty hunting rhinos in protected reserves, the price of rhino horn skyrocketed. The escalating prices meant that poachers had access to more sophisticated equipment, as well as the ability and means to bribe corrupt officials. The temptation for huge financial rewards outweighed any risks.

Poaching methods have become increasingly brazen and barbaric, leading to terrible suffering and gruesome deaths. Automatic weapons used to be the traditional method for slaying the beasts. A rhino would be tracked, sprayed with machine-gun fire and then the horn would be removed. But even more sinister methods are now being used. Since the automatic gunfire attracted attention to their nefarious activities, poachers are now incapacitating rhinos with high-caliber rifles. Or even worse, tranquilizing them and cutting off the valuable horns while the animal is still alive. The rhino wakes up in a pool of blood with half its face cut off. Bulls, mothers, and calves—all just left to die a slow, cruel death.

Hundreds of rhinos every year are lost to poaching. "South Africa has the highest rhino population and therefore the highest poaching statistics. Wildlife poaching is on the rise overall, with Tanzania losing up to ten thousand elephants per year, so we are not the only target," said Les Carlisle, group conservation manager at &Beyond.

In response, Phinda became the first ever private game reserve to donate rhino to another country when it translocated six white rhino from South Africa to the safer environment of Botswana's Okavango Delta in 2013. An additional one hundred rhino are scheduled for future translocation from South Africa to Botswana's remote wilderness through a joint effort with &Beyond and Great Plains Conservation. Perhaps the safe haven of Botswana, with its excellent security system and dedicated anti-poaching team, will provide respite for this endangered species.

At the current poaching levels, deaths will overtake births and rhinos could be extinct in two decades. Why is it that all too often we wait until it is too late to act? Previously we have managed to save rhinos just in the nick of time. We saved the white rhino from below a hundred animals in the early 1900s to the estimated 18,900 that "flourish" today. And we rescued the black rhino, whose numbers plummeted from 70,000 animals in 1970 to around 2,500 by 1993, a decline of ninety-six percent in just over twenty years! With regard to the current crisis, again global outrage will erupt like a fiery volcano, pressure will be placed on governments, and conservation authorities will try to step in.

But it is important not to get complacent and think that poaching is a cyclical process. Without a concerted effort right now, rhino and elephant poaching will continue until not a single animal is left. Commercial poachers are indiscriminate and lack foresight. They want to make as much money right now as possible. If there are no more rhinos left, they will move on to the next hot commodity. The poacher's vocabulary does not include the word sustainability.

Conversely, corruption is a word that poachers know well. Commercial poachers thrive by bribing the very people who are tasked with saving our wildlife: conservation officers and government officials. Rooting out this corruption, which provides easy access to our wildlife and immunity from prosecution, is one of the most important challenges in Africa's conservation movement and the fight against rhino and elephant poaching.

The old Zulu proverb "Do not speak of rhinoceros" takes on an even different meaning today. Many game rangers and conservation officials exercise great caution when using their radios, for fear of poachers trolling the airwaves. When a rhino is located, it is referred to by an alias or a code word. Those remaining solitary creatures live in total ignorance, perched precariously on the brink of extinction, existing under cover of disguised nomenclature.

Africa has a way of bringing out the best and the worst in people, with the fate of the rhino remaining in human hands.

"Kwathi ke kaloku ngantsomi ... "

And now for a story ...

Of murder most foul ...

... And we do not know how it will end.

FIGS, FOUNDATIONS, AND THE FUTURE OF AFRICA

But how wonderful when the tale is told,
And the message that is meant for us
Opens like the scents of a mountain-flower!
MAZISI KUNENE,
"Changes"

Siyimkhiwan' esikhumukil' esikhweni.
We are figs that have become detached from the main plant.
ZULU PROVERB

I AM DOING FINE UNTIL THEY hand me the farewell card. Reading through the kind thoughts and best wishes for my future, drives home the reality that I am leaving Phinda. I vow that this special place, where I experienced great adventures and deep friendships, would never fade from my memory. Each entry on the handmade card brings back memories of special moments, special places, special people.

Life at Phinda has been a wild ride. Most of the white rangers and staff stay for a year or two, then move on with their lives, so there is a constant turnover. Now it is my turn to leave.

I look at the people surrounding me, congratulating me on my new opportunity, with tears in my eyes. I shake off any sentimental nostalgia. I know I will be back. Nothing can keep me away from Phinda for long.

I met my future wife, Rebecca, while vacationing in the South Pacific on the romantic islands of Fiji. Even though Rebecca lived in Los Angeles, there was an immediate bond. During our long-distance courtship, we took turns visiting each other's country. Rebecca discovered that Africa wasn't like Disney, where everything was planned, scripted, safe, and predictable. I found myself over-whelmed by the big cities in the US, where people drove on the wrong side of the road and everything was planned, scripted, safe, and predictable.

Even though I wanted to marry Rebecca, I wondered what the future of this relationship would hold — the wildlife guy from Afri-ca and the busy executive from LA. There was definitely a change in the wind. It was a courtship and marriage that spanned five con-tinents and diverse places like Fiji, Los Angeles, Chicago, London, Columbia, Ecuador, Florida, and a lot of South Africa. Our lives would take many twists and turns.

Our first stop was London. Neutral ground for a South Afri-can and his American girl to settle. Rebecca continued her career in management, and I quickly maneuvered my way back to Phinda. I entered the MSC program at Middlesex University, my goal to complete a thesis in sustainable environmental management.

It wasn't just coincidence that the subject of my research im-mediately led me back to Kwazulu-Natal. My thesis focused on the relations between the local reserves and the communities: "To-wards Sustainable Conservation: Community Perceptions of Game Reserves in the Maputaland Region of South Africa." An opportu-nity to return to Phinda for two months! What a great way to spend time with my mates from the reserve.

Norman helped me establish connections to accomplish my re-search. I needed a guide and interpreter for my community visits. Someone who spoke both English and Zulu. Someone who knew the geographical and political makeup of the areas surrounding Phinda and the neighboring Mkuze Game reserve. Someone who was as skilled in dealing with people as Norman was in tracking wild animals.

The obvious choice was Jackie, a Zulu who worked at Phinda in the hospitality department. Jackie spoke flawless English. Well respected and with many local connections, he was the perfect intermediary to set up meetings in the surrounding Maputaland communities. He showed up early every morning, a big smile on his face, always organized and ready to go.

Instead of packing a Land Rover with a rifle, safari gear, and upscale snacks, we headed out with a schedule, a tape recorder, and a list of questions. We left the fenced confines of the reserve and traveled to Mnqobokazi, KwaNgwenya, Nibela, or Mduku, the communities closest to Phinda and Mkuze. Even though I was only with Jackie a short time, we developed a deep friendship as we bounced along the unpaved roads, avoiding the wandering goats and cattle. In typical Zulu style, laughing at everything.

Jackie was thin and, like Norman, not very tall by Zulu standards. He had a jovial personality and was always smiling, which is why he did so well in the hospitality industry. Nothing was ever too much trouble for Jackie, and he could always be found running around Mountain Lodge catering to some guest's trivial need.

I spent my days gathering information with Jackie and my evenings transcribing and translating the material. I conducted over three hundred interviews, asking questions about views on wildlife, poaching, tourism, and interactions with the reserve management. I even asked the participants if they had ever been inside one of the game reserves and poached animals themselves. I was surprised that some participants answered in the affirmative. This indicated to me that Jackie's presence—and the blessings we received from the tribal authorities—provided some level of comfort in providing honest answers.

I wanted to find out whether attitudes toward game reserves would correlate with attitudes toward wildlife, poaching, and conservation. The apartheid era was associated with South African conservation policies, exacerbating tensions between the impoverished peoples and the wealthy game reserves. My aim was to find out how profound this level of mistrust was in the communities surrounding Mkuze and Phinda. The results of our research showed that there was a radical difference in attitudes toward a private reserve from which the communities received significant direct benefits versus the state-run reserve. Poaching was minimal at Phinda but rampant at Mkuze. Game fences were respected at Phinda but pulled down at Mkuze. It was clear that we needed to "get the balance" right for community conservation. My thesis in a nutshell.

Before graduation, I received the news that Jackie had died from AIDS. Another blow. The whole time I worked with him, there was no indication that he was sick. Coming so soon after Rockerman's death, this changed my perspective on life forever.

My research eventually opened the door to an amazing career opportunity at Africa Foundation in Johannesburg. As the managing director of the organization, I oversaw our work in six African countries and was ultimately responsible for our work in the communities that surround Phinda. It was clear I couldn't stay away for long. The mission statement is clear:

> Africa Foundation facilitates the empowerment and development of people living in or adjacent to protected areas in Africa, by forging unique partnerships between conservation initiatives and communities.

A key Africa Foundation aim is to help break the cycle of poverty by tapping into the financial benefits that international tourists bring to Africa's wildlife areas. We sought to support projects that combined to provide a "conveyor belt" of resources from pre-natal care all the way through to university scholarships. During my tenure, we started a clinic, built over forty classrooms and schools around the area, created income-generating projects like vegetable gardens, and installed water tanks.

I hand a ripe fig to each visitor, but the fruit isn't a snack. As the managing director of Africa Foundation, I use the figs to tell the story of one of the wonders of the natural world, the life cycle of the fig tree. Today's guests are visiting our headquarters to learn more about the efforts to sustain unique partnerships between conservation initiatives and the local communities. I tell this story hundreds of times, but it never loses the ability to captivate.

Like a fairy tale, it is a story of immovable giants dependent on tiny winged creatures. A tale of courageous males with crushing jaws who sacrifice their lives for the indomitable females with pockets full of treasure. A tale about a race against time to detect the subtle fragrance of invisible flowers and deposit precious cargo. All to maintain a cycle of life for the massive trees that support a menagerie of wildlife from ants to bats to birds to elephants to humans. All reliant on a delicate sequence of events involving heroism, determination, and mutual need.

The story starts deep within the confines of a fig fruit. This pod is not actually a fruit, but a fleshy flower with its petals and stamen inside and inverted, invisible to the eye. At the base of one of these stamens, a tiny egg hatches. Our heroine emerges, a female fig wasp no larger than a comma on this page. At the same time, a male fig wasp is actively searching, crawling through the hundreds of florets, instinctively seeking her out in the floral garden. Somewhere, hidden among the flowers, he finds her in the darkness of the fragrant fruit and mates with her. But unlike other species, where the male rides off into the sunset after doing the deed, he must complete one final act of heroism before he dies. He must create an escape hatch for our heroine.

As with all fairy tale heroes, he is designed by nature to complete his mission or die trying. Our superwasp has strong jaws but no wings. His attention turns to the outer wall of the fruit and he ceaselessly gnaws his way through the fig. During her romantic exploits within the fig, our heroine has collected pollen in pouches on her breast. She crawls through the tiny opening created by the slender male, just large enough for her to escape with her valuable cargo.

She emerges out of the fig fruit and immediately flies off in search of another tree. But it isn't as easy as just finding the closest tree. She must find a tree receptive to the specific pollen she is carrying, a tree exuding just the right delicate fragrance to lure her in. Her life cycle is short, only a few days, so she is in a marathon guided by scent.

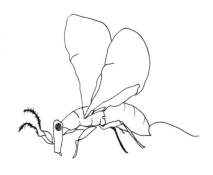

Her mission will not be complete until she locates the target fig flower, deposits the contents of her carefully guarded packet, and lays her eggs. It is a colossal task, as she must find and penetrate a microscopic opening in the bottom of the fig, much smaller than the one from which she emerged with the assistance of her mate. Her only entry back into the fig is through this one-way passage—a natural opening that is especially narrow so ants and other insects cannot enter.

Our heroine is a teeny but determined little thing. She squeezes through, breaking off her wings and antennae in the process. Once again, she finds herself in the dark interior world of the fig fruit. Inside the floral garden, she seeks out the stamen and deposits the pollen from the previous flower to germinate. She then lays her eggs at the base of the flower, completing the cycle to hatch new fig wasps. Our heroine's journey is complete.

The fig and the wasp are entwined in one of the most striking examples of coevolved mutualism in nature. There are approximately eight hundred species of fig trees worldwide and a matching eight hundred species of fig wasps worldwide. Each species of fig tree is pollinated by a specific species of fig wasp. If we lost one species of fig wasp, we would lose one species of fig tree and visa versa. There are cases where pesticides wiped out the fig wasps and the fig trees still exist today, unable to ever reproduce. Correspondingly, the loss of a fig tree species has brought about the extinction of the corresponding species of fig wasp.

If you look at fig trees from a distance, you will notice that they can survive in diverse landscapes. Their deep and strong roots take hold in rich and poor soils, in woodlands and plains, near rivers and on top of rocks. From a distance you see a safe haven, one that cannot be easily uprooted, not even by aggressive elephants. Many small animals make their homes in the holes and crevices, seeking shelter and protection.

The shy leopard might perch on the branches, waiting for an opportunistic meal. On closer inspection, you notice the constant flow of activity as animals come to the tree for sustenance. Everything from small insects to birds and bats, monkeys, antelope, and elephants, all come to feast on the fig fruits or rest in the shade. These immovable giants create a small ecosystem, so dependent on those tiny, brave winged creatures. Wiping out the fig wasps or the fig trees has a ripple affect on the surrounding wildlife.

It is at this point in the story that I pause and bring attention back to the fig fruit everyone is holding.

"Look at this fruit, with its secret garden inside, an invisible place where heroic deeds take place. This fruit needs the tree to develop. The massive tree must grow from the small fruit seeds inside this pod. The wasp is the intermediary, necessary to pollinate the tree and continue the cycle. None can exist without the other," I say.

There is an analogy here. The fig tree stands for conservation, with many branches. The fig fruit symbolizes tourism and the money it brings into the equation. The delicate job of the fig wasp represents the communities; however, this role has been most often overlooked. The tourism dollars are necessary to sustain the conservation efforts. When supported by the local communities, the system is in balance and the equilibrium maintained. That's the way conservation needs to be done around the world.

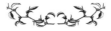

"Ultimately conservation is about people. If you don't have sustainable development around these (wildlife) parks, then the people will have no interest in them, and the parks will not survive," Nelson Mandela said.

Prophetic words for someone at a time when the winds of change in the conservation industry were just starting to blow. Until the 1990s, the idea of bringing people into the process was a big no-no. National parks were for wildlife and rich tourists, not the local people. The locals were forcibly removed from their homes to make way for the wildlife.

Our challenge was to overcome a culture that for over a hundred years had bred severe animosity between the locals and the South African authorities. For example, in order to protect the black and white rhinos, the government adopted a militaristic approach. Any poachers were shot on sight. No questions asked. Radical battles raged in wildlife areas of South Africa, and some battles continue today. There is a distinction between commercial poaching and subsistence poaching. Commercial poachers are heavily armed and go after the big game—elephants, rhinos, lions, etc. Subsistence poachers set snares and capture just enough to fill the pot for their families.

So what we are trying to do through community conservation nonprofits like Africa Foundation is heal over a hundred years of mistrust. By allowing the benefits to flow back into the local communities, we want to ensure that communities take ownership of their natural wildlife resources and land. Africa Foundation has become an indispensable link between the local communities, wildlife, and rich tourism. The tourism dollars flow through the nonprofit conduit, providing jobs and support for education and health care initiatives. To be truly sustainable, the communities, the wildlife and the tourism must coexist mutually, like a three-legged pot. If one leg corrodes, the pot falls over.

This vision is easier said than done and the deep mistrust of conservation and tourism by local communities is the biggest obstacle. During my years working at Africa Foundation, we documented and strategized ways to spread the message to donors and guests at lodges. We had the opportunity to reach some of the wealthiest people in the world, who were touched by both the wildlife we were trying to save and the local people who contributed to its maintenance. We would encourage the guests to venture out into the community, to see the people outside the reserve setting, so that they would become aware that people are part of the wildlife process and that communities in turn would slowly learn to trust the tourists that came to see the wildlife in *their* communities.

When I was a ranger at Phinda, I would take guests out of the reserve with Rockerman, and then Norman, and into the communities. We would offer free community trips after the morning game drive. Africa Foundation would pick everyone up and drive into the local environs, where they could meet families and share a traditional meal, a chance to experience Zulu life firsthand. This was not a contrived paternalistic approach but an opportunity to show how community development is best conducted in Africa. We visited clinics and schools and showed how the three legs of the pot worked together.

I also remembered from my thesis research that many local people never set foot in a reserve, and had never seen some of the wild game that roamed freely within its boundaries. At Africa Foundation, we set up special conservation lessons for school children from the local communities to take a safari ride through Phinda and introduce them to the wildlife that was on their doorsteps but from which they were largely separated by game fences.

Our mission was to aid the surrounding communities in three areas: education, healthcare, and income generation. Our format was simple. Ask the people what they needed and identify exemplary community champions to take ownership of the projects. Because in most cases, if you ask people if they want something, they will say yes. "Do you want soccer balls, money, etc.?" Of course. But is this what they really need?

So instead we would change the question from "Do you want this?" to "What do you need?" and have the community identify the scope of all of our projects. Everyone — the school governing bodies, tribal authorities, health care committees — would assemble and brainstorm. They would then present us with a list of prioritized needs specific to their community. We knew there would be no sustainability if the people did not take ownership. Our organization had to be run from the grassroots up and not from the treetops down.

So we began working on projects that would provide both immediate and long-term results. How can something so simple as a barrel change people's lives? It can when it's designed to carry water easily over long distances.

The hippo roller is a large plastic drum that can be filled with water and rolled by the handle connected at each end of the barrel. Traditionally, it was the women's responsibility to bring back water from a remote source, and involved carrying large containers on their heads. This simple convenience eliminated the head and neck strain on each individual. Children could even fill the containers and roll them home. It provided an immediate way to improve quality of life for rural dwellers.

I spent time showing investors and influential people how it all tied together. Projects like Mrs. Zikhali's school. She had started a classroom with sixty kids under three trees. If it rained, there would be no school that day. But Mrs. Zikhali had a vision and would not be discouraged. She knew that if she built a school, the government would provide teachers. But she needed funding and community support. With great persistence, she contacted foundations like Africa Foundation and devised a plan. The adjacent game reserves like Phinda needed local people and resources to survive. Setting up an educational environment would benefit the local communities and also provide the neighboring reserves with a talent pool.

Mrs. Zikhali's school functions as an example of a community project that has long-term benefits for the area. The original three trees that served as outdoor classrooms still exist, but now they provide shade for her school of over twenty classrooms, one thousand students, and twenty-five teachers. An amazing success story. A whirlwind of energy, she was determined to do whatever it took to move the students from under the trees and into a real brick-and-mortar facility. Professor Richard Boyatsis documented her story in his book *Resonant Leadership* as an example of never giving up on your dream. She continues to set an example for others to fulfill their hopes and dreams.

In addition to the bricks-and-mortar education projects, we selected students and provided them with bursaries to study medicine, education, and business. In return, they would be required to pay this forward by working during their vacations and breaks—teaching in the schools if they were studying education or working in the clinics if they were studying medicine. We had a ninety-five percent success rate of students graduating. Students who would become the future leaders in their communities. Leaders who would take ownership of projects and continue the cycle.

In 2008, the year after I left this great organization, Africa Foundation was awarded a World Savers Hall of Fame award for establishing medical clinics. The closest medical clinic to Phinda's neighboring communities had been twenty miles away and difficult to reach due to inefficient public transportation. But through the construction and renovation of two local medical clinics, the game reserve provided free treatment and health care to thousands of residents, including pre- and postnatal advice, nutritional and hygiene information, and HIV/AIDS counseling.

I took a special interest in the AIDS projects, having lost Rockerman and now Jackie to this disease. Education and medical care were critical to saving lives, promoting positive health and lifestyle in conjunction with retroviral drugs. But efforts needed to go beyond dealing with the aftermath. To prevent the spread of the disease, &Beyond, Phinda's parent company, recognized that programs had to change people's attitudes toward the use of condoms, encourage a more sympathetic approach toward those who had contracted the disease, and change sexual behavior patterns in a largely polygynous society. Knowing I had played a small part in supporting these efforts helped somewhat to ease the pain of seeing my closest friends pass away so quickly.

The reserves continue to grow and to attract affluent visitors. Wildlife conservation efforts are increasingly not just a product of tourist money but an integrated effort with the local communities. The local people fill the jobs on the reserve; they do not have to leave for the city to get an education and decent medical care. Guests learn that their trackers are often former poachers, now conservationists. Their skills are in demand by a new audience, tourists. They can fill their family's pot by earning money for food, not stealing it. Their wives are also often employed on the reserve as hospitality hosts, cooks, and housekeepers. A sense of pride emanates from being a part of the conservation efforts on the reserve. We are breaking the cycle of poverty one project at a time.

The years I spent at Africa Foundation were some of the most fulfilling of my life. But as time moved along, wanderlust set in. In spite of having a wife and children to support, I decided to leave the security of a good and fulfilling job and take on a new and risky venture. I had always wanted to tap into my love of birding, and Richard and I decided to start a birding tourism company called HoneyGuides. The trips were run throughout southern Africa with individuals and small groups of dedicated birders hell bent on increasing their birding life lists at all costs.

MINES, CRANES, AND MANES

As the birds return to their nests
Your shadow stands alone
By the setting sun;
Gesturing to receive the harvests of the earth.
MAZISI KUNENE,
"Journey into Morning"

Wamfak' ekhwapheni.
He put him under the arm.
ZULU PROVERB

I AM ABOUT TO TAKE MY binoculars down when I see it. A large African black-maned lion comes padding straight toward me through the moist plain, leaving a trail of glistening droplets clinging to the grass in the morning light. From a vehicle, the sighting would have been splendid. On foot, terrifying. I know from my past experience with male lions at Phinda that they will hardly ever confront a human, preferring instead to run away. But this one keeps coming, albeit nervously, and uttering a low call, not unlike the moaning at the end of a full roar.

He is about three hundred yards away and showing no indication of changing course. I back away from the open floodplain and head for the safety of the car, returning up the rugged path through the thick brush. My experience as a game ranger reminds me to walk slowly, turning to face the lion constantly.

Each time I retreat the lion moves forward, each time I stop, he stops and looks straight at me. I retrace my steps very, very carefully back up the path. Even in the heat of this drama I am instinctively glancing down, reading the tracks in the soft dirt, when I see the worst thing imaginable. Over my footprints, there are the unmistakable fresh tracks of more lions, or to be precise, lionesses. Bugger.

The realization quickly sinks in that I am trapped between a male lion and a pride of lionesses, quite possibly with young. I must have walked right past them on the way down to the marshland in search of wattled cranes.

I am thinking I have a choice. I can turn around, confront the big boy on the open plain, and make a major detour toward the vehicle. Or I can try to negotiate my way off the path and straight through the thick bush in the direction opposite to where the fresh lion spoor was headed, thereby evading both the male and the rest of the pride. Both options have their drawbacks, and I have seconds to weigh up the pros and cons.

The first option requires a healthy dose of courage to overcome the primeval knowledge that facing down a large cat one on one, armed with a pair of binoculars, is a supremely bad idea.

The second option requires precision maneuvering through the acacia trees. One slipup and the bush can grasp me in its talons, rendering my limbs useless and holding me in place like a fresh buffet for the lions. There is something about the determined mindset of the male that makes me nervous, and I choose to take my chances in the thick scrub. And just as I back off the path, I hear it.

GgrrruuuUUUUURRRRRRR!

A low growl, almost inaudible at first but rising in volume as it progresses. I feel a tightening in my upper body as my heart contracts, my stomach knots, and my lungs stop breathing. I try to get a fix on the location of the soft drawn-out warning, the escalating sound that vibrates through the core of my being.

All of my senses are heightened as I scan in the direction of the growl. Then my eyes are diverted to the swishing of a black tail tip about ten yards from me, deep in a thicket. And then another tail. And another. Pent-up maternal aggression and protective instincts coiled up like feline jack-in-the-boxes and primed for release in an explosive charge of claws, teeth, and muscle.

I glance over my left shoulder and see that the male lion is still advancing. Just padding along as before, but now alarmingly close.

I miss Norman. And my rifle. If there were two of us, I would be okay. If Norman or Rockerman were with me, they would grab my belt and guide me back through the trees, making sure that I'm not impaled and ensnared while I face off the lions, shouting and waving my arms to make myself look larger than life. If a tracker was with me, we could shout down the lions in unison. If I had a tracker, he probably would have spotted the lions on the way in and I would not be in this real-life nightmare. Too many ifs. And I am too alone.

But my Zulu brothers have not left me completely defenseless, having taught me the ancient skills of bush craft and survival. To know when to face danger and when to back off. With the male lion advancing on one side of me, I persist in my decision to enter the unforgiving acacia forest. I back into a branch and feel the thorns resisting my progress, digging into my shoulders, ferociously tearing flesh as I keep moving in an attempt not to get permanently trapped. I block out the fierce pain, concentrating instead on positioning each foot softly but firmly as I wedge my tall frame through the thorn trees. The short hike down to the marshland a few minutes ago now becomes an interminable journey backward to safety, as I forge a new passage through the forbidding undergrowth, step by painful step.

BBWOAARR!!

My movements trigger a charge, and a lioness bolts from the thicket, coming at me low to the ground, weaving with her mouth open and forelegs outstretched. She is a blur.

"Hamba isifebe! Haaamba!"

"Fuck off, you bitch!" sounds braver in Zulu.

It is my voice, but at the same time, it is the voice of every tracker I worked with, every mentor who taught me the ways of the wild. Over the past years I had learned so many lessons, so many laws for self-preservation. I was not intending to go down without a show. Africa is drama, pure and simple. Living. Dying. The only difference is how you react in the moment. It is more than steely nerves; it is pure instinct.

I had come to this no man's land in the middle of Africa, in a country that had recently come out of a prolonged war, walking over volatile ground riddled with land mines ... because of a bird. I was here to look for wattled cranes for a repeat guest of mine. Normally, this was not where I would take a guest to view wild animals and birds. As a professional wildlife guide and former game ranger, the safety of my guests and the wildlife we are viewing always take priority. But some of my charges have a high tolerance for danger, and even higher expectations of locating rare wildlife sightings.

My British guest, Harold, had traveled with me previously on guided excursions around the Cape to look for the last remaining African bird species that he needed for his list. Having worked in North Africa for many years and traveled the continent extensively, Harold was no stranger to adventure. He had seen close to two thousand bird species in Africa, a remarkable feat, considering that there are approximately two thousand six hundred species on the continent.

I had guided him, one of my favorite guests, on several birding trips. Although in his early seventies, he had the constitution of a rock. Every night, he would down half a bottle of whiskey and I would sometimes have to help him to bed. The next morning, he would wake up bright eyed and ready for another day of adventuring.

I had been thrilled to find the wattled cranes on the wetlands, knowing Harold would appreciate seeing these wonderful birds. We had driven almost eighteen hundred miles north from Cape Town at the tip of Africa via the barren western coast of South Africa, by way of the Kgalagadi Transfrontier Park, a massive desert wilderness conservation area that spans Botswana and South Africa. Entering the sparsely populated country of Namibia, one of the finest wildlife and birding regions in Africa, we headed to the northernmost end, where the land converges into a bizarre finger called the Caprivi Strip. It was here that we found ourselves in the Mahango Game Reserve. Four rivers surround the area, creating a wetland paradise for close to five hundred species of birds. Its river and delta systems are a maze of swamps and marshlands amid lush savannahs. The fenceless borders between the game parks allow for the free movement of animals.

A naturalist's paradise, but it came with hidden risks. The remote road network consisted mostly of old routes created by the South African military during the Angolan Civil War in the 1980s when the armed forces used the strip as a rear base. My father had been forced to serve in the Angolan war and had trod through similar terrain. He had been involved in a struggle that pitted men of all races against each other, foreign governments driven by conflicting motives of greed, power, and patriotism. Years later I was walking over the same ground, but with a very different goal. I was here for the wildlife, but keenly aware of the dangers of intruding on this idyllic landscape.

Caprivi. Not exactly an African-sounding name. Like so many other places in Africa, its name had been derived during the period of colonialism when Africa was divided up like a patchwork quilt. The Caprivi Strip was as long and narrow as the German chancellor's signature on the treaty, General Count Georg Leo von Caprivi di Caprara di Montecuccoli. Imagine a culturally isolated 280-mile stretch of land no wider than twenty miles across in some places, jutting out like a panhandle on the northeastern side of Namibia, sandwiched right between Zimbabwe, Angola, and Zambia to the north and Botswana to the south. Subject to numerous disputes over the years, the Caprivi Strip had become a lawless frontier.

The year was 2001, and the Namibia/Angola border area still reeled from the effects of a protracted and dirty war. Off the beaten track, concealed land mines waited patiently for the macabre opportunity to blow off an elephant's leg or maim and kill anything that had the misfortune to awaken them from their slumber. Unseen and quiet, they added to the long list of potentially fatal African encounters. And sometimes, just when a path was well traversed and deemed clear of land mines, an undetonated mine shifted position, the rain and mud carrying it from its previously unsuccessful ambush site to a new and more fruitful hunting ground.

Most of the dangerous African animals will give a warning before they attack. A growl, a mock charge, or some other indication of what's to come. The land mines kill indiscriminately, without notice. The animal populations themselves—elephants, birds, lions, hippos, and herds of ungulates that had been decimated during the quarter century of recent conflicts and illegal hunting—were just starting to recolonize and reestablish their habitats. But they were still wary of human intrusion.

Arriving early that morning, we parked a short distance from the floodplain. Mahango Game Reserve was not your average bird-watching location. It was so remote that days could go by without a single visitor entering the reserve. Bizarrely, Mahango was a place where visitors were not prohibited from leaving their vehicles but were free to approach the wildlife on foot. This was bizarre, because there were lions. There were elephants. There were leopards. There were buffalo. And there were crocs and hippos.

I had taken every precaution before heading out alone into the wilderness to scout for the cranes. Harold had been eager to come along with me to locate the birds. I recognized that look in his eyes, a birder ready to nail down a new species for his list. But the procedure was always safety first, so I had to put the brakes on.

"Listen, I need to check the floodplain. If the cranes are there, I will come back and get you. Stay put and do not leave the car," I warned. I'd guided other trips here so I knew that these large birds liked to congregate on the vast delta just out of sight. Taking a guest down to these fairly inaccessible wetlands required extra caution.

Now Harold was waiting patiently in the car, wondering if I

had spotted the cranes. It had been a relatively short walk to the wetlands, but I needed to pass through some thick bush between where our car was parked and where the cranes were known to gather. I was greeted by the early morning smells. A mix of rising heat and the recent rains produced that wonderful smell in the air, a mixture of wildlife dung, aromatic grasses, and mud. It was a sweet smell, strangely unique to the African bush. I inhaled deeply as I made my way down the veiled and narrow path. Through the cruel foliage of the encroaching acacia, I could just make out patches of the open marshland.

Carefully negotiating the thick bush, I heard the plaintive yelping of an African barred owlet, a tiny, gorgeous little raptor that can fit in a teacup. Every small bird's worst nightmare, barred owlets often snatched unsuspecting birds as they roosted at night or at dawn and dusk. Owls always delight birders, especially when they can be seen well during the day, so I stopped for a few minutes to triangulate the bird's call. I got a fix on it sitting on a limb up in a massive fig tree.

Barred owlets are partly diurnal, so it was not wholly unexpected to find this diminutive raptor at this time of the morning. The sighting would add to my interpretive story for Harold when I brought him down to see the cranes. I mentally recorded its location before proceeding down the path.

My training as a game ranger reminded me to always read my environment. I looked down, examining the tracks. Reading it almost like a newspaper. Who's been here since last night? What's been happening? There were warthog tracks. There was the odd impala track. There were lion tracks. Smoking Ponies! But I looked at them closely, pushing my fingers in the dirt and feeling that the mud inside the tracks had hardened somewhat. One set of lion tracks veered off into the thickets, and I noticed how several other animal spoor were imprinted over the big cat's tracks. Probably at least a day old. So I carried on.

Emerging from the shadowy trail, I was greeted by the spectacular vista of the open floodplain. Right before me, immediately, I saw the cranes. Not one of them. Not two of them. But forty wattled cranes. An impressive sight, as these are the tallest cranes in Africa, standing almost six feet tall with a wingspan of nine feet. There are only about seven thousand left, thinly distributed across a very large range. Excellent! I viewed them just long enough to count the birds and mentally prepare my interpretation for Harold.

And then they took off! The whole lot of them! All forty, up into the air and gone. The entire flock of cranes silently departed, leaving just a bare vision of the reeds and grasses. I was looking through my binoculars and thinking to myself, "Shite! How am I going to break this news to Harold? Double-shite!!"

I should have been more careful not to spook them.

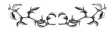

Now I'm trapped between a lion and his pride, and I'm experiencing the sickening, stomach-knotting effects of a charging lioness.

Lions are social animals that thrive as part of a pride, usually comprising a male or several males with a group of related females and their cubs. They do not normally hunt humans but will defend their territory against intruders, especially other predators. Males are fiercely protective, marking their territory with urine and secretions and warning upstart males with their far-carrying roars. Fights to the death between males are not uncommon. But it is the aggressive lionesses who are particularly dangerous to humans, even more so when young cubs are involved. A lioness will not hesitate to attack just about anything in defense of her little ones. I need to be very careful. I raise my hands and make myself as tall as possible as I shout down the charging lioness.

"Hamba! HAMBA! HEEEEYYYYY!"

The female stops abruptly, close enough to spray dust all over me. I notice the snarl creases on her face and her flattened ears. Growling, she retreats back to the thicket. I breathe and inch farther toward the car. I can feel a broken tree branch jutting into my lower back and I shift around the tree, blindly feeling my way with the back of my body and not daring to avert my gaze from the cats.

Now the male, perhaps emboldened by the lioness's charge comes at pace. I lunge forward and stand my ground, shouting and waving with outstretched arms. During a lion charge, it is vital to shout down the charge from start to finish, never wavering or becoming silent. The louder, deeper and longer, the better.

"HEEYYYY!!!! LEAVE ME ALONE!! I'M HERE FOR THE FREAKING CRANES!! I'M JUST A FUCKING BIRDER!!"

He stops some distance from me, growling, and slinks away behind a bush. Laboriously, I work my way back through that thick, heavy, and painful bush. Other lionesses now join the first female and come at me.

"HEEEYYYYY!!! PISS OFF!! WHHHOOOAAAA!!!"

Each time they charge, I stand my ground. They retreat and then I move back, only for them to charge again. This real-life game of cat and mouse continues. They charge. I swear. They retreat. I take a few painful steps through the thorns. And so it continues as I make my way right up to the vehicle. The lions finally stop, allowing me to open the door and disappear inside.

I glance at Harold and notice that his eyes are as large as dinner plates. The windows in the car are down, so he has heard everything quite clearly. Every feline outburst, every matching shout. I can only imagine what he must have pictured as he sat alone in this desolate location. He has come for wattled cranes, and he is getting a lot more than he bargained for.

I ease down into the front seat, absolutely shaken, and collapse. Harold's deeply tanned leathery face is completely ashen, but he brings me back to reality with his clipped British accent.

"The things we do for birds!"

"Weeee??!!" I reply.

I gun the engine in reverse and shoot out of there. Now that I am back in the safety of the vehicle, the adrenaline subsides and I revert to my role as fearless guide. I drive off to relocate the birds, not missing a beat.

We are birders on a mission, not easily deterred by hidden mines, elusive cranes, or dangerous manes.

BIRDING ON THE EDGE

Summer approaches
Bringing with it the birdsong
And the round sounds of festivals
The seed that was cold, breaks open.
MAZISI KUNENE,
"Summer"

Akukho langa lishona lingenandaba zalo.
No day passes without its affairs.
ZULU PROVERB

"DO YOU KNOW WHY THIS bridge is so wide?" I ask Harold as we park the car on the side of a substantial bridge spanning five hundred yards across the dry riverbed.

"The river below takes its name from the Herero word *okahandja* meaning 'two rivers that meet to form one large one,'" I continue on as we grab our binoculars. "The Okahandja bridge is built to withstand the torrential summer rains that transform the wide depression into a raging torrent."

The sun beats down on the tarmac, reflecting the heat back as we scan for birds. On the opposite bank, we can just make out a flock foraging in the riverine trees. I am excited, as even from a distance I can tell they are wood hoopoes. In perpetual motion, they are entertaining birds to watch as they climb tree trunks like woodpeckers and hang upside down while probing for grubs with their long, curved beaks. I wonder if this is the rarer of the species. There are two species of wood hoopoes in Namibia, and we are trying to find the subtly colored violet wood hoopoes, rumored to number as few as two thousand birds in the wild. Its habitat has rapidly deteriorated due to the expanding human population. The violet wood hoopoe relies on nesting cavities in trees along riverbanks like this, trees that are harvested for fuel or killed when the manipulation of dams alters the river's natural course.

We are determined to get a positive ID on these birds, but it's difficult from a distance, as they are in constant motion. There is an art to using binoculars—you must spot the bird and keep your eye on it. Note if there are any landmarks nearby, like a crook in the tree, a bright leaf, even a cloud overhead. Then raise your binoculars to your eyes. Repeat until you find the bird, often a moving target. It requires concentration to look for small distinguishing marks, like the shape of the beak or the color of the feet.

Engrossed with following the birds, Harold and I use our binoculars to glass the trees, and move quite a ways from the car in our attempt to get closer views of the wandering flock. Now late morning, with the sun baking the river sand, the resulting hot air rises to meet us on the bridge. It feels as if the overpass is a giant frying pan atop a rapidly warming stovetop and we are the eggs in the pan. As we move closer to the opposite bank, the flock moves tantalizingly farther along the edge of the river. We are both perspiring heavily as we lock our sights onto a particular individual near a dead limb. Yes! I definitively point out the dark violet coloration and larger size that distinguishes this species. It is often confused with the much more common green wood hoopoe, also known as the red-billed wood hoopoe, a bird that I am very familiar with from my time at Phinda. Harold is happy that we have just seen one of the harder species to find in this bird-rich country, and we turn to make our way back to the car.

I suddenly realize how far we have wandered away from the vehicle. Birding has a way of grabbing you like that, holding you in the passion of the moment, all attention on the trees, the sky, the birds. No thought of heat or cold or pain or wind or thirst or hunger or even trespassing through someone's property. Now that the thrill of the quest is over, our attention turns back to the mundane;

we are dreading the long walk over the pavement in the punishing sun, back to the car. Beyond the heat-haze I can just make out what appears to be a man walking alongside our vehicle. He stops for a while and appears to be looking inside. My pace starts to quicken as I see him bend down and pick something up from the side of the road.

"James, we're being robbed!" shouts Harold, alerting me to what I already know.

As I start running, I see the obvious movement of something being hurled against the window, shattering the glass. The thief quickly reaches into our vehicle several times, loading his pockets and rucksack.

Now I am shouting at the top of my lungs, running full-speed to the other side of the bridge. I have closed the gap to a hundred yards. The thief glances up at me, evaluating my progress and dives one more time into the car. He takes off down the embankment and into the riverbed, burdened by expensive spotting scopes and other valuables. I follow him as he disappears into the woodland that rises up out of the parched substrate.

He is fast. But I can run really fast too. My Polish grandfather's nickname was Bocian, which is Polish for "stork," because of his long legs. A national sprinter, he missed out competing for his country in the Olympics due to the outbreak of World War II. I have inherited those storkish legs and know that I have a strong chance of catching up to the criminal, who is now out of sight, carrying a greedy load of our possessions. The thick, thick river sand impedes my progress so I kick off my shoes and follow the thief's tracks. My lungs begin to burn, and I find myself gasping like a fish out of water. I come across my tripod, obviously discarded by the fleeing criminal in an attempt to lighten his load.

I run over thorns and barely feel them. My years of walking barefoot have resulted in hard, calloused soles that are now serving me well. Minor thorns are not an issue, but now I curse loudly as I pause to pull out a massive acacia spike that has penetrated the thick skin. Shaka Zulu, the famous Zulu chief, would train his warriors to run over beds of thorns like these. If they cried out, they were executed. It's a good thing that the Zulu king is not around to hear my painful yelps.

Back on the bridge, Harold watches dumbfounded as I have

once again left him to fend for himself while I am off facing yet another unexpected danger. Harold realizes the seriousness of the situation. I am running into unknown territory, chasing an obviously experienced criminal who could be luring me into a trap. He does his best to provide me assistance, attempting to flag down two men in a passing pickup truck. The vehicle carries on, its occupants seemingly oblivious to the drama unfolding below the bridge. But Harold's zealous signals for help do not go unheeded. The 4x4 takes an abrupt turn into the riverine woodland, as the Afrikaners are quick to notice the broken window, the shattered glass and the stout gentleman frantically waving and pointing, clear signs of trouble brewing below the bridge. Reinforcements are heading my way.

Harold continues waving down passersby and somehow manages to stop a traffic policeman. Before he can explain the situation, the policeman cites him for parking illegally.

"Too bad about the window," he says as he inspects it casually. "This happens a lot. You shouldn't have stopped on the bridge."

The cop lacks any sense of urgency and proceeds to write us a ticket as Harold rapidly explains the serious situation that has unfolded and continues to unfold. Unmoved by my birding companion's desperate pleas for help, the bureaucratic policeman shakes his head and starts explaining that it is our fault that we have been robbed because we have broken the law. The loud, unmistakable sound of a gunshot interrupts his lecture.

Namibia has always been one of my favorite birding destinations. I loved bringing guests to this sparsely populated and wild land. The dramatic scenery of the Skeleton Coast, the many thousands of flamingos at Walvis Bay, the abundant wildlife of the Etosha Pans, and the cultural diversity are just a few of this country's spectacular attractions. In particular, I loved the challenge of finding my birding guests the "special" birds of Namibia. The specials included endemic birds like the dune lark and over a dozen other enigmatic and near-endemic species. The Herero chat, Damara rockjumper, and Hartlaub's francolin are several of these near-endemics, birds that have over ninety percent of their populations in the country.

Once again, I was accompanying Harold, one of my favorite birding guests. For some reason, I always seemed to attract travel companions with a high tolerance for danger. I seemed to be a magnet for risk takers, who like me, would do anything to locate an endangered species, watch a silly mating ritual or hear the echoes of mysterious calls from deep in the bush. Risk takers who were also resilient and quick on the uptake when we found ourselves in perilous situations.

Harold and I had driven up from Cape Town via the West Coast region and spent several days in the Kalahari Game Reserve before moving on to Augrabies Falls National Park. This park is renowned for its scenic canyons and for highly sought-after birds like the Orange River white-eyes, cinnamon-breasted warblers, rosy-faced lovebirds, and dusky sunbirds. Like Table Mountain, the rocky terrain is also home to the dassies, great table fare for the resident black eagles.

The peregrine falcon nests in the crevices high above the falls. These raptors are not just the fastest flying bird in the world but the fastest animal on earth, three times as fast as the cheetah. They prefer nesting in the heights with access to wide open spaces, where they dive at speeds up to two hundred miles per hour, catching smaller birds in midair. Its hunting skills made it the favored bird of falconers for hundreds of years. The peregrine, which translates to "wanderer," nearly caused Harold's demise.

One morning we headed out to the gorge where the Orange River thunders down, the waterfall creating a "place of great noise." The park has several viewpoints over the gorge where it's possible to observe the wildlife up close. It was at one of these outcroppings that we decided to look for a peregrine falcon's nest, hoping to catch a glimpse of a nestling or two, perhaps view its legendary hunting prowess.

The roar of the falls was deafening, so I motioned Harold to wait while I peeked over the edge. He took a step backward, then stumbled and twisted to get his footing. But it was too late. To my horror, he was gone in a flash, just slipped out of sight. I could only watch as he fell down toward the falls.

"Holy crap!"

I had never lost anyone before, in all my years of guiding guests. There was that terrible sinking feeling as I peered over the edge into the eight-hundred-foot abyss, looking not for a graceful falcon but for the heavyset gentleman who had just been standing next to me. Every guide's worst nightmare.

A few yards below the rim, Harold had somehow landed on a small ledge, just out of sight. There he was, jovial and stoically British as always, but clearly in a lot of pain. He had just missed plummeting hundreds of feet by landing on this tiny sliver of rock. I had to summon the park officials to help lift him out of the gorge. This was no easy task and required reversing a *bakkie* close to the precipitous edge and carrying him up over the rocks to the waiting vehicle. Miraculously, he only suffered a twisted ankle and bruised hip. Undaunted, Harold bounced right back. After a gallon of whiskey and several days rest, he was ready to continue our journey into Namibia. Birders are a unique lot. It takes quite a bit to cancel a birding trip.

We crossed the South African/Namibian border and drove straight to Windhoek, founded around 1840 by an Afrikaner settler aptly named Jonker Afrikaner. We stopped briefly for refreshments, passed quickly through the busy capital city, and headed toward the coast. I had booked us into a wonderful birder-friendly bed and breakfast in the quaint town of Swakopmund, but first we had to cross the Okahandja Bridge. This was a known location for one of our target birds, a rare near-endemic. Little did we realize that this was a place where fervent birders also became targets.

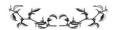

I hear the shot and the bullet whistles overhead. It's a lucky break I am not injured or killed. This time, the weapon has not been discharged accidentally by a rookie trainee. I am caught in the middle of a gun battle between a thief and the Afrikaners who have arrived in their 4x4 *bakkie*.

I dive headlong into the sand at the sound. I have heard enough gunshots in my life to know that this one came from close by. I remain flattened to the ground, trying to get a fix on the shooter's location. My reinforcements, in the form of the two farmers, are also trying to locate the source of the gunfire. From my prone position in the dirt, I can see their 4x4 about thirty yards from me, shrouded by a cloud of dust. The two large white men in khaki fatigues are crouched behind the open doors, using them for protection as they aim their firearms. Almost in unison, they fire two shots toward a thicket of tangled dry scrub.

A flash of blue T-shirt bursts from cover about forty feet from me. The thief-turned-gunman is once again on the run. Now is my chance to move; I know he will struggle to shoot backward while he is navigating through the brush. I jump up and attempt to close the gap on the miscreant, determined to salvage the cameras, wallets, scopes, and everything else he stole from our vehicle.

I am gaining on the thief. As he senses he is outnumbered, he drops his firearm and makes a last ditch attempt to flee. I rugby tackle him as hard as I can, making sure I grab his torso, arms and all, in case he has any further nasty surprises for me. Swiftly, the two khaki-clad farmers come to my aid and assist in getting the protesting man under control. As the farmers truss him like a pig and load him into their vehicle, I retrieve our stolen possessions and the perpetrator's gun. I thank them profusely for their help on the ride back.

I see Harold on the bridge, waiting with a policeman. The cop has come alive at the sound of gunshots and is now full of gusto. He immediately takes control of the situation, arresting the thief and writing up a statement from the two white farmers. My new allies are free to go, their role in the adventure complete.

In our newly air-conditioned car, Harold and I follow the cop and his reticent passenger to the police station, where we wait for about twenty minutes. A senior police official appears in the waiting room, beaming as he approaches Harold and me.

"You guys have done us a great favor by capturing this man. He is a known criminal here, and we have been looking for him. We need you to testify and make sure that he is put behind bars for a long time."

I explain to the official that we are on a planned tour and cannot be held up here for days.

"Not to worry," he says. "When will you be coming back this way?"

"In about three weeks," I reply.

"Okay, we will set the court date for the day you pass through here again. Would that work?"

I turn to Harold. It's his decision whether we take time from his birding trip to testify in court.

"Shall we make sure that the Okahandja Bridge becomes a safer place for the sake of future birders looking for violet wood hoopoes?" I ask.

"Absolutely," replies Harold without hesitation.

Three weeks later, we kept our promise and returned to Okahandja. We sat in court and testified to the judge about our crazy ordeal at the hands of the brazen thief. The police official was there and he thanked us for keeping our commitment.

Many people think of birding as a passive pastime. No! That's *bird watching. Birding* is an active pursuit, full of unknowns and excitement. To me, there's nothing better than a healthy dose of birding on the edge.

GOLDEN BIRDS

The intense eyes of the ocean
Drew me into the blue dwellings of the sea lion.
I threw my cloak of the dream into the wind
Into the hands of a passer-by.
MAZISI KUNENE,
"Uncontrollable Feeling of Ecstasy"

Uhambo nqumqunda lubhoko.
A journey is a thing which blunts the walking staff.
ZULU PROVERB

THERE IS A BIRD THAT makes an almost perfect pet. It's brightly colored, curious, friendly, playful, affectionate, inquisitive, intelligent … but raucously loud. It is rumored that there may be as few as eighty left in the wild.

The high demand by the legal pet trade resulted in a drastic decline in the population the last few years, as conservation authorities seriously dropped the ball with regard to the protection of these enigmatic parrots. Nearly extirpated, they can be found only in pockets along the river in Guyana and possibly neighboring Brazil. It is thought that only one viable wild flock of these amazing birds remains.

My goal is to locate that flock of sun parakeets, aka sun conures, and capture it on film. We head up the river from the tiny village of Karasabai, right on the Brazil/Guyana border, with the local guides. The longer we look, the more frustrated I become. There are none to be found. We have gotten up way too late, and in the heat of the midmorning sun, I am getting irritable.

"Just wait a bit and we'll make our way back down the river," the guides reassure me.

I've lost hope and am finding it hard to stay positive. Locating a flock of birds, especially one with so few numbers, takes all my concentration. My eyes scan the green canopy, looking for anything yellow, any golden specks that might indicate we are close.

Eventually, far, far in the distance, we spot these bright, bright yellow birds, flying above the canopy in a tightly knit flock on the Brazilian side of the river.

Yes! Sun parakeets!

The final challenge is getting my large cameraman on shore, as it is difficult to shoot from the boats. I am exhilarated to find one of the rarest wild parrots in the world, our first Golden Bird. Its golden color seems symbolic of our hopes for filming a birding TV show in Guyana.

This small country was long considered to be the home of El Dorado, the fabled lost city of gold pursued by early adventurers. I am personally hoping that we will strike our own gold with the show. But in the midst of filming in late October 2008, we had heard the shocking news that the bottom had fallen out of the stock market back in the States. Rebecca and I had risked all of our savings on the show, and now the financial climate was grim for starting a new endeavor. But now deep in Guyana, I am determined not to let this news distract me, as we are on a whirlwind tour to film the rest of the episodes. Energized by our successful search for the sun parakeets, we begin the arduous journey back to the center of the country to search for our next Golden Bird.

I am no longer taking people out birding. I am now bringing the world of birding to the people.

Spirits had been high when I landed in Guyana several days earlier with two cameramen and loads of equipment. A quick trip took us from the airport to the Georgetown Botanical Gardens right in the middle of the capital and largest city. My goal was to get acquainted with the variety of endemic birds we would encounter on our upcoming journey. The colorful parrots, parakeets, and parrotlets, all perched in the nearby trees, clamored noisily for attention. The cameras were rolling as one cameraman frantically filmed the plethora of bird species and the other recorded my spontaneous interpretations.

"Parrots are superbly adapted to feeding on nuts," I explained as the camera captured a red-shouldered macaw in a nearby palm tree. "Their bills can be compared to a handyman's toolkit, complete with a wrench, vise, and screwdriver. The upper and lower beaks work together, not only to husk nuts but to drive under hard objects, cut fruit from branches, and excavate holes in trees."

But it wasn't just the brilliantly colored birds that got our attention. Our local guide pointed out a flock of nondescript black birds in the field nearby. This was a terrific opportunity to feature him on camera and spotlight some local interpretive knowledge.

"That is one of the species here, a smooth-billed ani. It is commonly known as the jumbie bird, because in local folklore jumbies are the spirits of the deceased," the guide said somberly. "It's believed that whenever these birds are around in large quantities, somebody has died or is about to die."

"Hope it's not one of us!" I said, thinking about the strenuous adventure we had planned, traversing miles of rainforest by four-wheeler, boat, airplane, and on foot. We would be eating strange foods and staying in primitive lodgings. I knew firsthand what it was like to suffer the fevers and chills of malaria, to endure the swelling and toxemia from spider and tick bites. I had witnessed the peril of a poisonous snakebite. I wasn't worried about myself so much, but my main cameraman, Jeff, had never been on a grueling trip like this where he had to carry his own heavy equipment into the jungle so far from the comforts of civilization.

"Oh no, no. Just folklore, it's not actually true," my guide reassured me, speaking into the camera. "Just a belief that's passed down from generation to generation. So no need to worry. You'll get back in one piece."

I promptly forgot about the prediction as we left the park. Little did I realize that those jumbie birds were there as a warning sign for me. Heading into the heart of Guyana, deep into the jungle, I had more pressing matters on my mind. These first episodes would set the pace and tone of the future of a series on birding, a subject that most TV networks avoided like the plague. I was determined to show a wider audience how exciting it could be, using a camera instead of a gun to capture the essence of the thrill of the hunt.

"What makes you think *Birding Adventures TV* can succeed where others haven't?" a famous American birder once asked me—a very good question. And one that I could not answer except I knew I would not be content unless I tried. That yearning I first experienced with the Black Eagle on Table Mountain—and other experiences like it—were strong enough to propel the show into reality. It started with a dream, awakening me in the middle of the night.

"We're starting a bird-watching TV show," I told Rebecca.

It was 3:00 a.m., and I had just woken with a revelation. But Rebecca was still asleep.

"Okay," she murmured. "But can we chat about this at a more respectable hour?"

In the morning, she asked me what I had been dreaming about. Her initial reaction was that it was a crazy idea. But she had no objections to my looking into the possibility. I started making inquiries, and through pure serendipity, everything quickly fell into place. *Birding Adventures TV*, or BATV, was one step closer to reality. Here we were in Guyana, the perfect location to film exotic birds. I hoped my formula for the show worked, blending my passion for bird watching with the American public's expectation for high-energy entertainment.

My first introduction to the drama and power of viewing wildlife on television was through David Attenborough's nature series. As a young boy, I read all of his books and remember being glued to the television set watching his documentaries. I absolutely idolized him. David was a man of action, who combined his extensive wildlife knowledge with magnificent storytelling. Standing in raging rivers or atop mounds of bird droppings, hanging off the side of a boat or clinging to the tree canopies by rope and winch, he was always right in the middle of the activity. He promised high adventure to his readers and viewers, and never disappointed. More important, he wasn't afraid to show the darker side of nature, exposing the grim truth about vicious predators and their prey. Exactly the type of realistic programming that sparked my imagination and captivated me as a boy.

The spark was fanned into a flame at Phinda through a chance encounter. Imagine my delight when purely by luck of the draw Norman and I were assigned to guide a private tour one day. We prepared our Land Rover and drove up to meet our guests, a distinguished gentleman and his wife. With a distinctively British accent, he introduced himself as John Attenborough. My heart skipped a beat. I just had to ask if he was related to my childhood hero and star of nature adventure shows, David Attenborough.

"Why, yes. David and Richard are my famous brothers," he told me. He was obviously proud of his family connections.

Norman and I guided John and his wife through some of the best sights at Phinda. We saw many beautiful birds, including elusive Narina trogons, pink-throated twinspots, and African broadbills. Norman was superb. His instinctive tracking skills were phenomenally tuned into the rhythm of the reserve and we were able to locate many of the rarest species and all of the Big Five. I didn't need to contain my enthusiasm when guiding John. He was accustomed to his brother's exuberance for wildlife.

One evening, just as we were returning to the car park at Forest Lodge, Norman signaled me to stop. Ever vigilant, he had picked up the tracks of a big male leopard veering off from the car park toward the guest rooms. We quickly turned around and headed out on the little service road between Forest and Vlei Lodges. Norman knew that this male was taking a shortcut through the lodge and would more than likely come out on this track. It was more a footpath than a proper road and for some odd reason was named Whale Beach Road. It meandered through one of the prettiest patches of cathedral sand forest on the reserve.

That evening, bright moonlight reflected off the white sand of the forest floor, sand as smooth and shiny as the back of a whale in the ocean. From his perch in the tracker's seat, Norman scanned for tracks. Just as we rounded a sharp turn flanked by the massive, fluted trunk of a *balanites* tree, I nearly bumped Norman into our quarry. A few yards in front of us, this massive male leopard was just emerging from the low scrub. I quickly reversed gear, and Norman hopped in the seat beside me for obvious safety reasons.

We came round the turn again, cautiously this time, to see the leopard padding casually toward Vlei Lodge, totally ignoring the vehicle inching its way behind him. He was too busy scent-marking his way down Whale Beach Road. He would go from bush to tree, marking his territory by lifting his tail and spraying urine — the higher the better, letting others know just how big he was.

With the bright moonlight, fairy-tale-like surroundings, and the sounds of the nocturnal forest creatures, this was one of my favorite memories of Phinda. And I think John and his wife appreciated it too.

This chance encounter led to a friendship. On one of my visits to the UK, John gave me the news that he'd set up a get-together with his brother.

"Go to this address. David's expecting you," John told me.

No way! I was so excited, a chance to finally chat with my hero face to face.

I arrived at the address, expecting to see a large country estate surrounded by big gates and walls. To my surprise, it was a modest British countryside house with a small fence. There were no guarded pathways, no high security walls, no vicious dogs. I knocked at the door, expecting a butler. But David answered the door himself.

"Come in. I've been waiting for you."

He ushered me graciously into his sitting room. While he made tea, I admired his extensive collection of natural history books, fossils, and other artifacts from his travels. We spent the next hour chatting about his path to success. How he left a well-paid career with the BBC to follow his passions. The joys and difficulties in traveling, filming, and narrating nature shows with real wildlife, not just captive zoo animals. The challenges and responsibilities mankind faces in preserving the world around us. My time with David passed much too quickly.

The memories of this visit would stay with me a long time. Hearing David speak about his adventures, seeing the way he was able to follow his dream yet live a simple and happy life, inspired me. I returned to Phinda, but my view of the world and its possibilities had subtly changed. Somewhere deep inside, a seed had been planted.

I thought long and hard about David's shows and his formula for mesmerizing audiences. When I got to the States, I was taken aback by the realization that quite a few Americans had not heard of him. It dawned on me that, while he was a household name in almost every corner of the Western world, he did not appear to have the same widespread reach in America. I was not quite sure of the reasons for this. It might have been that the sudden appearance of new wildlife TV shows, no doubt spawned out of the success of David's shows, had saturated the airwaves. Perhaps it was the reluctance of American networks to air the BBC's productions. Or perhaps it was that the US audience was so massive and so diversified in its tastes that no one person could capture it all. I had grown up with and absolutely loved David's shows, but I quickly realized that a sizable proportion of the American TV audience thirsted for sensationalism, even when it came to wildlife TV.

In sharp contrast to David Attenborough's documentary style, Steve Irwin's show focused on the Australian's cavalier approach to handling dangerous animals. *The Crocodile Hunter* debuted in 1996 and soon became a worldwide sensation. Steve was a master showman, and his bushman persona captivated the viewing public, but there was a price to pay. His critics often found his brashness and unconventional approach to handling wild animals disturbing, and his presentation of facts occasionally misleading.

I too always believed that nature and wildlife should be left largely untouched. But in retrospect, Steve inspired a whole new generation of wildlife advocates due to his hands-on approach, and I now think that the educational value of his work far outweighs any negatives that his critics might throw out there. He attracted a huge US-based and global audience with his energetic narrations of high adventure, profusion of action, focus on conservation, and compelling stories. There was definitely something unique and interesting about him, and I completely related to his level of passion and energy. My show would debut in 2008, two years after the charismatic Australian's untimely and dramatic death. Crikey!

My goal was to differentiate myself from both David and Steve while incorporating the best mix of their styles. My focus would be on birds in interesting locations around the world, but I would also present the surrounding flora and fauna as part of a larger environmental picture. All the while conveying academic facts in an entertaining format, buoyed up with my natural excitement and enthusiasm. And, like Steve, I would occasionally go against my better judgment and handle an animal for the camera.

I was not trained in any type of film, media, or acting, yet I felt confident in this new endeavor. I had an unquenchable desire to find rare birds, combined with a background in nature interpretation, a head full of facts, and lots of experience relating to people. I'd been guiding for so long that the role of nature show host came effortlessly to me. So now, instead of talking to my guests in the Land Rover, I would be speaking in front of a camera. If I felt an awkward moment, I'd just tell myself, "Look at the camera. You're talking to your guests. Just be natural. Don't hold back. Just let the excitement fly."

I try to do everything in one take. Other hosts do multiple shots, but for me the first is almost always the best. It can be a bit of a negative to do the take again, as my initial patter is the most natural. I find it tough to recreate the same scene with an equal amount of energy. A loud truck passing by, an airplane overhead, even the background noise of the wind can interfere with the filming. I always hope for a successful first take and I'm usually lucky.

So my formula for the show was simple. First of all, to explore the best birding destinations on the planet. The habitat could be an exotic island, remote jungle, or even a city park, as long as the indigenous birds and wildlife were interesting subjects for the viewer.

In one of David Attenborough's early episodes, he tried to track down a rare bird — the white-necked rockfowl, aka *Picathartes gymnocephalus* — in Sierra Leone. It was a particularly difficult challenge for him, and it took several episodes to find the bird. His frustrations at trying to locate it actually held the audience glued. The lights went on for David when he discovered that the suspense only made him and his show more popular. I planned to foster anticipation, but since I was on a limited budget and a tight schedule, I hoped that my search for birds in the wild would be successful on the first attempt. So my activity would focus on my search for a Golden Bird, a highly sought-after, rare, or unusual bird species that would captivate the viewers' attention and have them wondering whether I would find the bird. I'd bring the audience into the experience with the drama of the quest.

In each destination, I would feature local experts. There are so many talented naturalists out there, waiting to impart their knowledge, and BATV would provide a vehicle for them. Besides, I'm not a worldwide authority on birds, and I need all the help I can get! I'm not sure if anyone else struggles with this, but I get so caught up in the moment and excitement of seeing a new bird that I will blurt out something like "Freaking magnificent woodpecker!" when what I mean to say is "Magellanic woodpecker!" So employing local talent is a vital part of keeping the on-screen presenter honest.

The show would provide a window into the lives of the people through interviews, sampling the food, and engaging in local cultural ceremonies. Then I'd incorporate a fun segment with an unexpected twist, usually with some physical activity on my part. Without being preachy, I also planned to integrate an emphasis on conservation, highlighting the importance and urgency of preserving the planet's incredible wildlife.

Finally, for each episode I needed to find an amenable lodge or tourist bureau with promotional dollars to cover the cost of the show. Presenting a birding adventure for potential visitors or armchair viewers that encompassed all of the above was a lot to do in twenty-two minutes of airtime, interspersed with the eight minutes of commercial sponsor time I hoped to get.

There was a lot to pull together on that first trip, aided by my soon-to-be trusty travel companion and primary videographer, Jeff. A man with dubious credentials and a dodgy past, Jeff had an uncanny knack for filming and editing. At close to seven feet tall and weighing as much as two male ostriches and a cassowary, he was not your average cameraman. And excessive birding makes him nuts!

This was not my first trip to the neotropics. When I graduated with my master's degree, my future wife Rebecca thought it would be cool to take a little trip to celebrate. After spending two years in London, I was ready for a serious adventure. I found the city confining and the constant gray skies depressing. My restlessness must have been palpable.

This offer from Rebecca to see a bit of the world resonated immediately. She gave me a choice between India to see tigers or Latin America to see birds. Having always longed to visit the continent with the world's highest bird diversity, the decision was easy. We would go to Central and South America. It would be a terrific opportunity to expand my birding life list, which had been neglected while I was studying. In truth, it was a chance to revive my selfish, fanatical pastime—chasing birds around the world. No need to twist my arm to get out of London and back to nature.

After a whirlwind tour of Costa Rica, we met up with Richard White, my mate and partner in mischief from Phinda. Richard was now a bird guide at Sacha Lodge in the Amazon in Ecuador and had a French girlfriend. One evening, on a whim and over a few stiff drinks, the four of us decided to go deep into the Amazon for a bird-watching and fishing trip. I always secretly wanted to visit Cuyabeno, one of the most bird-rich parts of the Amazon and the most unexplored and remote. If there were a brochure, the list of things to do at Cuyabeno would include rainforest hikes, bird watching, caiman spotting, sport fishing, and camping. Richard and I knew up front that there would be no accommodations whatsoever. But the poor girls had no idea where we were going, how isolated it would be, or the level of basic amenities they would have to do without.

The first clue for them would have been the bus trip. Piling in with all of our gear, we noticed that one of the large side windows was missing.

"Oh, that was shot out by rebels last week," the driver informed us in Spanish, Richard translating.

"Rebels?" we asked.

"Yes, we will pass near the Colombian border," he said. "I'll show you the spot."

This was to be the first of many unnerving incidents for the girls. Perhaps they should have asked to look at a brochure before committing to the trip, but it was too late now.

The bus stopped at the drop-off point along the river, where our local guide was waiting. He did not speak any English, but Richard could communicate with his limited Spanish. We would take a motorboat part of the way. After a few hours, we would transfer into tiny, primitive dugout canoes.

This was when the adventure began. As evening descended, we paddled deep into the jungle, our primitive canoes gliding silently through the murky waters. Yellow spotted turtles surrendered their warm, sunny rocks, cocoi herons hunted along the riverbanks, and vultures circled overhead. Giant blue morphos butterflies lured us around each bend into the sunset. The mood became one of complete enchantment. This would be a spectacular trip, I mused, just like old times heading into the wilderness with my good mate Richard.

The magic stopped when we reached what was to become our lodging for the next week. The girls were horrified. Nothing but tents in the middle of the jungle! A primitive outhouse. Definitely no bathing facilities. Not quite the romantic retreat that the girls had envisioned. And there was no turning back. We were entirely alone in the middle of the jungle. Our planned return to civilization would be in seven days' time, when we paddled the dugout canoes for several hours back to the rendezvous location to meet the motorboat.

A typical day for Richard and me would consist of waking up at 5:00 a.m. to go birding deep into the jungle. We would see the most amazing species, like pavonine quetzals, red-necked woodpeckers, and blue-backed manakins. We might return at midday and then head out for more birding or take the canoes out fishing. Then, at night, disappear into the darkness, looking for owls. It was just nonstop birding and fishing the whole time, supplemented with a dash of mammalian wonders like the tiny pygmy marmoset that is the smallest monkey in the world, or the pink river dolphin.

On one of our rare boat excursions with the girls, Richard enthused about the unexpected treat of seeing the dolphins nearly every day.

"This is an incredibly unusual sighting," he said, reverting to his guide persona. "The dolphins are concentrated in the main river channels on account of the low water levels.

"Look at their necks, how flexible. The unfused vertebrae in their spine give them the ability to probe in and around tree roots and submerged structures in their aquatic environment. When one comes up look at its tiny eyes, way smaller than other dolphins. They rely heavily on echolocation to locate their prey and get around."

He couldn't resist the chance to tease.

"There is a cool Amazonian legend that these dolphins are actually shape-changers. They sneak up on local women on the riverbanks and change into men to impregnate them. Then they revert to dolphins and disappear back into the water."

Richard's girlfriend was not impressed.

"Well, ze *dauphin* might actually be a better option for ze girls," she snapped to nobody in particular.

Her words should have been a sign of the way things were headed. Richard and I were oblivious to the trouble that was brewing in paradise, because for us guys, everyday was just pure bliss. There were not enough hours in the day to absorb it all. Not so for the girls. The days dragged interminably while their loving boyfriends came and went. A typical day for the girls would be to wake up to find strange insects and critters in their tents. Richard and I would often leave the tents unzipped in our haste to depart. After debugging and decrittering their sleeping quarters, there would be no hot water or showers. Then they would sit around all day, with nothing to do, surrounded by the strange sounds and rustlings in the jungle. It was remote with no other people around for many miles. The girls would often freak out.

The very first day, a blood-curdling scream came from the outhouse. On her first excursion to check it out, Rebecca had a run-in with a nasty-looking, seven-inch-long bug that resembled a giant cross between a spider and a scorpion.

"It's only a tailless whip scorpion," I tried to explain. "It's harmless and actually serves to keep the insect population down, using those sharp pincers to catch and crush more dangerous critters. It won't hurt you."

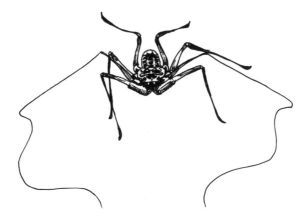

But the girls weren't buying it. And besides, Rebecca remembered the tales of my encounter with the puff adder in the outhouse at Phinda. Best to avoid places that were damp and dark, where one was unnecessarily exposed. Both girls refused to go in there, preferring the open jungle for their necessary ablutions.

"What do we do if we see a snake?" they asked.

"Catch it for us so that we can ID it!" we replied.

"And what's that roaring that comes from nowhere and everywhere?"

"Howler monkeys. No need to worry."

"Can we take a dip in the river and cool off?"

"Yes, of course! But make sure you don't have any cuts or graz-es. Piranhas have been known to take a bite every now and again. Watch out for caiman. And avoid quiet backwaters, because that is where electric eels like to hang out."

"Is that all?" they asked in horror.

"Oh, and don't pee in the water. There may be candiru fish in these parts. You know, those slim translucent fish with back-ward-facing spines that lodge in body orifices and need to be surgi-cally removed. You certainly don't want that!

"Also, you may want to check the leaves for any large ants when you head into the jungle to pee," we would continue mis-chievously. "They say the sting of the bullet ant is excruciating and lasts for twenty-four hours!"

Looks of horror, disgust, and disdain. Murderous looks would be a better description. It took just a few days for them to get fed up with us. We were totally disorganized and inconsiderate. No wonder they revolted. Mutinied.

One day, Richard and I arrived at camp ecstatic. We had re-turned from a superb day where we saw the pearly antshrike, a rarity that was seldom encountered by birders. In contrast, the girls survived yet another horrid day. A torrential downpour soaked all their recently cleaned clothes, and by now, they were completely miserable and ready to head back. Richard and I were hit with the news that the girls wanted to leave. Simultaneously, we were told we were being dumped; they were breaking up with us.

"You guys are so selfish, just a couple of *skollies*," the girls told us. "We didn't sign up for this. We're done."

"Perfect. How are you going to get out of here?" we replied.

Dead silence. They had no choice but to retract their statements. They knew that the only way out was with us. They would just have to grin and bear it. And to their credit, they did. Yes, I was a selfish, fanatical wildlife guy. It's a wonder Rebecca put up with me. But I had fallen under the spell of South America. I knew I would be back someday. But probably with different traveling companions.

I thought of that last trip, and the importance of choosing one's traveling companions. For an extended wildlife expedition, one needs to take people who not only appreciate nature but can also endure the privations required to experience it in the most remote locations. Difficult circumstances can bring out the best and worst in people.

My cameraman, Jeff, had experience with the nature part, but I wasn't sure about the birding-in-remote-locations part. This wasn't like filming in a zoo. Or filming a fishing expedition, where the fish are held captive at the end of a line. Searching out birds takes a keen eye and quick reflexes. Often, after hauling heavy equipment in the heat and humidity and setting up for inconvenient shots, target birds nonchalantly fly away or disappear behind a leaf. The success of my show depended not just on finding the Golden Birds but getting them on film. This trip would definitely be a test of Jeff's mettle.

It was absolutely wonderful in Guyana, the "land of many waters." Even though the trip was focused on birding, much of the action was in or around the water. We started our journey at the powerful Kaieteur Falls, one of the world's most spectacular waterfalls, with a drop twice that of Victoria Falls and four times that of Niagara Falls.

I frolicked with giant river otters and swam among the *Victoria amazonica,* gigantic water lilies that grow to nine feet wide. I had a chance to search for and catch the endangered black caiman, one of the largest reptilian predators, at night.

Jeff and I both were avid fishermen, so I was thrilled with the opportunity to navigate the rivers, fishing and catching peacock bass, payara and piranhas. But these water adventures were secondary to my mission, which was to search out rare and endangered birds and capture the quests on camera. Our aim was to produce three episodes each featuring a highly sought-after species. From the over eight hundred bird species in Guyana I needed to select which parrots, toucans, eagles, woodpeckers, cuckoos, crows, or cotingas would fascinate my audience.

I chose three Golden Birds that were truly difficult to locate, three birds that were symbolic in some way of my goals for *Birding Adventures TV*. The endangered sun parakeet would highlight the need for conservation. The strange appearance and odd behavior of the cock-of-the-rock would provide sheer entertainment. For pure drama, I would finish with my personal quest for the mythical harpy eagle.

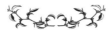

After finding the sun parakeets along the riverbank, I turn my sights toward the depths of the jungle. What starts out as a meander turns into a major excursion, a military-style hike that takes us through savannah, forest, rivers, and swamps. Due to recent rains, our planned two-mile trek somehow turns into an eight-mile hike. It is a real test for the crew carrying all their heavy equipment, all the cameras, binoculars, scopes, and paraphernalia. We hike down hills and vales, navigating our way through spider webs and dense mist, the thick jungle all around.

We are heading to a place deep in the jungle. A place inhabited by eagles, owls, snakes, jaguars, and one of the most incredible, outlandish birds on earth. Trekking for mile after mile through nonnegotiable bush, our destination is an area of boulder-encrusted mountains. The boulders and the open ground between them are the perfect nesting and lekking site for the stunningly colorful Guianan cock-of-the rock, our Golden Bird for the second episode.

Jeff, my primary cameraman, is feeling the effects of nonstop traveling in a strange place. He has such severe cramps that we have to rest and rehydrate him quickly before beginning the task of locating the birds. After getting Jeff's leg cramps under control, we round a mound of granite taller than Jeff himself. There it is — a lek of the gaudily colored males.

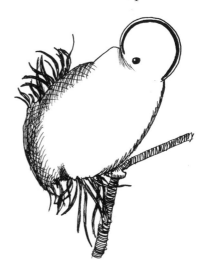

The male Guianan cock-of-the-rock is so beautiful words cannot describe it. This bird is all about orange, from the tip of its bill to the sides of its feet, one of those uniquely plumed birds that is highly regarded by any warm-blooded birder. It could also be considered the face of Guyana. With the male's brilliant orange colorings, complete with an attention-grabbing Mohawk, it's no wonder it graces the covers of so many tourism brochures. And while the radiant plumage of the male makes it one of the most sought after and easily identifiable birds of the tropics, the female's less-than-striking brown colorings don't attract equal attention, but watching the females interact with the males at the lek is a rare experience indeed.

Luckily for my physically exhausted camera crew, these birds like to inhabit the lowest stratum of the forest for their competitive mating displays. Once we reach their lek on the open ground, filming these beautiful orange birds is relatively easy. A second Golden Bird in the bag, so to speak. Smoking ponies! We are almost finished.

The thrill of spotting the sun parakeets and the cock-of-the-rock is exhilarating, but my last adventure will be the grueling quest to find the legendary harpy eagle. There is something very special about ending my inaugural three-part TV series with a bird I had yearned to see since I was a small boy.

The future of my show is in the hands of my local guides, the Amerindians who know the jungle so well. They found the hidden paradise where the cock-of-the-rock strutted and nested. They navigated the labyrinthine rivers to seek out the sun parakeets. Hopefully they will locate the harpy as well. And so it is with great anticipation that I head out from the small village of Surama deep in the heart of Guyana once again with my crew and local guides to try for a glimpse of this mythical creature.

The best chance of seeing harpy eagles is undoubtedly at known nest sites in countries like Brazil, Guyana, or Suriname. This particular expedition of mine is touch and go, because although the local guides previously staked out a nest, the youngster is already fledged. The sighting is not guaranteed, since the eaglet is spending more and more time away from the nesting tree.

My worst fears are realized on the initial attempt when we hike over a mile into the forest only to find an empty nest and not a harpy in sight. I return to the lodge disappointed. My time in Guyana is running out. I hope and pray that this last Golden Bird, the one that I most long to see, won't elude me.

THE EAGLE CALLS MY NAME

I was seized by the ecstasy of the song,
I was carried away by the travelling winds.
The northern summers came to hear me
Halfway they met me and they kissed my fingers.
They showed me the path to the ancestral shrines.
MAZISI KUNENE,
"The Return of Inspiration"

Yinja yomoya.
He is a dog of the wind.
ZULU PROVERB

MARTIN AND I WALK DELICATELY along the narrow but well-worn path. It is a trail that he knows well, because he made it years ago when he was a boy. We reach the stream and remove our shoes to inch our way along the old submerged limb from a kapok tree, just visible under the swift-moving waters. I follow Martin's lead as he confidently balances on the underwater bridge.

"Many years ago, my brothers and I created this crossing," says Martin. "It started with the violent storm ..."

Gusts of wind. A flash of lightning. An explosive crack. Followed by the dramatic sound of the large branch plummeting one hundred fifty feet down through the layers of the canopy. A myriad of forest life also hurtled down, down, down. All the epiphytes, insects, arachnids, reptiles, and amphibians that normally sought sunlight in the towering tree, high above the canopy, were now catapulted to the depths of the forest floor when the lightning bolt cruelly severed the massive limb from the old kapok's body. The tropical outburst subsided as quickly as it came. The curious boys, then merely teenagers, found the fallen bough. Along with the men of the village, they manhandled it into place fording the stream. This branch, once part of a highway across the roof of the rainforest, is now our sole means of crossing the river.

We are close now. The calls of screaming pihas punctuate the humid air like invisible missiles.

Pee peee hah! Pee peee hah!

The males are advertising their sex appeal with this three-syllable call, one of the most recognizable sounds in the Amazon. I strain to look up, scanning for the dull gray birds emitting these piercing cries. High above us, the old tree camouflages the birds well within its shadows of muted greens.

Martin is suddenly quiet, his face intent on listening to the sounds of the forest. He motions for me to stop. I also turn my senses to the surrounding area, breathing deeply the aroma of the Amazon, a hothouse full of lush growth and decomposing matter. Suddenly the hairs on the back of my neck perk up intuitively, as they always do when I know I'm being watched. Sensing that something other than the harmless pihas is watching our every move, I realize there is no point in going any farther. We need to locate our quarry from our awkward position, perched on the old kapok limb, fording the jungle creek. Arching my neck, I scan the dappled canopy, blinking once as a rare ray of sunlight pierces the sea of green. As the swift, cool waters rush over our clasping feet, I feel a burning predatory glare pulling my gaze to the right. And upward.

There they are. Sitting ten feet apart in the old kapok, on a branch just below the dark scar where the severed limb once stretched into the sky. Breathe. And now wait. Martin whispers to me that they will relax as they always do … if we remain still. After several minutes, we are relieved to notice that a plaintive calling diverts their stare. We listen transfixed as both birds answer their young one in unison. Almost a ducklike quacking.

Crack-crack-crack. Crack-crack-crack.

Martin speaks softly. "You're still here!"

And, as if on cue, the young harpy eagle flies in and joins the wary parent birds. A single large feather seesaws down. Martin stretches out his hand, plucking it deftly from the air.

Martin grew up in the tiny Amerindian village of Surama, deep within the heart of Guyana's tropical rainforest, in an area called the Rupununi. His Makushi parents named him Martin—which wasn't surprising, because Guyana is the only English-speaking country in South America. But to any outsider this would seem strange—an English-speaking local community in the backcountry of a remote nation.

The word *surama* means "place of spoiled barbecue," derived during a tribal conflict between the Makushi and Carib peoples many, many years ago. Surama village is situated in a picturesque mosaic of savannah, forest, and hills of the Pakariama mountain range. Cut off from the rest of civilization, Surama is the only world that Martin has ever known, and like other members of his community, he has become deeply in tune with his surroundings.

The two hundred–odd residents live a basic life according to the laws of nature. Like all other boys in his village, Martin grew up hunting the animals that abound in his jungle home. Birds were definitely not off the menu, but Martin remembers clearly the moment that changed his life.

The village boys often hunted together in a pack. And like all packs, there was a pecking order. The youngest of the group, Martin was often teased for his lack of hunting skills. Time and time again, Martin's brothers and friends would return to the village with agouti, birds, and other small animals for the pot. But Martin would always come back empty handed. It wasn't so much that he could not hunt. In fact, when the boys split off from the hunting party to pursue their individual quarries, Martin would sneak up on animals closer than any of the other boys. His intuitive connection with the wild enabled him to get within striking distance, but he never dispatched his primitive but effective weapons. He would quietly track the animal through the thick forest. Stop. Listen. Smell. Watch. Almost invisible, his small dark form blended with the foliage as he sneaked up to study the animal.

His problem was that he spent too much time studying them. Observing the colorful macaws flying gracefully in pairs, even within a flock. Spending hours watching a tarantula molt and shed its exoskeleton. Amused by the antics of a tree frog, defying gravity with the help of the adhesive discs on its legs.

But the constant teasing of his peers was beginning to wear on him. He knew that this day he would need to prove himself and make a kill. He was resolved to bag the best meal for dinner. Today there would be no time for watching birds, spiders, or frogs. He needed to bring home meat for the pot. His small but sturdy frame bent over to examine the trail for signs of game. Collared peccaries! A whole band of them! The hoof prints were clear in the soft mud, easy to follow. None of the boys had ever bagged a peccary, and Martin knew that if he returned with one of the dangerous hogs, the teasing would cease.

Armed with nothing but his bow and arrows, Martin tracked the native pigs. Taking great care to merge with his surroundings, he was more shadow than boy. The peccaries have razor-sharp tusks and are extremely dangerous. Martin was not much larger than a peccary himself and could easily become a victim of a deadly charge. A telltale musky odor lingered in the humid air. He stopped to listen. There was a snuffling sound coming from the undergrowth, a mix of grunts and hoof beats. The band of peccaries was rooting for their morning meal.

A young peccary lagged behind the rest of the foraging group. Martin began to stalk it, silently creeping over the carpet of rotting vegetation until he was within twenty-five feet. He took an arrow out of his quiver and positioned it, drawing the bow back carefully, steadying it against his body. The sweat trickled from his brow as he had second thoughts  about killing a subadult. The peccary was so close as it meandered out of the shade and into a beam of sunlight. He couldn't miss. His keen eyes focused on his target while he estimated the force and angle needed to bag the young pig. In that brief moment of hesitation, Martin realized he wasn't the only hunter on a mission that day.

The big female harpy swooped in, and for an instant, the young pig was shrouded in darkness as the spread of eagle wings blocked out all light. Her deadly talons struck their mark. Two over the peccary's snout and skull, and the remaining two embedded in the animal's neck. The young pig squealed briefly, alerting the foraging porcine band.

The forest erupted. Peccaries ran for cover in every direction. Martin was held spellbound, the shock of losing his prize to a more efficient hunter replaced by the sheer marvel of the power of the giant eagle. The piglet struggled for a short while, but death came quickly. Then as silently as she arrived, the large eagle just took off empty taloned, leaving the peccary for the astounded young boy. Perhaps sensing Martin's presence, the aerial giant disappeared into the canopy.

When Martin returned that day he was a hero. A peccary was valuable meat to the community, and he was never teased again.

And that was the day he vowed to protect the eagles forever. Martin finished telling me his boyhood story as he handed me the harpy feather.

It was 2008, and Martin, now middle-aged, was my guide as I embarked on my maiden trip to film this third episode of the first season of my TV show. Ever since that life-changing moment on Table Mountain as a young boy witnessing the power of the black eagle, I have longed to see a harpy eagle, one of the largest, rarest, and most powerful eagles in the world.

There are many enigmatic bird species that birders and wildlife enthusiasts long to see but none quite so highly sought after as the harpy eagle. While the rarity of a particular species might be the sole reason for fanatics to seek out a species, the rarity of harpy eagles is only one of a handful of reasons so many birders drool at the mere mention of its name.

Consider the fact that it is a contender for the title of largest eagle in the world, although there may be a few Steller's sea eagles, martial eagles and Philippine eagles that would give it a good run for its money. This apex predator of the rainforest has a maximum weight of around twenty-five pounds and a wingspan of six to eight feet. These massive wings—believe it or not—are relatively short in relation to its body size, a unique adaptation for weaving among the branches of thick forests.

Consider for a moment the power, skill, and equipment required to pluck adult howler monkeys and sloths from the rainforest canopy. Harpy eagles have feet the size of large human hands and talons longer than the claws of a brown bear. The "flying wolf" is armed with useful tools designed not only to kill but also to carry prey that weighs half their own body weight.

Or consider the fact that it is a stunningly beautiful animal. Its pearl-gray and graphite coloration is subtle but definitive, and every aspect of its physical makeup points to a creature that has reached the pinnacle of evolutionary perfection. Above the heart-shaped face, a uniquely beautiful double crest can be erected at will, giving the bird a decidedly fierce appearance.

Finally, consider the fact that even its nomenclature speaks volumes about the bird's presence and personality. The name "harpy" comes from the Greek word *harpazein*, which means "to snatch." Harpy eagles are named after the harpies of ancient mythology who were part-human, part-raptor personifications of the destructive elements of wind. The wind spirits that seized souls and carried them off. I was reminded of Dante's famous fourteenth-century epic poem:

> *Here the repellent harpies make their nests,*
> *Who drove the Trojans from the Strophades*
> *With dire announcements of the coming woe.*
> *They have broad wings, a human neck and face,*
> *Clawed feet and swollen, feathered bellies: they caw*
> *Their lamentations in the eerie trees.*

I was grateful for Martin's help. Without him, I knew that my search for this enigmatic species would be futile. Few people have seen these birds in the wild, and searching with a local guide who is familiar with the terrain and habitats was critical to the success of my show.

The Amerindian guide reminded me of my years spent with Norman and Rockerman back home at Phinda. As I set up the scope and video equipment, I remembered seeing crowned eagles hunting vervet monkeys in the sand forest with Norman. Then there was the time Rockerman spotted a massive martial eagle feeding on a young nyala. Birds so strong and fierce that they can kill large mammals. I had seen the two most powerful African eagles, and I marveled at how lucky I was to film their South American counterpart, a continent away in the remote rainforest of Guyana.

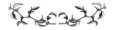

High above me, the eaglet is not about to be upstaged by my memories of African eagles. He is feeding on something large, probably a sloth, a peccary, or a monkey. Closer inspection reveals the remains of a capuchin monkey. Known for its intelligence, the capuchin is most often recognized as the organ grinder's pet, the clever performer who does tricks and collects coins. But in the forest, survival requires more than street smarts. This arboreal dweller is also a favorite meal of the harpy eagle.

Without warning, the parent eagles fly off, leaving the youngster alone with his meal. While the eaglet is preoccupied, we cross the creek to seek out a better position for filming. This is one of the birding highlights of my life.

I am mesmerized as the young eagle tears voraciously into the carcass. The camera rolls the whole time, capturing every nuanced movement. My mind recounts everything I've ever read about harpy eagles, arguably the most sought-after eagle species on the planet.

I begin to outline a story I can relate to the camera, the narrative glue needed to bring this moment to life for my armchair viewers. It's really all about the superb design of this aerial apex predator. The short wings for weaving, the long claws for grasping, the keen eyes and ears for hunting, its appearance of half ferocious woman, half vulture-like creature. And here I am in Guyana, one of few places left on earth to see these eagles.

The camera continues to roll. A shooting pain interrupts my mental run-through and narration of harpy eagle knowledge. I instinctively grab the back of my neck. Staring upward, not wanting to miss a moment of drinking in the sight of the youngster feeding in the fork of the majestic kapok tree, I am developing a severe case of warbler neck. This is a real affliction birdwatchers suffer as a result of looking skyward for long periods of time, their necks extended in an unnatural position.

We finish filming the young harpy and reluctantly head back, drenched in sweat. My cameraman is waiting for me back up the path, setting up to capture the on-screen interpretive footage necessary to complete the segment.

"Imagine the implications for the villagers of these remote jungles if harpy eagles were double their current size!" I say enthusiastically to the camera. "They would be hunting humans in the villages nearby."

Smoking ponies! The show is a wrap.

We are finished and must leave this paradise in the South American jungle. I will miss Martin. Our stories are parallel but continents apart. We both had close encounters with the apex predators of the skies at a young age, our lives changed forever by witnessing an eagle in the grip of the hunt. It is somehow fortuitous he was my guide on this trip.

There is much to think about on the plane back to the States, and my head is spinning. Three Golden Birds in the bag. The elusive sun parakeets. The colorful Guianan cock-of-the-rock. And my prize sighting, the mythical harpy eagle. Three episodes to edit and produce.

My dream of producing a birding TV show is now a reality. I'm already jotting down additional exotic BATV locations and potential sponsors I need to contact.

Flying high, I am just so happy, looking forward to seeing my family after a long trip. I am not prepared for the abrupt turn my life will take.

A few days later, I find myself paralyzed in the ICU of John F. Kennedy Hospital in Palm Beach, Florida.

"You need to make sure that anyone close to him comes right away," I overhear Dr. Goldenberg talking in hushed tones to Rebecca, my wife. She is visibly shaken, and I can hear her sobbing. "There is a strong possibility that he won't make it."

Although in excruciating pain, I am fully lucid and aware of my surroundings. The Heparin drip and Coumadin pills have caused my lower spine to hemorrhage. I cannot move my legs, feel my feet, wiggle my toes. I have lost the ability to walk.

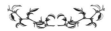

How I came to be lying in the ICU of JFK Memorial Hospital listening to the fragility of my life is a frantic journey along the border of life and death. It began with the pain in my neck while viewing the harpy eagle in Guyana. Then, the evening after I returned from Guyana, I was in a car returning to a Chicago hotel from a talk I had just delivered on African wildlife.

Suddenly I had the most intense migraine. I never got migraines, so I knew there was something wrong. Vertigo overtook my body, and I lost my sense of balance. It felt as though the car was negotiating an earthquake. Then I felt radical tingling in my left arm. The thought flashed through my mind that maybe I was suffering a heart attack.

I immediately asked the astonished driver, who had been one of the guests at my talk, to take me to the nearest hospital. The doctors suspected some kind of tropical disease and conducted a lumbar puncture to examine my spinal fluid. I spent the night in the Chicago hospital. In the morning, they released me and told me

I probably had a sudden-onset migraine. I flew back home to West Palm Beach in Florida that afternoon, unaware that I had likely suffered a series of mini-strokes.

That evening, lying in bed at home, my symptoms reappeared. I was in radical pain, worse than before. Rebecca immediately rushed me to JFK Hospital. The new doctors ruled out the obvious suspects — severe migraine, meningitis, malaria. They then thought it could be a tropical disease from Guyana. When the barrage of tests came back negative, the tropical disease doctors were left scratching their heads.

Three days after admittance, the hospital staff finally decided that my symptoms were consistent with someone who had suffered a stroke. Dr. Goldenberg, a well-respected neurologist, was summoned to my bed in the ICU to run a series of tests. A contrast-dye MRI of my brain revealed the doctor's worst fears. I had suffered an intracranial vertebral arterial dissection, or VAD. This occurs when the walls of the artery to the brain split or tear, severely reducing the flow of blood to the brain. When it heals, a clot forms and in most cases results in a major stroke and death. A rare condition usually found only through autopsies, it's the foremost cause of strokes in young and middle-aged people. I was only thirty-eight.

"How did this happen?" I ask.

Just a few days ago, I was in South America. Swimming, fishing, hiking through the Amazon, listening to screaming pihas, seeking out Golden Birds. Now I am immobilized in the ICU, the only sound the beeping of medical equipment and soft voices.

The doctor ticks off the causes. "Neck strain from injury, trauma, extreme extension of the neck … We need to start treatment right away. You have less than fifty percent blood flow to your brain right now. At best, you may be paralyzed the rest of your life. At worst … "

The doctor does not need to finish the sentence.

I sense how close to death I am.

That neck pain in the rainforest, looking upwards for hours at the prized harpy eagle. Warbler neck would have been a blessing.

This ferocious pain is much more sinister, as if the harpazein is trying to snatch my life from me.

In order to stop the bleeding from my lower spine, Dr. Goldenberg decides to take me off the Heparin drip, but the risk of stroke is now greatly increased. I am caught in a catch-22. Put me on blood thinners and I bleed uncontrollably. Don't put me on blood thinners and I will more than likely have a major stroke as the dissection heals, forming a tissue blockage of my artery. This is the critical juncture of my treatment.

Dr. Goldenberg opts for a balanced approach, carefully monitoring the seepage from my spine, while thinning my blood as much as he can, through the Coumadin pills, to reduce the risk of another stroke.

"Your family is waiting to see you," he says. "We'll start treatment within the hour."

I understand the gravity of his words. I must say good-bye to my family, possibly the last memory my young children will have of me.

How do you say farewell to a five-year-old? A three-year-old? A two-year-old? What words do you use to express your hopes and dreams for their future? Knowing you might not be there for them? How do you leave them with a lasting memory of your love for them?

The hardest part for me is being conscious the entire time and hearing the crying, the hushed voices, the palpable tension and sadness in the air. It is all so cold and clinical. I watch as they hook up the IVs and start the flow of drugs that will either save my life or kill me. My future will be defined by the delicate balance in the elixir flooding through my veins.

I am helpless, lying in that weird state between life and death. Fully conscious of everyone around me. The worry. The fear. I must be strong. And optimistic. I will get through this, I vow. I want to live. But my priorities have changed. Each of my kids gives me a long hug. The two youngest innocently begin to clown around until Rebecca reprimands them. I beg her to let them keep on. I want to see them happy, their shining, beaming, mischievous faces.

Before this, wildlife was the all-consuming thing in my life. It was everything I dreamed of and lived for. But near death experiences have a drastic way of waking you up and showing you

what's really important. I pray that I can get through this. I beg
God to give me eternal paralysis in exchange for the opportunity
to survive and see my kids grow up. I start my negotiations with
God. "God, if you get me through this, I promise to be your faithful
servant forever. I promise to never take your name in vain again."

In that ICU unit, I start thinking about how selfish my life has
been. I have always had wanderlust. Not just any wanderlust. The
selfish, all-consuming kind. As a child, I would run away from
home, driving my poor parents into a desperate frenzy. And it continues to this day. I don't know what triggers it. It just rolls in, like
a fog. I get bored and the desire to leave the comfy life I have built
overtakes me. It starts as an itch, then grows into a craving. All I
need do is call up one of my friends and we're off.

I remember when Rebecca was expecting our first child. She
was about seven months pregnant when Richard came to Cape
Town for a visit. We got drunk and started reminiscing about our
carefree days at Phinda, when we would spontaneously head out
on adventures.

"Let's go to the Kalahari," I said. "It's a bit of a drive, but a European redstart has shown up, and there are also a few rare larks I
need for my South African list."

When most people plan a trip through Africa, they organize for
weeks or months. Each leg of the journey, every aspect of the itiner-
ary is planned in advance, along with supplies and contingencies.
A reliable vehicle, usually a Land Rover, is a necessity. But not for
me.

Richard and I packed a few necessities into my old front-wheel-
drive VW Golf, meant for city driving. Binoculars and cameras,
fishing gear and tents. Snacks and beer and cigarettes. First aid kit,
spare tires, and jerrycans for fuel. Richard and I crammed as much
stuff as possible into the tiny car, everything we could think of in
an hour.

Then off we headed north to the Kalahari, the sole purpose of
our trip to find a vagrant European bird species that had overshot
its regular migration destination and a few different lark species.
Larks are not everyone's favorites, drab brown, hard to find, but a
great family of birds for experienced birders to add to their life lists.

We stopped on the way, adding Barlow's lark and red lark to
my southern African bird list. We arrived in the Kalahari after a

fourteen-hour drive, Cape Town then a distant memory. We were about to lose cell phone reception when I received an urgent message.

"I've gone into premature labor," Rebecca texted. "I'm in the hospital."

Now a good husband would have turned around immediately. Left the desert and the birds and driven at top speed to be by his expectant wife's side. And that was my intention. But, I must admit, I had to stop on the way back to spend a frustrating two hours waiting for a nice pair of Sclater's larks to come into a cattle trough to drink. With an unusually large bill and teardrop marks below the eyes, Sclater's lark was arguably the toughest of the three lark species that I needed, and I was totally exhilarated.

However, I returned to find an angry wife, pumped full of antilabor drugs. Which I am sure made her incredibly emotional. It certainly couldn't have been me and my preoccupation with birding that upset her! Rebecca should be awarded the gold medal for patience and endurance.

Wanderlust has always been the mistress in my marriage. I just can't escape it. It's been an obsession of mine since I was young. This was not the only time my yearning for adventure took precedence over family and friends. Lying there in the ICU, I firmly resolved that if I made it through this ordeal, my priorities in life would be forever altered.

Over the next few days, I lie with my immediate family and loved ones at my side. I see with new eyes how my obsession with wildlife has affected the people around me. I develop a new perspective about the relationships that mean the most to me. My life priorities are now shifting.

I spend as much time as possible with my family, trying to act positive, not knowing if I will ever see them again. My mum and dad fly over from South Africa. My sister flies in from the UK. Other family and friends are not allowed into the ICU, so Rebecca starts an online support page. Every day, she reads me all the good wishes from family and friends, many of whom I have not heard from in years.

Her entries in the support site reflect the dire circumstances of my condition.

> Nov 5, 2008 8:54 pm
>
> Today was a relatively good day. James is in considerable pain but there were no major upsets ... which is great. Tomorrow (Thursday) is a big day. They are giving him a baby aspirin. It seems OUTRAGEOUS for a 6′ 3″ man to be potentially threatened by a simple baby aspirin.
>
> Essentially, the baby aspirin thins his blood and he absolutely needs that in order to help his blood flow to his brain ... BUT the aspirin thins his blood and puts the hematoma at risk. The hematoma sits on the nerves of his spine and he is at risk of paralysis.... So the doctors said that if James' hematoma shows any growth tomorrow then he will need immediate back surgery. The surgery to remove the hematoma is very invasive and is risky. So we wait for tomorrow.
>
> James' visitation is extremely restricted as they try to keep his blood pressure and pulse controlled. He is not allowed to have too much stimulation because his brain needs rest. Kids are not allowed in ICU so he is missing them so much. But I have amazing support here and have been able to sit by him and hold his hand. I have been able to take a lot of time for him which has been so nice – I have not had one-on-one time with him in so long so we are actually finishing conversations. There are blessings in this time. There is awesome family support around us.... This has been huge.
>
> Please pray for James. Please pray for all the unknowns. There are all these one in a million incidences creeping into each situation and right now our prayer is that they stop and he heals. We need miracles.
>
> Love, Becks and Family

Nov 7, 2008 10:04pm

They gave James the aspirin today. The threat of a stroke or worse is a big issue with James. The blood thinner is important in bringing down this risk. But the neurosurgeon warned James that the time of healing is actually one of riskiest times for stroke. I think this set us back a lot because we really want to keep moving forward. We want to feel "out of the woods" and the neurosurgeon does not allow for that....

This morning before the pain came back, James was able to read all the messages we had printed off and with so much happiness and laughter. It means so much seeing his face smile at times like this so thank you all so much for giving him those moments.

I believe that great faith comes from great trials because even in the trials the purest life blessings emerge. For James, during this trial, he has seen so much love and he is peaceful about any path ahead. I have never seen him so weak but I have also never seen him so strong. It is amazing what a week can do. He credits this strength to love and friendship and he asks you to continue to pray or send your most positive thoughts. I see how uplifting they are to him in his lonely hospital world — and I am also deeply thankful for your gift of light to him.

Love and Faith,

Rebecca

It's a weird experience being fully conscious and alert but yet knowing that I am walking a tightrope, with my life barely visible at the end of the rope and death swirling everywhere in the valley below. Time is suspended as the drugs course through my veins. Family comes and goes. I am surrounded by love and prayers.

One day becomes two and then a week passes. Slow steady improvement, then relapses. Gradually, my condition improves somewhat, although I am still basically paralyzed from the waist down. I am told that if I recover my activities will be severely restricted. No more surfing. No more birding. No more tennis. No more active lifestyle. I may be bedridden for months. Maybe a physiotherapist can teach me to walk again.

After two weeks, the tests show a miraculous recovery. In most cases, the VAD forms a large clot, completely blocking the flow of blood to the brain. My vertebral artery didn't clot the whole way through but branched off and formed hundreds of little channels of rivers through my brain. The imaging shows a whole tributary of multiple arteries, oddly resembling the myriad waterways that form the Okavango Delta.

After endless days of hovering between life and death, I am going home.

> Nov 11, 2008 2:02 pm
> Hi Friends and Family:
>
> I am home! The last 2 weeks have been an incredible journey. It has been, and remains, a surreal feeling that something so small and freakish can turn a life around so fast.
>
> First things first, an update ... I am on bed-rest for 2 weeks and will be on blood pressure and anticoagulant medication for 6 months until there is no further risk of clotting of the vertebral artery. My doctors will be doing periodic angiograms/MRIs to review the healing of the artery but my headaches have greatly reduced and my blood pressure is down, both very positive signs. I am learning to walk properly again after the spinal challenge and am nearly fully functional, except for a little break-dancing kick from my right leg (which I may decide to keep for party purposes).
>
> There will be limitations for me going forward ... no surfing, contact sports — and hard-core birding! — but this a small price to pay for being able to see my beautiful wife Rebecca and the kids every morning.
>
> I want to thank each and every one of you for your positive thoughts and prayers. It's amazing what the power of collective thought can achieve — my doctors say my recovery thus far has been remarkable. Although there is still a ways for me to go, I'm confident that I'm on the mend and that this thing will only affect

my life positively going forward. To all of you, I love you all so much. A special thank-you to my sister Melissa for coming out from the UK and to my parents for making the trip from SA.

Becs, you are the BEST wife a guy could wish for. I love you so much. To all my friends, colleagues and &Beyonders you guys are all super-cool and I am eternally grateful for all your thoughts. Hopefully I can get back on the horse soon. Until then, take care and thanks again all.

p.s. I heard somewhere that long-boarding isn't surfing so I guess that'll be ok. ...

James

Today, as I write this, I am back to normal. I have beaten the odds. The tingling sensation in my left arm is still there from time to time. But I resumed my active lifestyle almost immediately after recovery, and for the last few years I have been surfing, playing tennis, and traveling the world looking for rare birds and amazing wildlife.

The cause of my near-death experience was looking too long at a harpy eagle! I've always had a premonition that I would die in some dramatic fashion—attacked by a lion, trampled by an elephant, gored by a buffalo, torn to bits by a shark. But coming so close to death because of excessive bird watching?! That is just too wimpish a death ...

And so it was that an eagle sparked my love and passion for wildlife and it was the wind spirit of another eagle that nearly took it all away.

MASTER OF THE SKIES

THE EAGLE

This morning he is perched in the same old tree
An extension of the earth
I watch him for a while and look with awe
At the splendour of his worth

Am I not privileged to spend this time
With a master of the skies?
As he relates to me a time before
The opening of my eyes

His words fall softer than the autumn leaves
Tales of a distant land
A place that instills deep within
A loyalty so grand

So alas the wind has come for him
As he spreads his wings to fly
To this warmer place he holds so dear
As Winter time is nigh

Now I watch the circling of his flight
As he climbs the thermal stair
A pilot of freedom and pure delight
Cradled by the air

JAMES ALEXANDER CURRIE

I SEE A MAJESTIC BIRD, SOARING in the distance. It alights on a fence post as if waiting for me. Through my birding scope, I can see that it is a golden eagle, the largest raptor in North America.

"Back in the van, everyone. Let's get closer to see this great bird!"

It is a beautiful morning in July on the salt flats in northern Utah. I am escorting a group on a birding tour. The trip coleader is Tice Supplee, director of bird conservation at Audubon Arizona. Accompanying us on the tour are others from the National Audubon Society and several sponsors of the show. It is here that I meet Bonnie Fladung, my future coauthor of this book.

I strike up a conversation with Tice and discover that she has recently been on safari in Africa. She remembers quite vividly her ranger guide and asks if perhaps I know him. His name is Norman Mabika.

Of course I know him! The other half of our tracking team at Phinda, the best man at my wedding, my understudy who wanted to become a ranger, like me. And who fulfilled his dream by becoming the "world famous Zulu Norman." Whoever was lucky enough to go on safari with him would remember him as one of the most fearless and entertaining guides in Africa.

I am delighted to hear that he is doing well, as I have been trying to contact him these past few months. Tice and I exchange stories and remark on what a small world it is.

I return home and throw myself into preparations for the busy fall season. There are destinations to coordinate for BATV, speaking engagements and schedules, and the all-important task of getting the kids ready for school. My days are a blur of activity until I am stopped dead in my tracks one morning. Catching up on correspondence, I open my inbox to see an e-mail from Tice. The content of the message jolts me to the core.

"I just found out from a contact in South Africa ... I am so sorry to be the bearer of sad news. ... Norman has passed away. ... He died from AIDS. ..."

The words jump off the page. I am jolted as if a Zulu spear has pierced through my heart. The old wound is reopened. First Rockerman, then Jackie. Then whispers of other trackers I knew. And now Norman. Can't be. Just can't be. He was such a strong character, so lively and vibrant and full of life. I am overcome with sadness at the loss of another close friend, at the thought of his grieving widow and children. What is happening to my country and my people?

While I have had many close brushes with death, some by chance and some by choice, I have been given a reprieve. But in what seems a brief passing of time, Norman is gone.

My adventures started with the magnificent black eagle and almost ended with the mysterious harpy. But the tale continues, as the mystical golden eagle beckons me forward.

I hear the eagle's cry as it arches back its head and beckons the dawn. I've always been somewhat disappointed by the meek nature of all eagles' calls. These top avian predators have high-pitched cries that hardly evoke images of fierce and powerful hunters.

But in my life eagles roar.

They roar deeper than any lion.

Louder than the throaty calls of tigers.

PLACE OF DREAMS

What will come last will be the truth
Since the beating of the heart outlasts
The nakedness of the bones.
Yes, in time we shall grow wise
Mazisi Kunene,
"World Wisdom"

Zimbila zantabanye.
They are rock rabbits of the same mountain.
Zulu proverb

PHINDA HAS A MYSTERIOUS HOLD on me and is calling me to return once again. This time, I am not on a journey to seek out wildlife or adventures. I am going because I am haunted by the faces of those who passed before me. Because I am haunted by the promises I made and never kept. I am going back to Phinda to make peace with whatever I shall find.

The last time I saw Rockerman, he was lying in a filthy hospital bed, a mere shell of his former self. His death had been fast and dramatic, his funeral a hazy memory. I barely remember speaking with his family; I was in such a state of grief. Young people just don't die! I made a deathbed promise to him, that I would look after his son. Yet I never so much as tried to contact the young boy in the years to follow.

I had also lost contact with Norman, as I grew busy starting my own family, my own business, moving a continent away. The last time I saw him, he was smiling and waving farewell to Rebecca and me as we boarded the plane with our young family.

Norman had a young family of his own, and I called out to him. "You take care of those handsome boys and teach them everything you know! I'll see you soon," I promised.

It was a false promise, as I soon became busy with my new life and responsibilities. By then, Rebecca and I had three young children and were settling into our home in Florida. I was establishing a business, which involved traveling and speaking. It was on one of these business trips to Utah that I met Tice, from whom I later learned about Norman's fate.

Why did the harsh African landscape have to take such promising lives? Why were the biggest threats from the smallest life forms? Not from lions, elephants, leopards, rhinos, and buffalo but from tsetse flies bearing nagana, mosquitos carrying malaria, and now the AIDS virus. Silent killers that worked internally, damaging the body from within, wearing it down bit by bit. Not large beasts that you could face down and blast with a Magnum .375. AIDS was an insidious killer, masquerading as flu, pneumonia, tuberculosis, and malaria and even blamed on witchcraft.

I lost both of my closest tracker partners to this killer disease, both young men in the prime of their lives, both my age with bright futures. Devastating blows.

Now I am heading back to seek out their families. What will I find? Rockerman's son would be a young man by now. Would he have his own family? Would Norman's two boys be aspiring trackers and rangers, inheriting their father's skills? Or will they have met the same dark fate, victims of this awful disease? I am hoping it is not too late to see Norman's and Rockerman's faces reflected in the next generation.

I board the plane with my family. It's been six long years since I visited Maputaland and my precious Phinda. I have mixed feelings. I am excited to show my three children the place where I had such incredible adventures. Where animals larger than life roam the savannahs and hunt freely, without fear of being hunted. Where I grew up and found friendships that I expected would last a lifetime.

It's one of the last places on earth where the vibrancy of life and the finality of death are separated by a veil so sheer you can almost touch it, like the diaphanous web of a golden orb spider. A web created out of one of the strongest fibers on the planet, yet capable of being destroyed by a simple barb. Like the thorn that grows on the wag 'n bietjie tree, which is common across many parts of southern Africa.

Wag 'n bietjie is Afrikaans for "wait a bit." Nearly every inch of every branch is covered with thorns, in pairs of two—one pair rapierlike, straight and forward facing, the other pair like an eagle's talons, recurved and backward facing. One of nature's mysteries, a branch designed so perfectly to grab you coming and going, to open up the veil to the next world. This is the branch used by the Zulus to transport the spirits of the dead to their final resting place in the household. Because the revered ancestors are always there, just beyond the veil. Brooding over each descendant with a watchful eye, offering advice in dreams, agonizing over galling behavior and rejoicing over good fortune.

I remember seeing a YouTube video posted by a recent guest at Zulu Nyala, where Norman was working. He is telling the story of the buffalo thorn, the wait-a-bit tree. He is standing tall, as tall as a short Zulu can stand, his white teeth flashing a smile, his words carefully crafted. There is no trace left of the rough and tumble poacher. His transformation to polished ranger is complete.

"The Zulus believe that the buffalo thorn is the tree of life," Norman begins. "Each branch is zigzag-shaped with many thorns. The forward-facing thorns are there to remind us to always have dreams and look forward. The backward-facing thorns remind us to never forget our past, where we come from, lessons learnt and the lives of our ancestors and close friends.

"If you have the misfortune of walking into this tree, it will pierce you with the forward-facing thorns, and as you jolt backwards in pain, the backward-facing thorns grab you, dig into your skin, and refuse to let you go." Norman holds up a branch and shows it to the guests.

"So if you walk into the buffalo thorn, don't beat a hasty retreat. Wait a bit. Take your time. Extricate yourself carefully. This is what life is like. It is not a straight road, and there are many twists and turns as we embark on life's journey."

I think about Norman and the buffalo thorn on the long plane ride. It had been quite a shock to learn, purely by chance, of his passing. Why didn't he contact me when he learned he was ill? Why didn't he respond to any of my attempts to get in touch with him? Surely he would have reached out to me, our friendship was that close. We were *abafowethu*, blood brothers, held together by the backward-facing thorns of the thorn tree.

How long had he been ill? Did he try to save himself by taking ARVs? Or did he delay in seeking out treatment? What became of his young family, his beautiful widow and handsome sons? Did their hopes and dreams disappear along with Norman, slipping off the forward-facing thorns of the buffalo thorn? My mind spins with questions, zigzagging through the possibilities, as I fly over the ocean and back to my homeland.

It's referred to as the "new sickness." The "you-know-what." The *amagama amathathu*. The "three words." Rarely spoken of directly, yet over one-third of the sexually active population of South Africa carry the HIV/AIDS virus, with the province of Kwazulu Natal especially hard hit. And it has taken the lives of most of the trackers I knew while I was on the reserve in the late 1990s.

AIDS is a slow-motion epidemic with a long incubation period between the initial infection and the onset of symptoms. A person can carry the virus for years and even decades with no indication, passing the death sentence along silently to unwitting partners. Like a house dismantled from the inside, leaving the structure standing and looking intact before the bomb is detonated, the HIV virus weakens the body until it crumbles in on itself, from whatever opportune infection happens to ignite the final sequence.

Until the acceptance of antiretroviral drugs (ARVs) in the 2000s, families witnessed the unexpected deaths of their family members and friends from a multitude of recognizable symptoms that did not respond to traditional treatments. It was a mystery how young, healthy people could succumb so quickly.

Funeral by funeral, on death certificates the cause was listed as infections or diseases they were familiar with. Tuberculosis, pneumonia, malaria, diarrhea, meningitis, cancers, skin infections, lung disease, unexplained weight loss. Diseases that commonly take lives in these poverty-stricken areas where medical care was scarce. The subtle difference was that these were people who would normally have survived, had their immune systems not been compromised. Day by day, young people were dying from these opportunistic infections.

AIDS was never talked about openly, and even today it seems to be taboo to openly address the topic. People are just *gula*, sick, and they never die of AIDS. People are almost too afraid to confront this silent killer, unlike anything they have ever known.

But confront it they must if there is any hope of prevention. The key is education at the grassroots level. But how do you tell people that their romantic interests could kill them? That a simple dalliance could set off a catastrophic series of events that affects individuals, families, communities, the whole society? That sex and childbirth, life-affirming activities, are now coupled with the fear of death?

How do you integrate Western health-care protocols and sexual practices—like using condoms for protection, or abstinence, or fidelity—into a society that for thousands of years relied on polygyny and their large extended family structures for survival? In a culture based on a patriarchal society, where one's manhood is measured by the number of wives and children one has, where multigenerational families are the norm, the ramifications of this disease hit hard.

When Rockerman died in 1999, there was a lot of ignorance surrounding how AIDS was transmitted. Back then, people thought it could be caught simply by touching an infected individual or breathing the same air. Or from a doctor's needle or a blood test. Victims were heavily stigmatized and ostracized. It would take years to educate the population that heterosexual relations were the primary method of transmission.

The latency of onset of symptoms further complicated the cultural awareness. Unlike most of the diseases that had a more immediate cause and effect, this sneaky virus defied all the rules. It lay dormant for years, slowly strangling the immune system, until an opportune infection took hold, usually within eight to twelve years of infection. The cause and effect were not immediately apparent.

The local healers, the *sangomas*, were the first line of health care, and their advice was highly prized. They were often capable of treating symptoms and infections with their herbs and natural remedies. But the sangomas had no knowledge that the bodies they were now treating were harboring an insidious killer that served as a conduit. The *muthi* they offered as a cure for the various illnesses would be ineffective, since the symptoms were just the outward signs of an opportunistic path to death through a weakened immune system. To the sangomas, who did not have sufficient knowledge of the underlying disease, unexplained death was attributed to the will of the ancestors, or possibly even witchcraft.

If the patient eventually sought out Western medical care, it was usually too late. They were already dying, often a difficult and prolonged death accompanied by fever, nausea, sores, nerve damage, and just generally wasting away. The hospitals were accustomed to dealing with acute conditions, like knife wounds, panga attacks, gunshots, snakebites, accidents. If you were streaming blood, they would patch you up. If a snake bit you, they would administer antivenom. They would have you up and out the door as soon as possible so they could minister to the next victim.

But back when Rockerman was dying, the hospitals and staff were not sufficiently equipped for dealing with the AIDS-related debilitating illnesses. Antiretroviral drugs were not available yet. The patients, even if admitted, received minimal care. Like Rockerman, they would be left to die a miserable and lonely death. And as in Rockerman's case, the underlying cause was seldom listed on the death certificate and a patient would be just another number, death usually attributed to tuberculosis.

It was 2001 when I learned that Jackie, the translator for my thesis project, had died of AIDS. By now, the disease was recognized worldwide, but South Africa was heavily in denial mode about the seriousness of the epidemic. Thabo Mbeki, then president of South Africa, was following in the footsteps of one of my heroes, Nelson Mandela, continuing Mandela's legacy admirably, and I really liked Mbeki as a president and as a person. Unfortunately, one of the dark moments of his presidency was the way he downplayed the rising HIV infection rates while exaggerating the toxicity of the newly released antiretroviral drugs, his position being that international pharmaceutical companies bent on making profits out of victims were spreading the disease.

Mbeki's controversial beliefs caused a delay in getting the needed drugs to the population that lasted years. Hundreds of thousands of people died, and the disease spread to epidemic levels as denialism filtered down from the highest levels of the government. Failure to recognize the disease, its cause and effects, continued to propagate stigma and discrimination at every level of society.

With the passing of Rockerman and Jackie, Phinda lost two amazing resources. Rockerman was a seasoned tracker who could read the animals and terrain like the back of his hand. Jackie was an educated interpreter who bridged the local culture and the foreign clientele he was serving. AIDS was killing the people trained to protect the wildlife and maintain the relations with the surrounding communities. Both had traveled a road from poverty to success, only to die in the prime of their lives, leaving behind grieving families, children and widows. Leaving a hole in the Phinda community and also in my life.

As the managing director of the nonprofit Africa Foundation in the mid-2000s, I continued to see firsthand the devastating effect and tumultuous impact on the lives of the people of Maputaland, an area with one of the highest rates of HIV infection in the world, over one in three adults, or forty percent of the adult population. So in the mid-2000s the statistics reflected the cresting wave. But the numbers and charts would never be able to capture the loss at all levels, from the personal tragedies to the void created by the loss of valuable skills and resources.

I would visit Mrs. Zikhali's school, bordering Phinda, and witness her patient care of all the children, especially the AIDS orphans. Her commitment to education started in the late 1980s and now included community outreach to families affected by the epidemic, making sure the surviving children had uniforms, food, and after-school care.

The local clinics supported by Africa Foundation at Mduku, Mnqobokazi, and Nibela were dealing with heavy caseloads of AIDS patients, offering confidential HIV testing at their Voluntary Counseling and Testing Centers, and supplying ARVs. HIV testing has always been and will continue to be a source of anxiety. Many refuse testing because it's better not to know, not to suffer the stigma of being labeled HIV positive. After all, there is no cure, and the ARVs are only given when your CD4 levels are sufficiently low. So why test until absolutely necessary?

At the same time, the role of the sangoma in the daily lives of the people was expanding to respond to the epidemic. Traditional healers are highly respected within their communities and understand the cultural impact of disease. Efforts were increasingly being made to train them to recognize the signs of AIDS, deal with the side effects of the ARVs, and provide emotional support. The sangomas were the answer to providing a crucial link between Western medicine and traditional remedies.

During the mid 2000s, ARVs became available. But even these life-saving drugs were initially only given when a patient was really sick. So while ARVs offered a lifeline, they are also a daily reminder that you are sick, carrying a deadly disease and dependent on Western medicine for survival for the rest of your life. There is no cure in sight and no preventive vaccine.

When Norman died in 2010, HIV/AIDS education and prevention programs were in full swing. He must have known ARV treatment was available. Did he get tested in time? In many cases, people postpone testing because they feel healthy. They will turn to the clinics when some opportune infection is running rampant through the weakened body. Did Norman wait until it was too late? Why didn't he contact me?

I had many questions and hoped to find answers.

This time I was not venturing into Maputaland as a rogue ranger looking for fun, or as a student delving deep into community attitudes and perceptions, or as the director of a nonprofit managing community projects. I was on a deeply personal mission, returning to search out the fate of my friends' families. While hopeful, the reality was that too much time may have passed. Africa has a way of swallowing up its dead and leaving no traces.

Before boarding the plane, I made contact with my old friend Benson to ask for help with my search. I trusted Benson with more than just my life, and our friendship had lasted through many years of distance. I knew I could count on Benson. He lived with his wife and family five minutes from the reserve in the Zulu village of

Mduku. I visited there often when I was a ranger. So often, in fact, that his young daughters teased me about being a substitute father.

Benson was well connected, with many friends and acquaintances in the community. Even though separated by vast distances, communication between the Zulu communities is fluid. The traditional bush telegraph is still active and now assisted by cell phones. If anyone could help me, it would be Benson. But when I arrived, he had mixed news.

"Nearly everyone at Phinda lost touch with the families of both of them," he informed me.

I was devastated, as I knew how easily people in rural Kwa-Zulu-Natal slip away into anonymity, especially if they leave their communities for some reason. Most rural people have limited access to technology, and Western ways of contacting someone are fruitless. Forget about e-mail, Facebook, and LinkedIn. Strangely though, even the poorest of rural people manage to secure cell phones, and I was hopeful that Benson would at least have a phone number for me.

He did have one piece of good news. By a crazy coincidence, his wife, Caroline, happened to be a cousin of Rockerman's widow, Jabu. She left the area following Rockerman's death and moved all the way to Richards Bay, one hundred miles to the south. But Caroline happily provided me with Jabu's phone number.

"Yes, the kids and I can meet you tomorrow," Rockerman's widow said.

What did she mean when she said she wanted me to meet the "kids"? Rockerman's last words to me were that I should please take care of his son. There had been no mention of more than one child, or if there was, I had forgotten. I am intrigued.

Jabu and the kids took a harrowing two-hour taxi ride from Richards Bay to meet me in the easily mispronounced town of Hluhluwe. I was stunned to be greeted by three beautiful young women, ranging in age from thirteen to seventeen. I had gotten more than I bargained for!

"*Uphi umfana?*" I asked Rockerman's widow.

Where is the young man?

She replied that Rockerman's only son had died as a young boy, presumably of AIDS, and that she was not the boy's mother. To make matters worse, the boy's mother died tragically in a car crash shortly after Rockerman's death. When she told me the young boy's name, my heart skipped a beat.

"Usicelo."

This was my African name, given to me by my isiXhosa professor at the University of Cape Town when I was eighteen years old. This was the name used by all my Zulu friends when they addressed me, and it became my entrenched Zulu name. Now I learned that Usicelo was also the name of the first of Rockerman's four children, born to a different mother in 1995, before he and Jabu were married. It was pure coincidence that we shared the same name, but I still felt incredibly humbled.

In a rare twist of fate, Rockerman did not live to meet my son, who was named after him. My son Joseph's middle name is Mavuso, Zulu for "one who has risen." And I, in turn, never got to meet his son who shared my name—Usicelo, Zulu for "the one who is requested."

Jabu introduced me to each of the three girls. Spending time with and learning about these beautiful kids was fascinating. How could I have lost touch with the blood of one of my dearest friends in the world?

Londiwe is the eldest daughter and wants to be a policewoman. Nokwanda, the one with the prettiest smile and who comes in first in her class, wants to be a schoolteacher. The youngest daughter, Ntombentle, which means "beautiful girl," wants to be a nurse.

I asked the girls what they needed, and I was touched to learn they wanted clothes and school supplies. Most Western girls their age would have asked for iPads, swanky clothes, or makeup. So we went shopping, as any dad and his daughters would do, and I watched proudly as Rockerman's girls picked out school clothes, calculators, and backpacks to further their dreams of becoming the teachers, nurses and policewomen of the future. We then all piled into the car and I drove them to meet Rebecca and my kids.

Why Rockerman never mentioned his daughters to me at his death, I will never know. Perhaps he felt safe in the knowledge that his wife would take care of the three girls but that his son was in some way vulnerable. Perhaps he was concerned that his son was his only male heir, and in his culture, as in many cultures, this was of paramount importance to him.

Either way, and whatever the reasons, I feel that I have let him down by not finding his boy sooner and offering up some sort of assistance. In many ways, it was too painful for me to be reminded of Rockerman's death, and perhaps this was my way of protecting myself from the grief of losing a loved one. Just move on and try to forget.

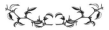

Later that evening, Benson sadly reports that nobody has heard of Norman's family for several years. The sole lead I have is that thirteen years earlier I traveled to a remote area of KwaJobe with Norman to meet his father-in-law, a Mr. Manzini. I know that his *kraal* is located far away in the community, close to the boundary of the Mkuze Game Reserve. That is all I know.

"Just ask anyone for Manzini's house," Benson says matter-of-factly. "Someone will be able to direct you there."

Benson's words are hard to believe because KwaJobe is a particularly large piece of community land that sits on the northern side of Phinda, sandwiched between Mkuze Game Reserve and the Greater St. Lucia Wetland Park. With a population of ten thousand and an area of over sixty-four square miles, the chances of locating Norman's family solely on a name seems daunting.

Now, with encouragement from Benson, I head out, armed with nothing but a last name and a general direction. As Rebecca and the three kids pile into the car, deep inside I am skeptical about finding any trace within this massive community. But we are off. Who knows what today's adventure will bring?

KwaJobe is a wonderfully beautiful piece of land that I visited frequently with Norman. The dirt track that accesses the community passes through Muzi Pan, one of the better birding sites in the area. We stop briefly to watch the flamingos, waterfowl, and African fish eagles, which abound in the nutrient-rich waters of the pan.

The sounds of grumpy hippos periodically punctuate the birdsong, and the banks of the pan shine golden-yellow, a reflection of the fever tree forests. The Zulu name for the fever tree is *umkhanyakude*, which means "shines from far," a much more accurate description than the English name, which is a reference to the early colonial belief that taking shelter under these trees gave one life-threatening fever. In reality, since the trees are mostly found near water, they share their environment with mosquitos, the true carriers of malaria.

I remember enough of KwaJobe to know that my best chance of finding the homestead is to stick to the main, severely potholed dirt road that traverses the entire community. This is the primary arterial route that locals use to go in and out. A map would have been useless, as none of the roads show up on commercial maps. As we weave along the winding dust tracks, I stop intermittently to inquire of any locals we pass on the road.

"Iphi ikhaya likaManzini?"

Do you know of the house of Manzini?

I am met with blank stares, as they try to interpret my Zulu, but I continue on. After too many hours of dodging wayward Nguni cattle, we hit the jackpot.

"Ja, I knew a Mr. Manzini," a young man on the side of the road answers. "But he died several years ago."

Drat! Still, it's a clue. I beg him to show me where the homestead is and offer him R50 for his troubles.

He smiles and happily squeezes into the car with us. We drive for several more dusty and jolting miles, finally arriving at the little farm that I remembered from so many years before.

Perched on the elevated banks of the Mkuze River, I recognized the place by the mixture of traditional and western buildings that is now all too common in rural Zululand. The main house was a western rectangular shape, and the two other secondary dwellings were constructed in the traditional, circular mud-and-thatch style.

When Norman and I visited over a decade ago, the adjoining garden was ripe with maize and pumpkins and traditional herbs for healing. The open *kraal* had held a small herd of cattle. Goats, chickens, and dogs roamed freely. The household was bustling with hope and energy.

All those years before, Norman and I had sat inside the main dwelling with Mr. Manzini. Over homemade beer and a simple meal, we discussed the old man's dream. He could see the success Norman had in the tourism industry and wanted to replicate it here.

A portion of the adjacent Mkuze Game Reserve had once been a Zulu homestead, and there was a traditional gravesite on this land. Mr. Manzini's ancestors were buried here. After the end of apartheid, the revamped reserve management recognized the local community's rights to this land.

Mr. Manzini's vision was simple. He wanted to build a tourist lodge on the community-owned portion of the land. The Zulus would educate visitors about their culture, embracing their heritage and sharing it with the world.

Employment in the lodge would provide a steady income for the locals and improve their standard of living. It would curb the exodus of young people looking for jobs in the white-ruled industrialized cities, like Johannesburg. Or becoming migrant laborers on farms or in the mines.

I had listened intently to his well-thought out plans, determined to help as much as I could. I even took the idea to business interests as far afield as Washington DC. But sadly, due to lack of interest from foreign investment and stonewalling from the management of the state-run reserve, the ambitious project never materialized.

"When two elephants fight, it is the grass that suffers" is a popular saying in eastern Africa. It's not just the people directly involved in the conflict who get hurt but the whole community.

So when this project was put on hold, the locals took out their frustration with violence. They entered the community section of the reserve, burned down the tourist shop and tore down the fences. The failure to acknowledge the rightful property claims of the KwaJobe people and support their efforts to engage in a project that would benefit the community had bitter ramifications and was another example of how the mistrust of over one hundred years of exclusion and lack of benefits is very hard to heal in an instant.

The memory of driving here with Norman and meeting with Mr. Manzini was fresh in my mind as if it were yesterday. But the years of neglect since his passing had taken their toll on the homestead. While the buildings looked much the same as they did the last time I was here, the gardens and *kraal* were strangely deserted. What clues would I find?

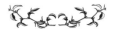

I negotiate a path between the scampering chickens and a single, malnourished dog. A bent old woman emerges from the simple dwelling. She is in the traditional Zulu attire of a colorful dress, beaded jewelry and a large red top hat.

"*Bakithi! Bakithi!*" she greets me.

I give the customary bow with raised hands, fingers pointed skyward as a sign of respect. I do not need to introduce myself. She remembers me from my previous visit with Norman. She takes my hands in hers and continues wailing.

"*Bakithi! Bakithi!*"

My ancestors! My ancestors!

Over and over.

This is a Zulu saying that is most often used to infer sympathy for someone when something terrible has happened. I return condolences for the loss of her husband.

"*Hawu Mama. Phepisa. Ngizwile kuba induna Manzini watshona. Ngiyajabula ukuvakasha futhi.*"

Mother, I'm so sorry. I heard that *induna* Manzini set. I am happy to visit with you again.

In Zulu there are several ways to talk about someone's death. The common way to mention a person's death is to use the verb *fa*, which means simply "to die." The word I always prefer to use for a loved one is *tshona*, which means to "set" like the sun. It infers that your loved one is not gone forever but that, just like the sun, he or she will rise again to a new day.

After offering my condolences about the loss of her husband, we talk about Norman. Since the old lady speaks no English, I speak in Zulu, trying my best to make myself understood.

"Where is Norman's widow, Fakazile, and the children?" I ask.

"She left with her mother and moved to Jozini," she replies. "I do not know the address."

In the manner of traditional Zulu society, Manzini had several wives. The woman I am speaking with is his first wife, or "head wife." She is accorded special status, which is why she may still live at the homestead, while Fakazile's mother, his second wife, moved on.

I am distressed to hear that Norman's family is living about an hour's drive farther north. It's late in the day, and we must return to our quarters. But this isn't a dead end. The old woman offers up

Fakazile's most recent phone number. She writes it down in a shaky scribble and I gladly take the scrap of paper from her.

"Fakazile is very ill," she tells me. "She has recently suffered a stroke."

Heartbreaking news that the mother of my friend's children is critically ill. How strange that someone so young could have a stroke. But then again, maybe not so strange, considering what had happened to me.

We bid our farewells and I leave in high spirits, knowing that the long and tiring day trip has not been in vain. We return to Benson's house to relate our adventure, and I dial the number, hoping to hear Fakazile's voice.

"The number you have dialed is incorrect. Please try again."

I am dismayed—after all we have gone through, the number is wrong!

Once again, Benson comes to my assistance, asking the trackers from KwaJobe to get the correct number. I thank him, and we return to our lodgings with heavy hearts.

The next morning Benson calls to let me know he has the number. What a miracle worker! The scribble on the paper was off by just one numeral.

I immediately call and am elated to finally speak with Fakazile. She recognizes me immediately.

"*Ngilinde isikati side kakhulu ukuva wena,*" she says.

I have waited a long time to hear your voice.

The morning shines bright as we pile into the car and head out. The roads are familiar now as we retrace yesterday's route, then veer northward toward the picturesque Jozini Dam. About a mile from the dam, Fakazile is waiting for us on the side of the road.

The kids and Rebecca join her, walking up the dirt track to the house. I follow behind in the car. It is quite something to see my kids walking barefoot in the African dust, the way all kids should grow up.

Inside the humble house, Fakazile introduces us to her mother and a small, shy boy. I recognize Norman's youngest son Siphephelo, who is now age ten and a spitting image of his father.

I am surrounded by memories of Norman. Pictures are everywhere, on the tables and mantel. This is when the floodgates open and I cry. Fakazile cries herself, recounting how Norman died right here in the house he had built for them. Brick by brick, he hauled the building materials in the car he had purchased with his gratuities from Phinda. Brick by brick, he built the house where he hoped to raise his sons to manhood.

"Why had he not contacted me?" I ask, looking at the picture on the mantelpiece of Norman and Rebecca and me on our wedding day in Cape Town, memories of happier times.

"Norman did try to contact you," she says. "He sent many messages to your e-mail address."

By then, Norman was a respected game ranger at a neighboring reserve where he had access to the Internet. But he had my defunct e-mail address, and all his messages to me disappeared into the ether.

I am devastated to learn that my good friend died without getting so much as a response from me. We were in touch fairly often at my old e-mail address and I was convinced that he had my new address. When my attempts to contact Norman by phone and e-mail failed, I suspected something was horribly wrong, but it would be a full year before I learned about his death.

I sit with Siphephelo on my lap as Fakazile fills me in on the goings on before and since Norman's passing. She is proud that both boys are excelling at school and tells how her eldest son Sibongiseni, now age fourteen, is living in Rustenburg with a preacher, trying to get a better education. Rustenburg has to be two hundred miles away, and I wonder how lonely it must be for a young boy to be uprooted from home without a mother or father.

She talks candidly about Norman's battle with AIDS, how he knew he had the disease and tried to go on antiretroviral therapy, but it was too late. ARVs can only be taken when the body is strong enough to handle the weakening effects of the powerful drugs. Norman's system was overrun and ravished by the disease, and his white blood cell count was too low for doctors to prescribe the ARVs. He died at home with his wife and boys at his side.

The story reminded me of my own brush with death, facing my young children and saying good-bye. How much more difficult it must have been for Norman, knowing there was absolutely no chance of recovery.

Before Norman's death, Fakazile was alarmed to learn that she too had contracted the disease. In her case, she was notified just in time and was prescribed the life-saving ARVs, but not without consequences. She suffered a severe stroke that basically paralyzed one side of her body and left her severely compromised in terms of being able to work.

It's important to take the ARVs as prescribed, often many times throughout the day, for the rest of your life. It's the only proven treatment for HIV, the only way to keep the viral load low. The strict regimentation can be overwhelming, and patients can experience "treatment fatigue." However, stopping the pills, even for a short time, can result in drug resistance within the body. Fakazile assures me that she will stay on her rigorous ARV regimen for the sake of her boys.

It is getting late, so we bid Fakazile and the family farewell. I promise to stay in touch.

"Salani kahle!"

"Hamba kahle!"

On the return that evening, I thought about Norman's sons, growing up without a male role model. There was no father or grandfather to pass on the traditions and customs of their culture, to relate the stories of their ancestors. The boys would never have the opportunity to hunt and track with their father, learn how to summon a leopard, answer a bird call, or discover the secrets of the plants and herbs. There would be no one to teach them how to build their own home brick by brick. No chance to present their own sons and daughters to a doting grandfather.

Africans say, "He who doesn't know where he came from doesn't know where he is going." No wonder many of the youth of Africa are lost. AIDS created a gap in this carefully constructed society, not just a whole generation of fathers and mothers missing, but a tear in the very connective tissue of their culture that cannot be repaired.

I always regarded Norman's family as my own and plan to stay in touch. Fakazile mentioned that Norman was buried at his parents' homestead in the remote mountain community of KwaNgwenya, situated in the Lebombo Mountains. I made a promise to myself that I would pay my respects there on a future visit.

Having reconnected with Rockerman's and Norman's families, I made a commitment to assist as much as I can, in spite of the distance between us. This is what you do for your kin. I am relieved to feel that my new promise does not come from a place of guilt but from a belief in the African tradition of extended family. There will come a day when I return to my beloved Phinda, when I can reunite with my extended families again.

Norman and Rockerman are gone, their lives inexplicably snuffed out. I always thought if death came to any of us, we would die spectacularly in the African wilderness. Lions, elephants, leopards, buffalo, rhinos—we faced all these dangerous predators together and lived to see another day unscathed.

Yet ironically it was the AIDS virus, a microscopic organism, that killed my friends. And it was a rare vertebral arterial dissection brought on by something as simple as extending my neck that had almost killed me.

But for some reason, I was spared in the lottery of death. Meeting Rockerman's daughters for the first time and reconnecting with Norman's family, I see the likenesses of my old friends in the new generation. Like their fathers, they have hopes and dreams for their futures. And perhaps, with education, foresight, and medical advances, they might be spared the devastation of Africa's newest plague. As I face the future, Norman's words still echo in my head:

> So if you walk into the buffalo thorn, don't beat a hasty retreat. Wait a bit. Take your time. Extricate yourself carefully. This is what life is like. It is not a straight road, and there are many twists and turns as we embark on life's journey.

PLACE OF DREAMS

There is a place
Where the dream is dreaming us,
We who are the shepherds of the stars.

It stands towering as tall as the mountains
Spreading its fire over the sun
Until when we take one great stride
We speed with the eagle on our journey.

It is the eagle that plays its wings on our paths,
Wakening another blind dream.
Together with other generations hereafter
They shall dream them like us.

When they wake on their journeys they will say:
Someone, somewhere, is dreaming us, in the ruins.

MAZISI KUNENE

ACKNOWLEDGMENTS

The authors are indebted to many wonderful people who have supported and assisted us in the writing of this book.

James Currie thanks the following:

To &Beyond and Phinda Private Game Reserve for the opportunity to live, love and learn.

To Richard White, Fraser Gear, Benson Ngubane, Walter Khoza, Kevin Pretorius, Kathy Pretorius, Karl Rosenberg, Graham Vercuiel, Mike Karantonis, John and Pippa Raw, Gavin Foster and Andrew Mortimer for your friendship and feedback.

Immense gratitude to Nikon for their belief in birding television.

To Fakazile Mabika and Jabu Ngubane for sharing Rockerman and Norman.

To my Dad for nurturing my independent nature and for his generous spirit.

Many thanks to my life partner, Rebecca, and our children Jemma, Joseph and Ella for their tireless support.

Bonnie Fladung thanks the following:

The staff at &Beyond Phinda Private Game Reserve who delivered the adventure of a lifetime. At Mountain Lodge, the enthusiastic team of ranger Darryn Gates and tracker Sifiso introduced me to the thrill of the game drive. At Forest Lodge, I was lucky to meet up with James's close friend Benson, who along with his tracker partner Jabulani, shared memories of James and answered endless questions. A special thanks to Grant Telfer for the tour of Inkwazi Ranger Training Camp on a day when luckily no snakes crossed our path.

I was fortunate to take a tour of the local Kwazulu Natal community with VR Nxumalo from Africa Foundation. He graciously imparted the mission of the foundation while we visited the

Khulani Special School, Mduku Clinic, Mbedhula Craft Market and the Nkomo Primary School, where the founder Mrs. Zikhali shared her story of hope.

For special insights into life in South Africa, I thank Michael Currie, who also clued me in that James writes poetry. Heartfelt gratitude to Magda Currie for her kind hospitality, encouragement, and for giving me a window into James's childhood in South Africa. And I am deeply grateful to James for trusting me with his stories.

Most importantly, thank you to my family. My daughter Margo who persevered through the many iterations. My son Sam - I taught him to read and write, and now he is my biggest critic. And my husband Dan, who said "Believe."

Both authors thank the following:

To Margo Gabrielle Damian, our brilliant illustrator who brought each chapter to life.

To the Mazisi Kunene Foundation for permission to include the inspirational poetry of the late Poet Laureate Africa 1993 and Poet Laureate South Africa 2005.

We wish to thank the many friends and family members who provided invaluable feedback at various stages of the project: Tom Cotton, Erin Fischell, Sarah Fischell, Suzanne Harvey, Daniel Hopkins, Barbara Jones, Norman Miller, Kevin Simoni, Renee Thompson, Sally Weiner Grotta, Lisa White, Mark Yonkof, and "our mystery reviewer somewhere on the continent."

A special thanks to Andrew Stewart, whose early comments and candid criticisms were instrumental in getting the focus right.

And a word of thanks to our copy editor Margery F. Tippie.

A certain amount of serendipity brought this book into existence. Thanks to Susan and Dan Gottlieb for hosting the magical evening of storytelling at the G2 Gallery in Los Angeles, and to Diane Shader Smith for her assistance. And to Anna, who lit the spark.

GLOSSARY

abafowethu *(Zulu)*   Brothers.

Afrikaner *(English)*   White South Africans of mainly Dutch descent who speak the Afrikaans language.

amabubi *(Zulu)*   Evil shades, spirits.

askari *(Swahili)*   Warrior; also used to describe a young bull elephant that protects an older, more dominant bull.

baas *(Afrikaans)*   Boss.

bahlekabafazi *(Zulu)*   Wood hoopoes; literally translated, means "the cackling women."

bakithi *(Zulu)*   A Zulu word meaning "my ancestors," but used as an expletive of disbelief similar to "Oh my goodness!"

bakkie *(Afrikaans)*   Pickup truck.

biltong *(Afrikaans)*   Dried, spiced meat that is similar to jerky.

blaauwbok *(Dutch)*   Blue antelope, now extinct.

boet *(Afrikaans)*   Brother; but used colloquially in South African slang between male friends.

boetie *(Afrikaans)*   Little brother.

boma *(African)*   Commonly used in South African vernacular, an outside enclosure for sharing meals or keeping livestock.

bru *(South African)*   Slang for "brother."

bumble *(South African)*   A game drive for the benefit of staff and friends (slang).

dagga *(Afrikaans)*   Marijuana; but also used interchangeably with *dugga* to describe old, mature buffalo bulls.

dassie *(Afrikaans)*   Hyrax, a small rodentlike creature.

dauphin *(French)*   Dolphin; Historical term for the heir to the French throne, derived from the dolphin on the coat of arms

dikkop *(Afrikaans)*   Literally meaning "thick head," but refers to a genus of nocturnal shorebirds called "thick-knees."

dugga *(African)*	Mud; also used interchangeably with *dagga* to describe old, mature buffalo bulls.
fynbos (Afrikaans)	A vegetation type found only in the Cape region of South Africa. Literally means "fine bush", a reference to the silky feel of many of these plants.
gula *(Zulu)*	Sick.
"Hamba kahle" *(Zulu)*	"Go well"; good-bye.
"Hambe" *(Zulu)*	"Go away."
hawu *(Zulu)*	Expletive indicating extreme surprise.
ibhubesi *(Zulu)*	Lion.
igwalagwala *(Zulu)*	Purple-crested turaco.
imbube *(Zulu)*	Lion.
impisi *(Zulu)*	Hyena.
induna *(Zulu)*	Chief, headman.
ingonyama *(Zulu)*	Lion.
ingulule *(Zulu)*	Cheetah.
ingwe *(Zulu)*	Leopard.
inja; (pl.)	Dog.
inkosi *(Zulu)*	Chief.
inkosikazi; (pl) **nkosikazi** *(Zulu)*	Wife; madam; lady; married woman; mistress
inkunzi *(Zulu)*	Bull or male animal.
inkwazi *(Zulu)*	Fish eagle.
inyathi *(Zulu)*	Buffalo.
inyoka (Zulu)	Snake.
isidingidwane *(Zulu)*	Fool.
isifebe *(Zulu)*	Bitch.
isilo *(Zulu)*	King.
isipokwe *(Zulu)*	Ghost.
isithuthuthu *(Zulu)*	Motorbike.
izindlovu *(Zulu)*	Elephants.
izinja *(Zulu)*	Dogs.
jambiya *(Arabic)*	Dagger.
jislaaik *(Afrikaans)*	Expression of extreme surprise.

kraal *(Afrikaans)*   Livestock enclosure or outside eating area.

"Kunjani?" *(Zulu)*   "How are you? How are things?"

Landie *(South African)*   Colloquial term for a Land Rover.

latte *(Afrikaans)*   Sticks that are placed close together in fence and wall construction.

mama *(Zulu)*   Mother.

mavuso *(Zulu)*   One who is risen.

mfowethu *(Zulu)*   My brother.

mhlope *(Zulu)*   White.

moerse *(Afrikaans)*   Very big, enormous.

musth *(Persian)*   A heightened hormonal state a bull elephant goes into when breeding.

muthi *(Zulu)*   Medicine, drug.

nagana *(African)*   Sleeping sickness in cattle.

ndlulamithi *(Zulu)*   Giraffe; literally translated, means "taller than the trees."

Nguni *(African)*   Refers to an African super-tribe or a type of Zulu cattle.

nkosikazi *(Zulu)*   A term of respect for a female. A queen.

Nutticrust *(South African)* A South African brand of cookie, excellent for dunking in tea.

okes *(South African)*   Slang for "guys."

osama *(African)*   Terrorist (colloq.).

panga *(Zulu)*   Machete.

pap *(South African)*   Maize porridge or samp.

phinda *(Zulu)*   "The return."

Puffie *(South African)*   Slang for puff adder, a type of poisonous snake.

"Qaphela" *(Zulu)*   "Be careful."

quagga *(Khoikhoi)*   A species of zebra, now extinct.

sadza *(Zulu)*   Maize meal.

"Salani kahle "*(Zulu)*   "Stay well"; good-bye.

sangoma *(Zulu)*   Medicine man, diviner.

sanibonani *(Zulu)*   Hello (greeting to multiple persons).

sawubona *(Zulu)*   Hello (greeting to one person).

shebeen *(South African)*   Slang for township bar or drinking house.

skinder (*Afrikaans*)   Juicy gossip.

skollies (*South African*)   Slang for ruffians; riff-raff.

sundowners (*British*)   Afternoon cocktails, usually imbibed as the sun sets.

tokoloshe (*African*)   A mischievous spirit that takes the form of a tiny man.

tshona (*Zulu*)   Set (v.); a polite way of referring to the death of a person.

ubuntu (*Nguni*)   Human kindness; spirit of kinship uniting mankind.

ukuhlwa (*Zulu*)   Darkness.

umfana (*Zulu*)   Boy.

umkhanyakude (*Zulu*)   Fever tree; literally translated, "shines from far."

umlungu (*Zulu*)   White guy.

umoya (*Zulu*)   Spirit or wind.

umthakathi (*Zulu*)   Witchcraft.

uSathane (*Zulu*)   Devil.

Usicelo (*Zulu*)   "The one who is requested."

ukhozi (*Zulu*)   Eagle.

ulwazi (*Zulu*)   Knowledge.

uyindoda (*Zulu*)   Man, husband.

veld (*Afrikaans*)   Bush, African landscape.

wag 'n bietjie
(*Afrikaans*)   Buffalo thorn; literally translated, "wait a bit." Used as the fleuron throughout this book.

wijd (*Dutch*)   Wide.

Xhosa (*Xhosa*)   A Nguni tribe that lives in South Africa; the tribe of Nelson Mandela.

yima (*Zulu*)   Stop, halt.

Made in the USA
San Bernardino, CA
09 April 2015